The Concept of Church

The Concept of Church

A Methodological Inquiry into the Use of Metaphors in Ecclesiology

Herwi Rikhof

Sheed and Ward/Patmos Press
London and Shepherdstown

Copyright © 1981 by H. W. M. Rikhof. First published 1981. All rights reserved. *Nihil obstat* Anton Cowan, Censor. *Imprimatur* ✠ Philip Harvey, VG, OBE, Bishop in North London, Westminster, 26 March 1981. Library of Congress Catalog No 80-84751.

British Library Cataloguing in Publication Data

   Rikhof, H. W. M.
   The Concept of Church
   1. Catholic Church
   2. Metaphor
   I. Title
   262'.02   BX1753

ISBN 0-7220-2618-8 (U.K. edition), 0-915762-11-0 (U.S. edition)

Printed in Great Britain for Sheed & Ward Ltd, 2 Creechurch Lane, London EC3A 5AQ, U.K., and Patmos Press, Box 833, Shepherdstown, West Virginia 25443, U.S.A., by Biddles Ltd, Guildford, Surrey.

Contents

Preface by Edward Schillebeeckx		xi
Table of Abbreviations		xiv
Introduction		1

Chapter I	The Church, Lumen Gentium and the Theologians	11
1.	The analysis of *Lumen Gentium*	11
1.1	The first schema: *Aeternus Unigeniti Pater*	13
1.2	The second schema in its various forms	18
1.2.1	The first version: *Concilium duce Spiritu Sancto*	18
1.2.2	The second version: *Lumen Gentium*	22
1.2.3	The third version: the constitution *Lumen Gentium*	25
1.2.4	The development in the three versions	28
1.3	The third schema: the constitution *Lumen Gentium*	29
2	The theologians	38
2.1	The arguments from content	39
2.1.1	The synthesis-view	39
2.1.2	'People of God' as the central term	49
2.1.3	Another term	55
2.2	The linguistic status of the terms	60
2.3	Conclusion	65

Chapter II	Metaphor	67
1.	Preliminary remarks	67
1.1	The requirements	67
1.2	A discussion among linguists	70

2.	A theory of metaphor	78
2.1	The general outline	78
2.2	The background	84
3.	Theories of metaphor	93
3.1	The word approach	93
3.2	The sentence approach	98
3.3	The category-mistake approach	108
4.	Two problems	112
4.1	True and false	112
4.2	Paraphrase	114
5.	Conclusion	119

CHAPTER III	THREE ANSWERS	123
1.	Narrative theology	124
1.1	Intermediary theology	124
1.2	Apologia for narrative theology	128
1.3	Metaphorical theology: reconstruction and coherence	134
1.3.1	'Narrative innocence'?	135
1.3.2	Criteria?	137
1.3.3	'History tells stories'	142
1.3.4	Conclusion	148
2.	Models	148
2.1	Models and metaphors	150
2.2	Transcendental realism	153
2.3	Models in theology	160
2.3.1	Metaphor and model	160
2.3.2	Models in theology?	163
3.	Thomas Aquinas	167
3.1	Aquinas' view of the structure of metaphor	167
3.2	Aquinas' view of the role of metaphor	171
3.2.1	The *Scriptum*	172
3.2.2	The *Summa Theologiae*	179
3.3	Reconstruction	187
4.	Conclusion	190

CHAPTER IV	METHODOLOGICAL CONSIDERATIONS	193
1.	Two levels of language	193
1.1	The fear of reduction	193
1.2	Theology: a form of paraphrase	195
2.	The definition of 'Church'	205
2.1	The arguments	206
2.2	Real definitions	211
2.3	The arguments reconsidered	214
3.	The practice of the theologians	220
4.	The basic statement in ecclesiology: a proposal	229
NOTES		239
BIBLIOGRAPHY		279
INDEX OF NAMES		297
INDEX OF SUBJECTS		301

voor mijn ouders

Preface

During and after the Second Vatican Council numerous articles, books, commentaries, and diaries appeared explaining its teachings, indicating the new starting-points and assessing the results of a particular council session or of the whole council period. After this first wave of publications and a subsequent period when less interest was shown in the council, in recent years we have once again begun to see studies of the council appearing, but these have a somewhat different character. The documents are read afresh, with an eye to developments since the council, and this reading is helped by the fact that various sources have become available. The lapse of time calls for an evaluation taking into account subsequent events. And it is quite natural that after some years the importance and significance of people and events is judged differently.

Dr H. W. M. Rikhof's *The Concept of Church* should be seen in this context. It starts with a reading of the Dogmatic Constitution on the Church, *Lumen Gentium*, and focuses on one important question: does the constitution indicate which term applied by it to the church should be central in future ecclesiological treatises developing the new insights of the council? It appears that the text gives no clear indication, but remains ambivalent. By means of analyses of the schemata and proposals preceding the final text, the source of this ambivalence is discovered in the compromise between two rather different approaches to the church.

A personal recollection may serve to highlight this point. During the sometimes heated discussions about the final version of *Lumen Gentium*, I had an exchange with the theologian who played a crucial role in preparing that version and in the processing of the amendments, especially those concerning the principle of collegiality. He told me: 'We have intentionally formulated some texts in an ambivalent way, so that the minority can accept the principle of collegiality.' To my first reaction that in this way the council would become multi-interpretable and in the end would be used in the opposite direction, he answered: 'In due course we will interpret the texts.' My response that I did not think this to be a fair procedure, and that moreover the fact that others – the official authorities rather than the theological redactors of the documents themselves – would interpret the constitution, and would do so in the direction of the minority position, was not taken into account in such a procedure, he brushed aside. His final comment on the whole matter was: 'Compromise is the only way to reach a degree of consensus.' In his introduction, Rikhof rightly sees a link between the ambivalences and lack of clarity created in this way and the quick change of mood in the period after the council – the change from an initial euphoria to a certain resignation and even indifference.

Rikhof's survey of a number of 'first wave' publications shows that the theologians who deal, more or less explicitly, with the question of the central term in *Lumen Gentium*, maintain unsatisfactory positions: they either remain too much within the compromise, or are influenced by certain presuppositions about images and metaphors. The ambivalence of *Lumen Gentium* on the point of the central term and the unsatisfactory reaction to this problem by theologians form the starting-point of his inquiry into the subject of metaphor and its role in theology and ecclesiology. These inquiries lead in turn to the proposal of a definition that can function as central and basic in ecclesiology: 'the church is the communio of the faithful.' Because of its formal character, this definition and its implications provide a framework of discussion by means of which the ambiguities of *Lumen Gentium*, created by compromise, can be removed and overcome, and the deep insights of that constitution further developed. But Rikhof's arguments and analyses, especially those concerning metaphor, the relation between narrative and argumentative theology, and the relation between religious and theological language, and the clarification of many theological concepts, help us to deal with much more than the problems in the documents of the Second Vatican Council alone: they can also be used for other theological treatises, whether about the Trinity or Christ, about the eschaton or the sacraments or any other subject. The importance of this inquiry far exceeds the particular field to which it is directed in the first instance, namely, *Lumen Gentium* and ecclesiology. We are indebted to Dr Rikhof for the many conceptual clarifications he has provided *in theologicis*.

EDWARD SCHILLEBEECKX

Table of Abbreviations

AAS	*Acta Apostolicae Sedis*, Rome 1909ff
AER	*American Ecclesiastical Review*, Philadelphia 1890ff
APQ	*American Philosophical Quarterly*, Pittsburgh 1969ff
Bijdragen	*Bijdragen*, Maastricht 1930ff
BJA	*British Journal of Aesthetics*, London 1960ff
BJPS	*British Journal of the Philosophy of Science*, Aberdeen 1950ff
Concilium	*Concilium*, London 1965ff
Dialectica	*Dialectica*, Biel (Switzerland), 1947ff
D-S	H. Denzinger, *Enchiridion Symbolorum* (ed. A. Schönmetzer), Freiburg-im-Breisgau 1963^{32}
DTh	*Divus Thomas*, Freiburg 1914ff
DThC	*Dictionnaire de théologie catholique*, Paris 1899ff
DVLG	*Deutsche Vierteljahrschrift für Literaturwissenschaft und Geistesgeschichte*, Stuttgart 1923ff
ed. (edd.)	edited by, editor(s)
EE	*Estudios Eclesiasticos*, Madrid 1922ff
ET	English translation
FL	*Foundations of Language*, Dordrecht 1965ff
FZPT	*Freiburger Zeitschrift für Philosophie und Theologie*, Freiburg 1954ff
GL	*Geist und Leben*, Würzburg 1947ff
HT	*History and Theory*, Middletown (Conn.) 1960ff
IKZ	*Internationale Katholische Zeitschrift*, Frankfurt-am-Main 1972ff
Irenikon	*Irenikon*, Chevetogne (Belgium) 1926ff
ITQ	*Irish Theological Quarterly*, Maynooth 1906ff
JAAC	*Journal of Aesthetics and Art Criticism*, Philadelphia 1941ff

JAAR	*Journal of the American Academy of Religion*, Missoula (Montana) 1931ff
Jurist	*The Jurist*, Washington (D.C.) 1941ff
Language	*Language*, Baltimore 1925ff
LTK	*Lexikon für Theologie und Kirche* (10 vols.) (ed. J. Höfer and K. Rahner), Freiburg-im-Breisgau 1957–63²
LTP	*Laval théologique et philosophique*, Quebec 1945
MTZ	*Münchener theologische Zeitschrift*, Munich 1950ff
Nous	*Nous*, Bloomington (Indiana) 1967ff
Philosophica	*Philosophica*, Gent 1963ff
PPR	*Philosophy and Phenomenological Research*, Buffalo (N.Y.) 1940ff
PR	*Philosophy and Rhetoric*, University Park (Pa.) 1968ff
PS	*Philosophy of Science*, East Lansing (Mich.) 1934ff
RL	*Religion in Life*, Nashville (Tennessee) 1932ff
RLT	*Rassegna di Letteratura Thomistica*, Rome/Naples 1968ff
RSPT	*Revue des sciences philosophiques et théologiques*, Paris 1907ff
RSR	*Revue de science religieuse*, Paris 1910ff
Scholastik	*Scholastik*, Freiburg-im-Breisgau 1926ff
SE	*Science et Esprit*, Montreal 1968ff
SJT	*Scottish Journal of Theology*, Edinburgh 1948ff
Soundings	*Soundings: An Interdisciplinary Journal*, Nashville (Tennessee) 1968ff
TF	*Tijdschrift voor Filosofie*, Louvain 1939ff
TG	*Theologie und Glaube*, Paderborn 1909ff
THAT	*Theologische Handwörterbuch zum AT* (ed. E. Jenni and C. Westermann), Munich/Zurich 1971–6
Thomist	*The Thomist*, Washington (D.C.) 1939ff
TQ	*Theologische Quartalschrift*, Tübingen 1819ff
trans.	translated by, translator
TT	*Theology Today*, Princeton (N.J.) 1944ff
TTZ	*Trierer theologische Zeitschrift*, Trier 1888ff
TvT	*Tijdschrift voor Theologie*, Nijmegen 1961ff

TWAT	*Theologisches Wörterbuch zum Alten Testament* (ed. G. Botterweck and H. Ringgren), Stuttgart 1970ff [ET: *Theological Dictionary of the Old Testament*, Grand Rapids (Michigan) 1974ff]
ZEE	*Zeitschrift für evangelische Ethik*, Gütersloh 1957ff
ZKT	*Zeitschrift für katholische Theologie, Innsbruck 1877ff*
ZPPK	*Zeitschrift für Philosophie und philosophische Kritik*, Leipzig 1837–1918

Introduction

'Cynicism' is probably the best way to describe my reaction to the use of metaphors in ecclesiology: everything seems possible and everything seems permissible. And judging from comments made by other people in recent years during discussions of my work, I am not the only one to experience such a reaction. Although a touch of cynicism prevents a theologian from acclaiming the kingdom of heaven too quickly and from forgetting the difference between the task of the magisterium and that of the theologian, too much of it kills any zest or zeal and thus theology itself, an indispensable critical function within the whole of the church. The argument I present in the following chapters will show, I hope, that there is an escape from this paralysing situation in ecclesiology, and that there is an approach and an opening to a truly theological treatment of the church.

I have decided to concentrate within the field of ecclesiology on *Lumen Gentium*, the dogmatic constitution on the church issued by the Second Vatican Council, and on Roman Catholic ecclesiology after the council, and I have made this decision on several grounds. In the first place some practical arguments dominated my choice: I had done some work previously in modern ecclesiology, and, by concentrating upon *Lumen Gentium* and on the reaction of theologians to it, I could narrow down the dangerously broad perspective and could reduce the abundant material to manageable proportions. But there was also an intuition that *Lumen Gentium*, by acknowledging and employing so many images and metaphors for the church, has created a new situation to which theologians have to find an adequate response. In the course of my analysis, this intuition was confirmed and deepened: *Lumen Gentium* has created a new situation, which must be viewed as a breakthrough and a fundamental change in reflection on the church.

The church occupies a central place in the documents of Vatican II and that is, compared to the documents of other councils, a new and important feature. But the way the church is seen forms an even more important point of difference with recent and not so recent official teachings. The self-understanding of the church expressed in these official pronouncements shows the influence of a way of thinking, whose origins can be traced back to the first separate treatises on the church in western theology that appeared around 1300.[1] This relatively late appearance of separate ecclesiological treatises was provoked not so much by inner logic or theological development, but more or even exclusively by political circumstances. The defensive attitude and the rather narrow focus on the jurisdiction and power of pope and hierarchy, which characterize these early ecclesiological works, was reinforced by the reaction to the Reformation. A more open and more theological approach to the church, never completely forgotten, gained influence in the 19th century and is linked to the names of J. A. Möhler and J. H. Newman.[2] At the First Vatican Council an attempt to combine the two approaches was not received favourably, and the revised schema, which shows predominantly the traces of the narrow approach, was never put to a vote, since the council was adjourned indefinitely due to the political situation.[3] The theological developments between the two world wars resulted in another attempt at integration: the encyclical *Mystici Corporis*. The subsequent history and theological discussions make it clear that it did not prove to be a successful attempt.[4] Certain key-terms figured in these approaches and integration-attempts: *societas* (or *coetus*) in the narrow approach, and *corpus mysticum* in the other approach and in the integration-attempts, although in different interpretations. *Lumen Gentium* can be seen as another attempt to face the problems raised by these two, rather different ways of thinking about the church. But compared with the schema of the First Vatican Council and the encyclical *Mystici Corporis* there is a major point of difference, for the transition from schema and encyclical to constitution is not a further development along the lines set out by these first attempts. In the first two texts the narrow approach dominates the reflection; in *Lumen Gentium* the open approach is fundamental. This change is echoed in the decision to quote a number of biblical images and metaphors for the church and in the way these are understood; the implications of the change are unfolded in (e.g.) that other important document of Vatican II, *Gaudium et Spes*. The genesis of the text of *Lumen Gentium* gives a dramatically compressed picture of this transition, with its fundamental turning-point: the first proposal follows *Mystici Corporis* closely, while in the subsequent schemata the other approach slowly gains dominance. But although the change is crucially important, it would be a simplification to suggest that *Lumen Gentium* has created an unambiguous situation. Like the previous texts, it is an attempt to integrate what cannot and should not be integrated, and consequently it does not present a coherent and consistent view of the church.

It is precisely this new and ambivalent situation which provides the theologian with opportunities and problems, with the possibility of developing systematically the fundamental insights of Vatican II and so of treating the church in a truly theological way, and with the necessity of deciding which term should be central to such a treatment. It is understandable that in previous periods the choice of a central term did not present itself as a special problem, since it was more or less obvious given the official teaching. Consequently, methodological considerations of this kind have not been at the centre of discussions about the church. But given the indecisiveness of *Lumen Gentium*, and given that reflection about the question as to which term is to be central has therefore become necessary for the stabilization of the breakthrough and the further development of the insights of Vatican II, these methodological considerations can no longer be avoided or taken for granted. In a first reading of the post-conciliar ecclesiology, though, I did not discover any growing awareness of this aspect of the changes; and a further analysis even revealed a disturbing confusion among theologians on this point, which, given the vital place of these considerations, must exercise a frustrating influence on the way they develop the insights of Vatican II. And so, in the course of my study, the wish to deal with this situation created by *Lumen Gentium*, and the hope that a discussion of the possible role of metaphor in theology might contribute to the advancement of a truly theological treatment of the church, became more and more important. And since I cannot deny my impression that the lack of clarity with regard to the central term has played a role in the rather rapid disappearance of the euphoria of the immediate post-conciliar period, I thought too that the choice of this particular problem might have some useful consequences for pastoral work, even if only indirectly.

As my reasons for starting this research were not completely clear at the beginning, my way of approaching the problems was not well defined. Looking back, I can see various suggestions that proved to be unhelpful and my relatively slow realisation of what now seems to be the best approach. In previous years I had come across I. Ramsey's way of considering metaphors in theology, which appealed to me and which seemed helpful in explaining and elucidating certain theological procedures. Ramsey develops Black's metaphor and model theory and adapts this for religious and theological language; his reflections on the use of models seemed at first to contain the key to the solution. But when I started to work along these lines all kinds of questions arose which made the usefulness of his understanding of model less obvious, and I was driven back to the metaphor-theory. At that stage P. Ricoeur's masterly book on metaphors, then recently published, provided considerable help in exploring the various approaches to metaphor and metaphor-theory. It has influenced my own thinking on this topic profoundly. On the basis of his analyses and arguments, especially his argument that a metaphor is a sentence, a predication, I have tried to develop a metaphor-theory as a preliminary to the discussion of the role of metaphors in theology.

Right from the beginning I have made the distinction between religious and theological language, between the language of scripture, preaching and prayer on the one hand, and the language of technical theological discourse on the other, and I have limited myself to an investigation of the role of metaphors in theological language. Although the importance and the implications of this distinction became clear when I was dealing with models and the relation between models and metaphors, the distinction itself proved to be at stake in some of the present criticism of academic theology. And so the problem of metaphors in ecclesiology appeared as an aspect of a much wider problem: the necessity, possibility and desirability of theology as distinct from preaching, of theology as 'science', as 'Wissenschaft'. A complicated problem. It seemed to me best to remain within my original scope and to present any possible contribution to that larger discussion from this perspective.

The absence of any distinction between religious language and theological language, or the refusal to acknowledge it, leads and has led to frustrating and dangerous demands. The eclipse of theological language leads, at worst, to a kind of blind, chaotic frenzy, and, at best, to a pious, irrelevant and watered-down Christianity. The eclipse of religious language results only too easily in an overcharge of theological language, in an employment for which it is not designed. Highly abstract words and technical terms do not provoke and are not meant to provoke the response of faith, should not be expected to do so, and so should not be criticized for failing to do precisely that. Only by investigating and determining the proper task of both types of language can these two deadly extremes be avoided. Since the emphasis in what follows is on the role of metaphors in *theological* language, the relation between religious and theological language is considered mainly from the perspective of theological language and of the tasks of this language; the role of metaphors in religious language is not thematized explicitly. My argument against allowing metaphors to play a crucial role in theological language is a specification of the task of theological language, but is not intended as a plea for a return to the dominance of theological language in sermons and catechesis, with the argument that metaphors are merely ornaments. On the contrary, my argument is an attempt to respond to the contemporary insights which stress – in addition to the emotional, aesthetic and didactic elements – the cognitive element in metaphors. This cognitive element is central to the determination of the task of theological language *vis-à-vis* religious metaphors: the theologian should not try to replace the metaphors with his or her kind of technical language, but should try to elicit and develop with the help of that language the richness buried in the metaphors.

My argument is divided into four chapters representing four consecutive steps. In the first chapter I trace the genesis of the text of *Lumen Gentium* and indicate at each stage which term is the central one, which term determines the view of the church. The overall conclusion is that *Lumen Gentium* does not have one central term, but two, namely 'mystical body of Christ' and 'people of God', and that their relation is not clear. In the second section I analyze the arguments of the theologians concerning the central term in the ecclesiology after Vatican II. There appear to be two kinds of arguments: arguments related to the content of 'mystical body of Christ' and 'people of God', and arguments about the status of these terms. In view of the new situation these last arguments are important, especially since presuppositions and conclusions seem likely to prevent any systematic theological development. The situation in ecclesiology created by Vatican II, and the insufficient and contradictory responses of the theologians to it, require a clarification of the role of metaphors in theology and, preliminary to that, a clarification of the meaning-mechanism and the function of metaphors in general.

In the second chapter, I state the requirements of a metaphor-theory, propose one, and compare it with some other theories. Here the arguments are directed at finding the required essential notions for a metaphor-theory.

In the third chapter I examine arguments for and against the central role of metaphors in theology: the arguments of narrative theology in favour of metaphors, the arguments of some philosophers of religion in favour of models, and the arguments of Aquinas against metaphors in theology. Since these arguments often rest upon an inadequate metaphor-theory, I restate and reconstrue the various positions on the basis of the theory proposed in the second chapter.

In the final chapter the conclusions of the two middle chapters are related to the problems discovered in the first chapter. In the first section I try to develop a view of the relation between metaphorical language and theological language using insights and arguments borrowed from the

Introduction

authors discussed in the third chapter. This general view does not lead to immediate conclusions with regard to ecclesiology, for there are two types of problems that have to be solved first: the question of definition which serves as a focus for the various arguments about the status of the terms 'people of God' and 'body of Christ' given by the theologians, and the discrepancy between their theory and their practice. In the final section I propose 'the church is the communio of the faithful' as the basic statement in ecclesiology. I have limited myself to outlining a rather formal structure indicating what kind of questions can and have to be asked and what kind not. Any further filling in requires biblical and historical studies and sociological, psychological, economical, political and cultural analyses of the contemporary situation – requires, in other words a type of reflection which is different from the introductory methodological considerations developed here.

My title, finally, is an expression of my conviction that it is possible to talk in a truly theological way about the church.

I have been so fortunate to spend three years at Oxford for my post-doctoral studies, thanks to 'Het deken Scholtenfonds' (Oldenzaal) and the N.K.O.V. who provided money for the first year, to the Z.W.O., and to the Provost and Fellows of The Queen's College who elected me to a Florey Studentship. Dr J. Annas spent much time and energy in critically reading and discussing the papers and drafts that have resulted in the second chapter, and Mr R. Harré has helped me in various ways to understand the role of models in science and has kindly read my account and application of his theory. I am very grateful to these people and institutions. And I am very grateful to those who have made these years not only academically fruitful but also thoroughly enjoyable in all those other areas of life. This study was concluded in December 1979.

HERWI RIKHOF
February 1981

The Concept of Church

Chapter 1

The Church, Lumen Gentium *and the Theologians*

This chapter contains two analyses both dealing with a problem fundamental to a systematic treatment of the church: the choice of the central term. The first analysis is concerned with *Lumen Gentium*. The Second Vatican Council has created a new situation and a new starting-point for theological reflection by issuing this dogmatic constitution on the church, which compared to previous teachings manifests a different approach to the church – to its nature, its tasks, its structure. Since part of the new situation is that *Lumen Gentium* does not itself provide a clear indication of the term it favours, the reaction of theologians to it and the answers they give to the question which term should be central become crucial to the theological development of the insights of *Lumen Gentium*. The second analysis concentrates on these reactions and answers.

1. *The analysis of* Lumen Gentium
Lumen Gentium is one of the central documents of the Second Vatican Council. Like other documents, the dogmatic constitution on the church was the result of a long and turbulent process.[1] The original schema was introduced by Cardinal Ottaviani, the chairman of the doctrinal committee, on 1 December 1962. He qualified it as a pastoral, biblical and accessible document, but expressed at the same time his fears that it would be received with the by-then customary criticism of prepared documents: viz, that it was not pastoral enough, not ecumenical, too scholastic, too negative.[2] The schema was discussed briefly during the last week of the first session and the criticism voiced was fundamental and devastating. The

schema was sent back to the committee to be rewritten. Before the second session the council fathers received a new text which was based upon a schema written by G. Philips and which in its original form had circulated among the fathers near the end of the first session. This second schema was accepted by the council fathers in principal as the basis for further discussion on 1 November 1963. The discussion in the aula was long and at times stormy. These speeches, together with the written comments submitted at various times, were used for the redaction of the third schema. This was discussed and accepted during the third session. On 21 November 1964 the final text was promulgated.

The first proposal and the final text express two rather different views of the church: the first describes the church in apologetical and juridical terms, while the other places the church in the context of the history of salvation. A quick first reading of the two texts reveals also a difference in what seems to be the central image or concept in the two schemata: 'mystical body of Christ' in the first, and 'people of God' in the second. A connection between the difference in view and the difference in central concept suggests itself with an apparent consequence, among other consequences, that an ecclesiology developing the insights of Vatican II must take 'people of God' as its central term. But a more careful second reading discloses a much more complex relationship. Only if the first proposal and the final text are seen as the beginning and the end of a development, while the various versions of the second schema are treated as transitory phases of this development, can the complexity of the whole process be grasped. For, apart from the apparent discontinuity, there is also an element of continuity in all the texts. The decision of the committee which had to rewrite the first schema, that it should not rearrange the acceptable material from that first proposal but rather adopt Philips' schema as a starting-point, does not contradict this observation, since Philips used much material and even complete chapters from the first proposal.[3] The features of continuity and discontinuity expressing the old and the new cannot immediately be discovered in the final text: an analysis of the text at its various stages can reveal the different layers, the transpositions and the constant elements.

The basic outline of the view of the church which provides the framework for the discussion of issues like the relation of church and state, the collegiality of bishops, the place of religious, the connection between the church on earth and the church in heaven, etc., is given in the first part of the different texts. For the present discussion, dealing with the view of the church and with the role of terms like 'mystical body of Christ' and 'people of God', these first parts are most relevant; the rest of the text is only referred to as an illustration of, or support for, the conclusion reached in the analysis of those first chapters. The analysis proceeds first by summarizing the main ideas in a paraphrase which mirrors as much as possible the original and sometimes abrupt connections, and secondly by pointing to important structuring elements, by answering the question which term is central, and by comparing the different texts.[4]

1.1 *The first schema:* Aeternus Unigeniti Pater
The first schema was handed out on 13 November 1962. The work on it was started some two years earlier when the theological committee instituted a subcommittee with the task of writing a constitution on the church based upon an outline accepted by the central preparatory committee. In frequent meetings and in contact with the theological committee the work was done. By March 1962 the schema was ready for inspection by the central committee which asked for some changes. It has been a complaint that the composition of the various committees did not sufficiently reflect the diversity of theological schools.[1]

The first proposal consists of 11 chapters and an appendix on the Virgin. The first chapter determines the nature of the church militant, while the second declares the church necessary for salvation and defines the conditions of membership. Chapters three and four deal with issues concerning bishops and priests, chapter five with religious, and chapter six with the laity. Chapters seven and eight are concerned with the magisterium and with authority and obedience in the church. The final three chapters discuss the relation between church and state, the need to preach the gospel to all people, and the ecumenical movement. Of these the first chapter is most relevant to the present discussion.[2]

The chapter on the nature of the church militant starts with a section on the plan of the Father to redeem mankind and to bring it into his kingdom by sending his Son. The Son will acquire through his death a people, for the Father does not want the redeemed to be separate individuals, but wants them to form a people, a new Israel under Christ the head (section 1). This plan is executed by his Son. Christ himself leads the people of God to eternal salvation in his capacity as teacher, priest and king. But he leads it via the leaders appointed by him; he entrusted to them the tasks, to be performed under Peter, of being teachers, priests and kings. This new people, this Israel of God, does not march like a confused mass, but like a column in close order, invincible, towards the end of time (section 2).

The next three sections deal with biblical names for this Israel of God. Like Moses, who called Israel in the desert 'the church of God', so Jesus calls the new Israel 'church'. And he calls it his church, not only because he acquired it through his blood, but also because he founded it upon Peter and his successors. To express more clearly the nature of the church Jesus has used, directly or indirectly via the apostles, different names and images that describe the mystical and social aspects: kingdom, house, temple, body, flock, bride, column and foundation of truth (section 3). But among these, 'body' occupies the first place. Inspired by Christ, Paul uses 'body' to state that Christ is the head of his body and that those who are baptized and take part in the eucharist are made into one body (section 4).

This is further developed in a long section in which five elements can be discerned. First, that the body is visible: because the church is a body, it can be seen. Secondly, that it is an organism with many members; these members are not at all equals, for some are superior to others. Thirdly, that apart from the social, juridical and ministerial relations, there is also an intimate relationship with Christ, which Christ has illustrated by means of the comparison with the vine. Fourthly, that the Spirit is the soul of the body. He gives graces and charismas and he constitutes the unity of the body. Fifthly, that some of the members are sick. Not all members are healthy in holiness; their sinfulness offends the church but does not affect the essential holiness of the church. The church is holy, because as bride of Christ it is constituted in holiness. As a mother the church cares for its members and helps them with its sacraments (section 5).

On the basis of this view the final two sections present two main conclusions. First, the hierarchical church-organisation and the charismatic church of love are one and the same. This is explained via the analogy with the mystery of the incarnation: as the human nature serves the divine, so the organisation serves the development of the mystical body. Secondly, the Roman Catholic Church and the mystical body of Christ are identical. There is one, holy catholic and apostolic church, and that is the Roman Catholic Church.

The question about the central term is not difficult to answer: the central term in this schema is 'mystical body of Christ'. The reason why biblical images are mentioned can further clarify this position of 'mystical body'. The images are introduced in contrast with the word *ecclesia*, 'church'. They reveal in a clearer and more precise way the nature of the church because they describe the social and mystical aspect of the church. This betrays one of the central concerns of the text: to acknowledge both aspects and to show their inseparable relationship.[3] 'Body' receives here a preferential treatment, since it expresses most clearly this inseparable connection. This concern to show both the mystical and the social aspect of the church determines, at least partly, the way 'body' or 'mystical body of Christ' is understood and explained. On the one hand, the text refers to Christ's relationship and intimate connection with the body, and to the role of the Spirit; on the other hand, the text mentions the visibility of the body, the social and juridical relations between the members. The analogy with the mystery of the incarnation is also used to emphasize the inseparable connection between the domain of the organisation and the domain of grace. The use of the analogy is also a sign of the 'Christus-prolongatus' view: the church is seen as a continuation of the incarnation of Christ, as Christ living on.[4]

But this concern explains neither the structure of subordination among the members nor the hierarchical interpretation of the gifts of the Spirit. These elements are determined by another concern, namely, that of identifying the Roman Catholic Church with the mystical body of Christ. The whole chapter leads up to this identification and its importance is indicated by introducing it as a solemn declaration of the sacred synod. The Roman Catholic Church is understood in a certain way, however: it is understood as consisting of unequal members (as a *societas inaequalis*). There exists a fundamental dichotomy between clergy and laity, between leaders and subordinates, between teachers and disciples. Related to this is the way the threefold function of Christ is employed: the function of priest, king and teacher is attributed to the hierarchy only, which implies a narrow interpretation of the church as the continuation of Christ. In the context of the analogy with the incarnation this leads to the statement that only the hierarchy is instrumental in the development of the body. Another element that is crucial to the understanding of this view of the Roman Catholic Church is the relation between the health or holiness of the body and the illness or sinfulness of its members. Their illness does not really damage or affect the health of the body. This presupposes at least a one-way dependance and some kind of hypostatization of the body.

The important role of 'mystical body of Christ' in this view of the church is also revealed in the rest of the schema.[5] In the discussion of issues like the necessity of the church for salvation, the conditions of membership and the union with other Christians, 'mystical body' or related terms like 'incorporation' and 'member' occur several times. The chapter on the laity contains an introduction which states explicitly the constitution and the aim of the church, and as in the first chapter, 'mystical body of Christ' is here the central term.

Besides, no other term is a serious candidate, certainly not 'people' or 'people of God'. It is used in the first chapter, but it is not mentioned among the biblical names and apparently does not express the mystical and social aspect. Despite the reference to 1 Pet 2:9 – in turn a quotation from Ex 19:6 – 'people' is not used here in its biblical sense: it is neither used as a salvation-historical term, nor understood in a maximal way. The first two sections do not present the plan of the Father in terms of the history of salvation, and Jesus' execution of the plan is not placed in a historical context, but introduced abruptly. There are more or less implicit allusions to a history of salvation – the comparison between Israel in the desert and the church – but these allusions are not fundamental and they do not indicate a continuity with Israel, but, on the contrary, a rupture. This is shown by the addition of 'new' to 'people' and 'Israel', a combination which does not occur in Scripture. 'People' is used, moreover, in a minimal way, for it is introduced to reject the suggestion of a solitary redemption: it refers to a multitude under leaders.[6]

The way the schema sees the Roman Catholic Church leads to internal tensions in the use of 'body'. The emphasis on the inequality of the members is not an obvious point in the understanding of the image, and there is certainly a contrast between this interpretation and that of Paul, whose uses of 'body' are referred to. Paul stresses the unity of the members despite their variety and emphasizes the equal importance and significance of all members (1 Cor 12:12–27; Rom 12:4–5). Moreover, the way the relations between body and member is seen with regard to health and illness is puzzling. It is difficult to maintain, certainly as a general principle, that the illness of one member does not harm the health of the body, though it would make sense to argue that the illness of one member does not imply the illness of other members as well. Yet the text states the improbable proposition. In addition, the problem arises how on this view the whole that is not affected by its members nevertheless affects those members. The hypostatization of the body leads to such a tension in the image that it destroys the image and renders it unintelligible.

Another point of tension is the use of other images at crucial moments: the image of the vine to indicate the intimate relationship between Christ and the church, the image of the bride to express the sanctity of the church, and the image of mother to specify the sacramental activities. The employment of this last image leads to the strange vision of the body conceiving its own members.[7] A final point of tension in the understanding of 'mystical body of Christ' is revealed by the analogy with the incarnation. Although 'body' and 'mystical body of Christ' are introduced to show that the social and the mystical aspect belong together, the use of the analogy shows a somewhat different understanding. The point incarnation and church have in common according to the analogy between them is that in both cases one nature or aspect serves the other nature or aspect. But if the social aspect of the church, the church as *societas*, serves the development of the mystical body of Christ, 'mystical body of Christ' must refer to the mystical aspect only and does not any longer include both aspects.[8]

1.2 *The second schema in its various forms*

There are three versions of the second schema. Of these the first one is Philips' original schema that was circulated during the first session. The second version is an amplification of that original schema; this amplification was accepted by the sub-committee as the starting-point for the new schema. The third version is the text that was sent to the council-fathers in two instalments before the second session.

1.2.1 *The first version:* Concilium duce Spiritu Sancto

Apart from an introduction which states the aim of the constitution, the text consists of four major sections. The first section 'What is the church?' comprises a chapter on the mystery of the church and a chapter on the necessity of the church for salvation and on the conditions of membership. The second section 'In whom does the church consist?' contains chapters on the hierarchy, the laity and the religious. The third section 'How does the church live?' is divided into chapters on the doctrinal life of the church, authority and obedience, and the spreading of the gospel, and the final section 'relationships in the church' consists of a chapter on the unity of all Christians and one on the relations between church and state. In these four major sections much of the material from the first proposal is used, rearranged or expanded. For the last two sections, this version corresponds very closely to the text of the first schema.[1] But there are also signs of a different approach. An indication of change is given in the introduction, where the aim of the constitution is stated to be that of enabling the church to announce the gospel in a better way, not just to the believers, but to all men living in the modern world. Instead of a defensive, apologetic stance a more

The Church, Lumen Gentium *and the Theologians*

pastoral and open attitude is adopted. Another indication is the title of the first chapter: instead of 'the nature of the church militant', the caption 'the mystery of the church' is now used. A closer look at the first chapter will reveal whether this different approach has influenced the text.

The chapter contains six sections, which can be grouped in three clusters: 1–3, 4–5 and 6. The first sections cover the plan of the Father concerning the universal church. He created the world and wanted people to participate in the divine life. He decided to redeem men fallen in Adam through the death of his Son and to gather an acceptable people to himself. Accordingly Jesus, after his resurrection, sent the apostles out to the whole world to be his witnesses. Those who are baptized enter into the church founded by the Lord and, united in faith and love, become witnesses of Christ. The church extends over all the regions of the earth till the end of time. The second section, on the people of God, qualifies the church further as Christ's church, as the people acquired by him, on pilgrimage towards the Fatherland. The next section describes Christ's presence in his church via the gifts of his Spirit, via his inhabitation of the hearts of believers, and via the eucharist and the other sacraments. The two following sections discuss biblical names and images. Section four mentions the image of the temple of the Spirit and discusses briefly that of the body of Christ. The life of the risen Christ is diffused in the members of the church so that those who partake of the one bread form one body with Christ. Therefore, the church is in a mystical way the body of Christ. Christ is the head and together with him we form a society constituted by visible connections. Section five continues by declaring that the church is also described as the bride of Christ or as the bride of the Lamb. The nature of the church is revealed by other images as well: it is the true spiritual creation of God, existing in heaven and on earth: the kingdom of God, the New Jerusalem, God's dwelling-place among men. The final section deals with the church in its terrestrial condition. There is only one holy, catholic and apostolic church, given to Peter and the apostles and their successors to tend; upon them Christ has built as a living instrument and sacrament of salvation the column and foundation of truth. This heavenly church, the community of grace and love, exists on earth as an organic society and is the Roman Catholic Church.

There are several differences between this first chapter and that of the first schema. A first point of note is the broad perspective within which the exposition of the mystery starts: the creation of the world and the connection between creation and redemption. One finds an echo of this in the description of the church as the new creation and in the mission of the church to the whole world, and in the observation that the church extends itself to all the regions of the earth. Another point revealing a broader perspective is the formulation that the church exists in heaven and on earth. The focus of attention is on the whole church. A second remarkable point is the way the relationship between Christ and his church is discussed. There is more interest in the relations of faith and less in organisational ties as the basis for calling the church Christ's own. Related to this is the difference in the treatment of the biblical images. The emphasis is on the mystery. 'Mystical body of Christ' is not discussed at length, while 'people of God' is given a separate section. There are no traces of the triumphalistic military language of the first schema. The sacraments and the Holy Spirit are mentioned in the context of both 'mystical body' and 'people of God' (cf the use of temple).

Despite these differences the new perspective is not fully developed, and, apart from the jerky organization of the material (see especially section 1), there are ambivalent features in the text which are signs of a superficial integration of old and new. The distinction between the church in heaven and the church on earth is not clear and not thematized. While the church is connected to creation, creation is understood more in spatial terms than in temporal categories. The lack of historical interest is especially clear in the way Jesus' role is introduced. Jesus does not appear in a historical context nor does his life seem to be important: it is only the risen Christ that appears in this version. A similar observation can be made about the treatment of 'people of God', for there is no reference to the Old Testament.

This insufficient integration and this incomplete development of an individual and new view is also clear in the rest of the schema. The other chapter of the first part follows more or less the order and the text of the second chapter of the first schema: the need of the church for salvation, the determination of kinds of relations, the conditions of membership, and unity with separated brethren. A new part is added about the non-Christians and the need to incorporate them into the Body of Christ. By this addition the structure of the chapter has become more coherent, but it shows also that it remains in line with the first schema. With regard to the hierarchical organization part II offers a more comprehensive text, developing and quoting old material and adding new, and instead of discussions of separate problems the result is a more coherent treatment. An introduction and chapters on the election of the apostles and on the bishops as successors of the apostles are added, and their threefold task of priest, prophet and king is developed in three chapters. With regard to the laity and religious this version offers only titles and refers to the text of the first schema, because, as the note states, it was well received by many council-fathers.[2] The chapter on the laity is placed before that on religious with the argument that first the whole *populus fidelis* should be considered. The new title indicates this: 'On the faithful, especially on the laity'.

This relation between the first version of the second schema and the first proposal can also be seen in the choice and treatment of the central term: this version uses 'mystical body of Christ' as its central term, but in an interpretation that is somewhat different from that of the first schema. It is not understood in such an elaborate organizational way, although the interpretation of body as society is clearly present as is also shown by the other parts. The importance of 'mystical body of Christ' in the rest of this version is revealed both in the quotations from the first schema and in the new parts in which 'mystical body' or related terms are introduced.[3] Moreover, there is no serious other candidate. 'People of God', although mentioned in a new short section, is not frequently used either in the first chapter or in the rest, and the way it is used may explain why it cannot function as a central term. It still refers to a part of the whole church, i.e., to those who do not belong to the hierarchy. The broad biblical understanding that could be discovered in the short separate section is not developed.

1.2.2 *The second version:* Lumen Gentium
The second version of Philips' scheme is an amplification of the first version and presented as such. It was written and circulated after the first session; in that period other schemata and proposals were circulated as well. The sub-committee 'de ecclesia' decided to take this amplification as the basis of its work (26 February 1963) and the doctrinal committee ratified this decision (6 March).[1] It consists of two chapters: one on the mystery of the church, and one on the hierarchical constitution of the church.[2]

This is the first time the programmatic title *Lumen Gentium* appears in the preface. Originally used by Pope John to refer to the church, it is used now to refer to Christ. He is the light of all nations and with his light the church hopes to illuminate all men. Together with the introduction of the term *sacramentum* in the preface, it shows that the focus of attention is no longer the church on its own but the church as pointing to Christ and to the unity of all men and their unity with God. There are also changes in the first chapter: a new section on the Spirit is added, so that the mystery of the church appears in relation to that of the Trinity. This is expressed in the final sentence of the third section, a quotation from Cyprian: 'a people brought into unity from the unity of the Father, the Son and the Holy Spirit'.[3]

As in the previous version, the first section tells of the Father, who created the world and who did not abandon men after the fall, but who gave them help in anticipation of Christ, the first-born of the new creation. He destined his Son, born out of the chosen people, to redeem all men through his death and to make his brothers sons of the Father; he was not to sanctify them in an individual way, but to make them into the people under one head. This holy church, started from the beginning of mankind and prefigured in the election of the old people and the old covenant, is manifested in the fullness of time (section 1). Sent by the Father to gather the sons of God, the Son founded a new covenant and began the new creation, the new people of God. As Israel in the desert was called the church of God, so this new Israel is called the church of Christ: he has acquired it with his blood, has filled it with his Spirit and has built it upon Peter and the apostles with visible means of unity. The congregation of those who believe in Jesus, the author of redemption and the beginning of peace and unity, form the church, the visible sacrament of that redemptive unity which extends itself over all the regions of the earth (section 2). The Spirit of life, through whom we have access to the Father, is sent by God into our hearts. The Spirit who lives in the faithful and in the church as in a temple, so that all are endowed with his gifts, renews the church constantly and leads it to unity with Christ the Bridegroom. Spirit and Bride say to Jesus: 'Come' (section 3).

The next three sections deal with various biblical images that describe the relationship between Christ and his church. Christ the priest, prophet and king has not abandoned his people after his resurrection, but has given it his Spirit and refreshes his people with the bread of the eucharist and of doctrine (section 4). The section on the mystical body, section 5, contains some new material; the variety of members and of ministries is mentioned, and there is a greater emphasis on Christ the head. In the sixth section 'kingdom' is replaced by 'house and family of God'. The final section, 'the church on pilgrimage on earth' states that the community of faith, love and grace, the mystical body of Christ and the visible society, are not two different things, but one. The analogy with the incarnation is mentioned: as the human nature served the divine, so the church-society serves the Spirit of Christ in building up the body. To the identification between the one, holy, apostolic and catholic church and the Roman Catholic Church under the direction of the Roman pontiff and the bishops in communion with him, is added that outside the Roman Catholic Church elements full of sanctity can be found. The section concludes with the remark that the church as sacrament of Christ is a sign for all nations of the evangelical poverty of Jesus. Three sections on membership conclude this chapter.

The expansion of the first version is done in two different and diverging ways. First, the view maintained in the first schema is strengthened, and, secondly, the new commencement of the first version is further developed. The first way is visible in the introduction of elements derived from the first schema and expressing the concern of that schema: the church is again called Christ's own because he built it upon Peter and the apostles and equipped it with the visible means of unity. The analogy with the incarnation is introduced again to clarify the relation between the domain of organization and the domain of love. And with the quotation of the analogy the problems already mentioned are introduced as well. The introduction of historical and eschatological elements reveal the other way. The time before Jesus is important and recognized as a part of the history of salvation, for help is given right from the beginning and because election and covenant are prefigurations of what is now manifested clearly. Moreover, Jesus is born out of the chosen people. The eschatological element is present in the image of the New Jerusalem and in the section on the Spirit, who with the Bride calls to Jesus: 'come', and in the title of the sixth section: 'The church on pilgrimage on earth'. The development is also apparent in the introduction of a separate section on the Holy Spirit: the history of salvation is seen now as the consecutive activity of Father, Son and Spirit.

Because of these diverging developments and trends the text of the second version does not present an integrated view. The role of the Spirit is only partly related to the church: he is in the first place sent 'into our hearts'. This one-sided emphasis is related to the division of the history of salvation into two parts: preparation and fulfilment. The eschatological elements present in the section on the Spirit and in the section on the pilgrim church are not fully integrated in the history of salvation. The lack of integration can also be seen in the organization of the text. Section 1 does introduce historical notions but does not present them in an orderly way, which results in an unnecessary repetition of the theme of the church existing right from the beginning of creation. Section 2 abruptly connects the broad perspective with the visible means of unity. Section 4 has in fact become superfluous because of the introduction of section 3 on the Holy Spirit, but is nevertheless maintained. The solution of introducing it in connection with the biblical images is clearly inadequate since no biblical image is discussed in that section. The threefold function of Christ remains a strange and alien element. There is also some tension between, on the one side, the insistence upon the fact that Jesus equipped his church with visible means of unity, which is related to the thesis of identification and the declaration that there is only one church, and, on the other side, the recognition of elements full of sanctification outside the church.

Given this situation a clear change of central image or concept cannot be expected: 'mystical body of Christ' is still the most important term for describing the church. Compared with the first version it receives even more attention, and it is introduced again in the crucial part on identification. While in the first version the heavenly church, the community of love and grace, was said to exist on earth as an organic society, now the identification between the visible society and the mystical body is added.[4] Moreover, the issues in the sections on membership, now part of the chapter on the mystery of the church, are discussed in terms of incorporation. 'People of God' is used in the first part of this chapter, i.e., in the context of the history of salvation, and it is used in combination with either 'old' and 'new', or with 'elected', and on one occasion Christ is mentioned as the head of the people. Of these the last and the combination 'people' and 'new' refers to the church. 'People of God' is only used in this part, and its occurrence in the section of Christ's presence in the church is, as noted earlier, not very influential, and its place is not strengthened by the fact that it is used in a superfluous section. 'People of God' does not return in the rest of the chapter, either in the sections on the biblical names or in the section on the pilgrim church: in those sections 'mystical body' is used. In the rest of the schema 'people of God' is only used a few times, and, when it is used, it is used in a material and general way.[5] 'Mystical body' on the other hand is used several times.[6]

1.2.3 *The third version:* Lumen Gentium
The text of the third version is the text that was sent to the council fathers in two instalments during the summer of 1963. It was only after the four chapters had been approved by the committee and the pope, and after the first two chapters had been sent to the council fathers, that the committee accepted the suggestion that chapter 3 should be split into a chapter on the people of God and a chapter on the laity, and that the new

chapter on the people of God should be inserted between the chapter on the mystery of the church and the chapter on the hierarchy. Neither the decision nor its implications influenced the text at this stage.[1]

Compared with the first chapter of the second version this first chapter contains one major structural alteration: the section on the presence of Christ has disappeared, although parts of it reappear in the section on biblical images. The structure of the chapter had been improved by this change, showing a straight line of argument: first the mystery of the church is related to that of the Trinity, next the biblical images for the church are mentioned, then the Roman Catholic Church is discussed, and finally the membership conditions of that church and its relation to other Christians and non-Christians are outlined.[2] The main difference with the previous version can be noticed in the treatment of the biblical images. The section on the mystical body can now be divided into three parts: an introduction, a part on the inner life and a part on the ministries.[3] The introduction contrasts 'people of God' with 'the mystical body of Christ'. Christ has raised the people of God to a new and higher state by conquering death. He not only gathers the faithful into one people, but unites his brothers called from all nations in himself and constitutes in a mystical way his body. The relation between Christ and the church is such that the life of the risen Christ is diffused in the members of the church: they form in and with him one body. For all we believers in Christ are baptized in one body and partake in this one body as in the one bread. We are united so that not only our bodies are joined to Christ via the sacraments, but so that we also form one body of faithful equipped with various organs and endowed with different gifts. Christ is the head and his fulness fills all. Due to his task, perfection and virtue Christ stands out above all members and organs that he directs.

The final part of this section turns towards the mystical body on earth: Christ distributed gifts of ministries to build up his body on earth. In different functions, especially in those of the hierarchy, the Lord himself acts as teacher, priest and king. The Spirit, one and the same in head and body, vivifies, unites and moves the body and is rightly called the soul of the church. The body on earth is connected with the head in heaven and the body truly represents Christ on earth and constitutes the beginning of the kingdom of heaven. The section on the other images mentions several new ones, giving the following list: flock, vine, field, family, temple and house of God, dwelling-place of the Holy Spirit, holy city, new Jerusalem, bride of the Lamb, new Eve.

The changes made in the first chapter reveal the same tendencies as those of the previous version: a strengthening of the older view and at the same time a further development of the salvation-historical approach. And, as in the previous version, there are signs of an insufficient integration. The introduction of the notion *ecclesia ab Abel* in the first section does clarify problems raised by the second version, but its place in the whole amounts to a repetition. The changes in the section on the mystical body result in a more orderly organization of the material, but in the mostly new final part the concern of the first schema returns. The statements that Christ acts through the hierarchy and that the heavenly Christ is represented on earth by the church reveal the influence of the *Christus-prolongatus* view. At the same time, the phrase 'germ and beginning' does not fit well into this way of thinking, because it belongs to the context of the history of salvation.

The first part of the section on the mystical body of Christ gives a clear indication of what is considered to be the central term of this schema. Christ has raised the people of God to a higher condition, namely, that of being his body: the people of God becomes the mystical body of Christ.[4] This difference between people of God and body of Christ implies that 'people of God' is understood either materially or as the people of the old testament. The formulation 'new people' is, on the argument given in the text, not an apt and adequate term for the church, but it is nevertheless used in this chapter.[5] If it is correct that Christ has raised the people of God to a new condition, it is not clear why the term should be used after this statement at all, but 'people of God' is nevertheless used, sometimes referring to the whole of the church, sometimes referring to the subjects, to the non-hierarchy.[6] Nor is it clear why in the outline of the plan of the Father his decision not to redeem men and women separately but united in a people is mentioned. One would expect 'body' here too. These tensions reveal that the place and the understanding of 'people of God' is ambivalent.

1.2.4 *The development in the three versions*
Taking these three versions of the second schema together and comparing them with the first schema, the following differences and developments can be noticed.

The official commentary, sent to the council fathers together with the text of the schema, notes that the church is presented as the object of faith and that more than just its external manifestation is described.[1] The primary interest is not the organization but the mystery of the church. This is the most salient point of difference between the first schema and all the three versions of the second schema. 'Mystery' is here not understood in the sense of 'puzzling' or 'obscure', but in the biblical sense of God's plan of salvation as disclosed in the history of salvation. The first schema does mention God's plan, but does not understand it in terms of the history of salvation. In the three versions one can discern a growing realization of what the implications of this difference in interest are. The relation between the church and the workings of the Trinity, the introduction of historical notions like the period between creation and Jesus' lifetime, the introduction of eschatological notions like the pilgrim church are signs of this growing awareness. Related to this is the change in focus, or the emergence of the 'transparency-view' of the church. While the first schema focuses upon the church itself in its current appearance, a change is noticeable when in the course of the development within the three versions the church is seen as a sacrament, as an instrument and sign, directing the attention to that of which it is a sign: the unity of men and their union with God.

But this point of difference is not fully developed. The history of salvation consists only of two phases. The activity of the Spirit, whose role has become more important, is not related to the church in the first place, but to the faithful. Furthermore, the texts do not make the most of the eschatological elements already present, like the church being the germ and the beginning of the kingdom of heaven, the church being on pilgrimage and the church calling, with the Spirit, to Christ:

The Church, Lumen Gentium *and the Theologians*

'Come'. The transparency of the church is therefore not complete. The triumphalistic language has disappeared, but the view underlying this type of language is still influential, as can be seen in the *Christus-prolongatus* view, the analogy with the incarnation, and the identification of the mystical body with the Roman Catholic Church. It is impossible to talk about a straight development on this point, since at least two of these elements did not occur in the first version but were introduced later.

There are also differences in the role and the use of biblical images. While in the first proposal images other than 'mystical body' were hardly mentioned, in the versions of the second schema other biblical images are allotted more space and importance. However, this does not result in a replacement of 'mystical body' as the central term, even though fluctuation in the interpretation of that central term can be noticed. In the first schema, 'body' was emphatically interpreted in the organizational sense; in the final version of the second schema, there is more attention for the inner life. But here again one cannot talk about a linear development, for the first version does use 'society' in relation to 'mystical body' but with less emphasis, while in the later versions more elements from the first schema return and in the final version with even greater emphasis than in the second one. A similar development can be noticed in the use of 'people of God'. In the first proposal it hardly occurs and is understood in a general way indicating the communal aspect of salvation. In the three versions of the second schema elements revealing a different understanding can be discerned, but this interpretation is not the prominent one. The first version dedicates a separate section to 'people of God', but the title has disappeared in the following versions.

1.3 *The third version: the constitution* Lumen Gentium

The third schema has taken into account all the spoken and written comments and reactions to the second schema. It consists now of eight chapters. During the discussions of the second session the four chapters of the previous schema were transformed into six, and since the council fathers also decided not to issue a separate constitution on the Virgin, but to dedicate a chapter to her in the constitution on the church, the last chapter was added. The seventh chapter on the eschatological nature of the church is a new one. It was discussed and rewritten during the third session.[1] The first six chapters were not discussed again but only voted upon.[2] Of this third schema there are again three versions, but since the changes in the relevant chapters are only small ones, mostly concerned with formulations, section-headings and references to scripture and notes, the final text suffices. Apart from the first chapter, the second chapter on the people of God is also relevant for the discussion. All elements related to 'people of God' and originally occurring in the first chapter are now combined with those elements concerning the church as a whole that appeared mostly in the chapter on the laity.[3]

In its final phase the text of the first chapter contains eight sections. After an introduction and three sections in which the mystery of the church is related to the mystery of the Trinity, a new section is inserted on the kingdom of God. The order of the two sections dealing with biblical images is reversed and the final section deals with the church 'at the same time visible and spiritual'. The sections on membership and on the relations to other Christians and to non-Christians are moved to the new second chapter on the people of God. Several sections of the first chapter have been extensively rewritten.

In the first section on the Father's plan of salvation two main elements can be discovered in the one line of thought: the universal church reaching from creation to the eschaton and the five phases in the history of salvation – the church is prefigured from the beginning, prepared in the history of Israel, constituted by Christ, made manifest by the Spirit and to be fulfilled at the end of time. The section on the mission of the Son is largely rewritten. An important new element is that the Son inaugurates the kingdom of heaven on earth. The kingdom of Christ is, in a mystical way, already present in the church that grows in the world. Another, and related element, is the unity with Christ to which all men are called and which is represented and effected in the eucharist. In the section on the Spirit a new emphasis on the role of the Spirit in the church can be seen. The Spirit is sent on Pentecost, leads the church towards the truth, unites it in community and ministry, organizes and directs it through different hierarchical and charismatic gifts, renews it permanently and leads it to its final union with Christ, the Bridegroom.

These three sections are again summarized in Cyprian's saying 'a people brought into unity from the unity of the Father, the Son and the Holy Spirit'. The theme of the kingdom of God is further developed in a new section. The mystery of the church appears in its foundation. Jesus started the church by preaching the good news, that is, the arrival of the kingdom of God. This kingdom shines through in his deeds, words and person. After Christ's death and resurrection the task to preach and establish the kingdom of Christ and of God is received by the church: the church is the germ and the beginning of the kingdom. The next two sections deal with biblical images. In a much expanded sixth section images from both the Old and the New Testament derived from pastoral and agricultural life, from building construction and from family and marriage are presented in an order of increasing importance. This progress culminates in the section on the mystical body, which can be divided into three parts. The introduction states that Christ has redeemed and recreated man by his death and resurrection, for by communicating his Spirit he constitutes in a mystical way his brothers as his body. The difference in treatment of 'body' in the Pauline letters is acknowledged for the second part refers Romans and Corinthians, while the third part uses Colossians and Ephesians. In the second part the emphasis is put on the community of the members, in the third on Christ the head. The community of members is first determined with regard to baptism and eucharist. Through baptism and the eucharist we become members of the body of Christ. The variety of members and functions is mentioned. The Spirit distributes different gifts. Charismas, though, are subjected to the authority of the apostles, for the grace given to them stands out above these charismas. The theme of Christ the head is developed under several heads: Christ's primacy in the church and in creation, the resemblance between head and members in death and resurrection, the influence of the head on the growth of the body via the distribution of gifts of ministries, the activity of the Spirit, the soul, who is one and the same in body and head, and the fulness of Christ filling the church.

The final section on the church 'at the same time visible and spiritual' sets out to show that Christ's church can be found here on earth in the Roman Catholic Church, albeit not yet in its final glorious state and not without ambiguities. The section proceeds by stating first that Christ has established his church, the community of faith, hope and love, as a visible structure. The society furnished with hierarchical organs, the visible gathering, the terrestrial church on the one hand and the mystical body, the spiritual community and the church endowed with heavenly gifts on the other hand, are not two different things but one complex reality. This is explained by means of the analogy with the incarnation. Then it is remarked that the church is one. Christ gave it to Peter to tend and to him and the other apostles to govern. This church constituted and organized as a society 'subsists' in the Roman Catholic Church, although outside this church elements of church can be found. The rest of the section is concerned with the ambiguity, by developing the theme of poverty and sinfulness and by ending with expressing the conviction that by the power of the risen Lord the church will be able to pursue its pilgrimage till the mystery of Christ is revealed at the end of time.

Chapter 2, 'The People of God', starts with a section on the New Covenant and the new people using material which previously appeared in the first sections of the first chapter. The following three sections give an exposition of participation by the people of God in the threefold function of Christ, although the full exposition of the participation in the kingship takes place in the next two chapters. In this chapter participation in the priesthood, i.e., the common priesthood of all the faithful and the ministerial priesthood, and participation in the prophetic function, i.e., the *sensus fidei*, and the charismas are outlined. After a section on the catholicity or universality of the church three sections are dedicated to membership and the relations to other Christians and to non-Christians. The final section discusses the missionary task of the church. Of these sections the first one is important for the present discussion, since it contains an outline of how the church is seen and reveals how 'people of God' is used.

The first section can be divided into three parts. First,

the realization of God's wish not to save men and women individually but gathered in a people is pointed out in the history of salvation. He has chosen Israel and made his covenant with it. It was a preparation for the new covenant that would include all men. This new covenant was instituted by Christ who called together a new people of God. Those who believe in Christ form, reborn not from flesh but from water and the Spirit, 'a chosen race, a royal priesthood, a holy nation, a purchased people' (1 Pet 2:9). Secondly, the special character of this messianic people is outlined in the following points: its head is Christ, its status the freedom of the children of God, its law love, and its goal the kingdom of God. Thirdly, this new Israel is called the church of Christ as Israel in the desert was called the church of God. Christ acquired it with his blood, filled it with his Spirit and equipped it with visible and social means of unity. God has called together those who believe in Christ as the source of unity and peace and made them into the church so that it is the visible sacrament of that redemptive unity.

Compared with the versions of the second schema, the final text represents an improvement in several respects. Inconsistencies have been removed between the trinitarian structure of the history of salvation, the eschatological elements and the elements of church outside the church on the one hand, and the underdeveloped link between the Spirit and the church, the division of the history of salvation into two phases and the identification of the one, holy, catholic and apostolic church with the Roman Catholic Church on the other hand. With these elements connected the result is a much more coherent view. The role of the Spirit is not limited to an internal principle in the heart of the individual believer, but is connected with the history of the church, for he is sent on Pentecost and he is connected with the whole of the church, since he distributes charismas and hierarchical gifts. The history of salvation as sketched in this text does justice to that role of the Spirit by acknowledging the difference between constitution, manifestation and fulfilment of the church. It also includes the eschatological elements. The eschatological nature of the church is developed by relating the church to the kingdom of God as germ and beginning of that kingdom. This in turn leads to the replacement of the identification by the phrase 'subsists in' and to the recognition not just of possible elements of church, but of actual elements of church, outside the Roman Catholic Church.

With regard to the biblical images, it is clear that the trend of the three versions of the second schema, namely, to pay more attention to these images, is continued and carried further: a great number of images is mentioned, and in a systematic way. The treatment of 'mystical body of Christ' is better structured. Although in the final version of the second schema and in the final text the external and the internal elements are discussed, the way they are discussed differs. While in the second schema the threefold function of Christ was introduced and related to the hierarchy, and while the church was said to represent Christ the heavenly head on earth, these references have disappeared; a relation of subordination, though, between the different gifts and functions is still present. This leads again to some tension when in the final section 'mystical body' is contrasted with the hierarchical society in order to say that they are not two different things. Here the relation is not formulated by saying that they are the same but by stating that they form one complex reality. This formulation presupposes, even more than in the previous versions, that 'mystical body of Christ' is understood as referring to the spiritual aspect only. This occurrence of 'mystical body' in the final section shows that 'mystical body' still occupies a central place. The expansion of the section on the other images does not imply that 'mystical body' has become less important. On the contrary, the role and place of 'mystical body' have been strengthened by the reversal of the sections. The change was undertaken with the argument that 'mystical body of Christ' is more than an image and that in a more profound way it leads into the mystery of the church.[4]

But before a definitive conclusion can be reached with regard to which image is central in the final text, the relation between the first and the second chapter has to be clarified. The disappearance of 'people of God' from the first chapter does not necessarily mean that it has lost all influence. The reasons which led the committee to write a new chapter and to place it between the chapter on the mystery of the church and that on the hierarchy can be found in a commentary attached to the text in which decisions and changes are explained.[5] There are two fundamental considerations: 'people of God' is understood to include pastors and faithful, and an exposition of the church as the people of God concerns the very nature and mystery of the church. To maintain the original order – first mystery, then hierarchy, then 'people of God' – would mean to destroy the unity in the treatment of the mystery of the church. The new order facilitates, moreover, the discussion of the role and place of hierarchy and laity within the whole and the discussion of other issues as well. So, chapters 1 and 2 form a unity. The argument for dividing the material over two chapters is a practical one, for to treat everything in one chapter would have made that chapter too long.[6] The division is not arbitrary, though: the exposition of the nature and the mystery of the church is so structured that in the first chapter the church is presented in all its amplitude, from the beginning of creation till completion at the end of time in heaven, while in the second the church-in-the-meantime, i.e., the church between the ascension of the Lord and his glorious return, is treated.[7]

But this last argument about the relation between chapters 1 and 2 is not convincing and raises questions about the precise meaning of 'people of God'. First of all, one cannot maintain that the first chapter presents only the church in its amplitude and that it does not discuss the church-in-the-meantime without doing injustice to the content and the concern. The church as germ and beginning of the kingdom of Jesus and God, the hierarchical gifts of the Spirit, Pentecost as the date on which the Spirit was sent, the organizational elements in the section on the mystical body, the concern not only to establish the church as an organization but also to relate the church to the Roman Catholic Church – these are all elements which become unintelligible if the chapter is not dealing with the church-in-the-meantime as well. Moreover, one would not expect terms like 'body', 'incorporation', etc to occur in the second chapter nor in the other chapters dealing with the church-in-the-meantime. But these terms are used. In the sections on Catholics, on other Christians and on non-Christians 'incorporation' is introduced, while 'members' and 'mystical body' are retained in other chapters.[8]

Remarkable in this context is Chapter 7, the new chapter on the eschatological nature of the pilgrim church. The first draft, which is part of the first version of the third schema, is mainly concerned with the connection between the church on earth and the church in heaven; in it, 'people of God' does not appear, while 'mystical body' plays an important role. In the final version, 'people of God' is mentioned once in a minor place, while 'mystical body' is still used several times.[9] The possible argument that 'mystical body' captures the whole church and is therefore apt in this context does not explain all occurrences of that term and does certainly not explain the absence of 'people of God' in this chapter on the eschatological character of the pilgrim church. The division as indicated in the note does also cause some problems with regard to the understanding of 'people of God'. If it is true that 'people of God' is only used to describe the church-in-the-meantime the term loses much of its biblical meaning; it is no longer used to refer to the continuity with Israel and no longer locates the church in the whole of the history of salvation.[10] Strictly speaking, the ascension of Christ would be the beginning of the people of God, which is in fact the way 'people of God' is used in the first schema. The link between the new approach and the change of terms would be questioned as well. If 'people of God' is used in its full biblical sense and if the first section of the second section, in which an outline of the history of salvation is given, is taken seriously, the division cannot be maintained. The remaining argument that can answer the question why 'people of God' is not used in the first chapter is a pragmatic one: the chapter would become too long. This seems neither a strong argument for such an important decision nor a completely correct one. One could argue that if the exposition of the church as the people of God had been integrated in the first chapter, repetitions could have been avoided in the two chapters and a much more unified picture could have been presented. In the end this integrated chapter would not have been much longer than the one on the hierarchy.

'People of God' is clearly an important term in the constitution on the church, but given the influence of 'mystical body' in the first chapter (and in the rest of the schema) and given this unsatisfactory answer to the question about the relation between the first and second chapters, one cannot maintain that 'people of God' has replaced 'mystical body of Christ' as the central term. The answer to the question: 'Which is the central term?', must therefore be: there are two terms that occupy a central place, 'mystical body of Christ' and 'people of God', and their relation is not decisively indicated in the text.[11]

This conclusion is not surprising if one sees the final text against the background of its history and genesis, both textual and non-textual, and if one acknowledges that the text is that kind of compromise which does not resolve all the tensions. This may be more obvious in the chapters on the bishops and in what happened in connection with the *nota praevia*, or in the chapter on the Virgin, but even in the first chapter this compromise character can be seen as shown earlier. The clearest example is the last section in the first chapter: the *societas* concept of the church and the *Christus-prolongatus* view, so prominent in preconciliar ecclesiology and in the first schema, are still present when the mystical body and the hierarchical organization are said to be one complex reality, and when an analogy is drawn between this complex reality and the mystery of the incarnation.[12] Nor is this conclusion surprising when one recognizes that the final text does not coherently present or thoroughly develop the new ideas and insights which were introduced in an ambivalent way by the first version of the second schema. The possibility of opposing interpretations and the ambiguity of structure of the final text, both on the level of the overall organization of the material and on the lower level of the sections, are signs of an unfinished process. The question of the nature of the church, for example, is again discussed in the chapter on the eschatological nature of the church, and the full impact of the eschatological perspective for the understanding of the history of salvation is not realized, for this history is still depicted as a process of continuous and organic growth without enough attention to moments of failure or even complete failure. This means that moments and possibilities of disobedience are not taken into account for the understanding of 'people of God'. And this view of history also influences the way in which the relation is seen between the church and the kingdom of God.[13]

Despite these shortcomings, *Lumen Gentium* has created a situation in which the development of a truly theological treatment of the church becomes possible. Although previously several attempts were made to realize such a theological treatment, the tendency to treat the church in a narrow apologetic way remained prevalent in official magisterial pronouncements. *Lumen Gentium* is the first magisterial document that, at least in the sections on the nature of the church, in principle breaks through the limitations of that mainly juridical and organizational view. The question now is whether theologians have taken advantage of this new situation and have stabilized this breakthrough by developing an ecclesiology, i.e., a truly theological treatment of the church. And since, in the development of any theory, a crucial element is the place and the role of the central term, and since too *Lumen Gentium* does not clearly propose such a term, the fundamental problem is what term theologians choose and with what kind of reasons when they reflect on the church in the light of *Lumen Gentium*.

2. *The theologians*

In the ecclesiological debates immediately before, during, and after the Second Vatican Council the methodological question which term should be taken as central had not yet assumed the most important role: issues like membership, collegiality, infallibility, and ecumenism received much more attention. But a number of theologians discussed this question, and in the discussion three types of answer were given: a majority argued for a combination of 'people of God' and 'mystical body of Christ', some for 'people of God', and others for the selection of a different term altogether.[1] The arguments they gave for these positions can be classified in three groups: arguments from content, arguments from the linguistic status of the term, and arguments on practical grounds. This last type of argument will not be treated separately in the following analysis, but will be included in the discussion of the other two types.

The analysis of the arguments from content will attempt to show that the arguments put forward by the theologians either in defence of the synthesis-view or in support of the view that 'people of God' on its own should be the central term, exhibit internal tensions or are incorrect, not so much on the basis of a detailed exegesis of the relevant passages from Scripture, but on the basis of very general considerations and presuppositions. The analysis of the arguments concerning the linguistic status of the terms will attempt to locate the underlying presuppositions about the nature and role of metaphor. These presuppositions will be seen to influence decisively final judgements about the solution to the problem of the central term.

2.1 *The arguments from content*

2.1.1 *The synthesis-view*

Of the theologians arguing for a synthesis between 'people of God' and 'body of Christ' several – namely, Congar, Schmaus, Philips, Ratzinger, and Küng – were involved in an official way with the work of the council. The general structure of the argument they put forward in favour of a synthesis is as follows: the analysis of the notions 'people of God' and 'mystical body of Christ' reveals that both have advantages and disadvantages when applied to the church, but by using these notions as complementary the advantages are kept while the disadvantages disappear. This procedure is necessary since the disadvantages attached to each makes an exclusive use of either term impossible. Congar's article on the church as people of God, written not long after the promulgation of the text of *Lumen Gentium*, forms a good example of this kind of argumentation, and since it contains those elements mentioned by most theologians and has influenced the position of other theologians it can serve well as the frame for our analysis.[1]

Congar's article is a kind of assessment of *Lumen Gentium*. In his opinion not all the intentions that led the committee to insert a new chapter on the people of God were fully realized in the final text, and not all the implications of the rediscovery of the biblical concept of people of God were integrated. He lists the following five points in order to show how important and useful the biblical concept of people of God is in talking about the church. First, by indicating the continuity between Israel and the church, 'people of God' locates the church in God's plan of salvation and in the history of salvation. The ideas closely related to this notion thus become available for the reflection on the church: the ideas of election, of service, of calling, of covenant, of promises and eschatology, the idea of a people belonging to God, i.e., called into existence to serve and praise the Lord, the idea of a messianic people that is the bearer of hope. By placing the church in the history of salvation a dynamic element is introduced, for it is a people on the way to the aim set by God. Moreover, from this perspective a correct approach to consideration of the relation of the church to the Jewish people is possible. Schmaus, too, sees it as one of the main advantages that the continuity in the history of salvation is expressed, and that central notions such as God's initiative in the constitution of his people can be used. Küng mentions these central ideas, with an emphasis on God's call as the decisive initiative for man's salvation: the church is neither a free association, nor does it come forth from the individual, nor does it have its origin simply in the common will. Küng also develops the relation to the Jewish people from this perspective. Beumer thinks it understandable that people want to introduce salvation-historical and eschatological elements into ecclesiology and thinks that 'people of God' elucidates that aspect of the history of salvation. McNamara remarks that the insights provided by 'people of God' prevent future interpretations of 'mystical body of Christ' in a salvation-biological way, and Harvey sees the connection with the history of salvation as one of the reasons for the growing importance and popularity of 'people of God'.[2]

Secondly, according to Congar the use of 'people of God' emphasizes that the church consists of people who respond to a call. Biblical figures like Abraham or Mary who respond to God's call can be seen as a type of the church. Although the view which presents the church only as a mediating structure over and against people is correct in a certain way, it is adjusted by this emphasis. Schmaus, Ratzinger, and McNamara articulate this point in terms of 'responsibility' and 'individuality': the church as people of God underlines the fact that those who belong to it are independent persons who do not lose their identity and creativity. Like Congar, Küng mentions the importance of the human decision to answer God's call, and he too points to Mary and Abraham as types of the church, but, unlike Congar, he does not want to leave any room for a supra-personal mediating institution. Schmaus maintains that 'people of God' indicates that the church is not just the sum of those who belong to it, but that it is a supra-personal entity.[3]

Thirdly, because 'people of God' connotes a people on the way towards the Kingdom, elements of failure and sin as well as the need of constant reform are introduced. The church as an institution does not, according to Congar, need to repent, but the people do. For Küng this connotation makes it impossible to idealize the church in any way: the church is not perfect but in constant need of reform. Harvey notes as one of the advantages of 'people of God' over 'mystical body of Christ' that 'people of God' enables one to mention both the holiness and the sinfulness of the church, which is an essential requirement for a true theological definition of the church.[4]

Fourthly, 'people of God' can express both the equality of believers as far as their Christian existence is concerned, and their inequality as far as function and organization is concerned. This point of equality is also mentioned by Ratzinger, Küng, and Schmaus. Congar mentions the equality on a par with the inequality, while Schmaus thinks that 'people of God' indicates some order, but not the hierarchical order instituted by Christ; Küng acknowledges some differences but regards these as secondary compared with the fundamental equality. McNamara notes as one of the first results of using 'people of God' for the church that it leads to an ecclesiology in which the visibility and the structures have a place.[5]

Fifthly, since 'people' often refers to the local community in liturgical and patristic texts, Congar thinks 'people of God' can also be used for the discussion of the relationship between the local churches and the universal church. Congar mentions this point in the context of 'people of God', while Küng, McNamara, and Ratzinger discuss these issues with the help of 'body of Christ'.[6]

In addition to these points concerned with content, some theologians notice that 'people of God' facilitates ecumenical dialogue, for it is a term known to Protestant theologians (so Beumer, Congar and Harvey) or see good possibilities for catechesis and pastoral work (so Congar). Schmaus thinks 'people of God' important because it corresponds well to the values so highly esteemed in our present democratic culture, while Ratzinger argues that an easy assimilation to democracy, as occurs in the discussion about democracy in the church, overlooks the spiritual transpositions and the difference between 'people of God' and 'people'.[7]

As has become clear, not all the theologians who defend the synthesis view recognize the same advantages in 'people of God' or draw the same consequences from these points. The advantages imply partly disadvantages on the side of 'mystical body of Christ'. But not all agree on these points either. Some remark that notions like history of salvation and eschatology do not belong to 'body of Christ' (Schmaus, cf. McNamara), but Beumer asks whether the historical and eschatological elements are not already present in 'body of Christ' via the idea of 'salvation-collectivism'.[8] Some remark that 'body of Christ' suggests the loss of personal identity, suggests that people are cells in an organism (McNamara, Schmaus, Beumer), but Congar adds to this point – that it is 'people of God' which most clearly expresses the people's response – that 'body of Christ' is equally well capable of accommodating these values. He adds also that 'body of Christ' expresses equally well the basic equality of the members and the functional and organizational differences. Schmaus sees here a difference of degree, since 'people of God' expresses this element best.[9]

Apart from the positive points in the notion 'people of God', all theologians mention elements which they think crucial to the understanding of the church but which in their opinion are lacking in that notion. Because of this deficiency, the argument runs, 'people of God' on its own cannot serve as a description or definition of the church. Congar mentions three major shortcomings, which are all related to the fundamental difference between Israel and the church.

First, Jesus is not just the Messiah but the incarnate son of God. Congar's central theme in the development of this point is that of heir and heritage. Only by becoming incorporate in Christ can we become co-heirs to the heavenly and eschatological possessions. The minor theme is that of God's promise to dwell among his people now realized, for he dwells in Jesus' sacrificed and resurrected body and in the community.

Secondly, while under the old dispensation the Holy Spirit was only revealed as a power active in certain persons at a certain time, under the new dispensation the Spirit is revealed as a person and as constantly present in the whole church: he is given to the whole church as the principle of life, he is the soul of the church-body. Sent on Pentecost, the Spirit is a gift to the apostles personally and to the church as far as it is not just the people of God, but the body of Christ.

Thirdly, while the people of the old covenant formed one people in the sense of an ethnic and social unity, the people of God of the new covenant form a spiritual unity constituted by faith and consisting of many peoples that keep their own cultures and identities. They form the *tertium genus*, the *corpus Christianorum*, a *corporatio sui juris*. This all leads Congar to the conclusion that under the new dispensation the people of God receive a status that can only be described adequately in categories of the theology of the body of Christ.[10] Similar points are mentioned by other theologians, but again with differences. According to Ratzinger, 'body of Christ' indicates the *differentia specifica* by which the people of God of the New Testament is distinguished from that of the Old Testament and all other peoples: the church is the people of God that lives from the body of Christ and becomes the body of Christ. This means that the notion 'people' receives a different meaning: its principle of unity is no longer blood but faith and baptism, its existence is no longer aimed at self-preservation, but at service.[11] Schmaus sees the differences in the arrival of the Messiah and in the fulfilment of the promises, although complete fulfilment has to wait till Christ returns. Schmaus differs here from Congar, who says it is not enough to see Jesus as the Messiah. The people of God of the New Testament distinguishes itself from that of the Old by its fraternal unity founded in Christ and in the intimate relationship with Christ, who is the way to the Father. This intimate relationship can only be expressed by 'body of Christ'. The church is the people of God because it is, and as far as it is, the body of Christ — this is the formulation Schmaus uses. It has consequences for the understanding of 'people', for ties of blood are no longer decisive, as only faith and baptism are important. This spiritual people consisting of many peoples should not be connected or contrasted with 'people' in its ordinary sense, but only with the people of God of the old covenant.[12]

Philips remarks, like Schmaus, that 'people', although referring to a structured whole, is not an adequate term for expressing the intimate character of the real community under the new dispensation: this community must be called 'body of Christ'.[13] But Küng thinks that 'people of God' and 'body of Christ' express both the unity of Christians among each other and their unity with Christ; at the same time he maintains that 'the concept "body of Christ" describes very fittingly the new and unique nature of this new people of God'.[14] McNamara writes that the new spiritual existence of Christians is realized by their incorporation into Christ; by entering into the body of Christ Christians become the people of God. But, unlike Congar, he does not think that the articulation of the role of the Holy Spirit calls for 'body of Christ'; on the contrary, he thinks that the role of the Spirit within the notion 'people of God' has been deepened and made more dynamic compared with the theory of the Spirit as the soul of the body.[15] Beumer qualifies it as a decisive disadvantage for 'people of God' that it leaves out an essential characteristic of the church as it exists – namely, its relation to Christ — and that the term itself does not mention Christ's name. He thinks, moreover, that the eschatological element is not clearly indicated in 'people of God', but that it is not obvious in 'mystical body of Christ' either.[16] Harvey, who quotes Beumer, apparently does not think that the meaning of 'people of God' changes, for he maintains that the people of God of the Old Testament and that of the New Testament are the same people.[17]

Of the theologians mentioned, Philips, Schmaus, and Congar discuss the issue of the central term with explicit reference to the text of *Lumen Gentium*. Philips states that the suggestion made by some commentators that 'people of God' replaces 'body of Christ' as the central term in the constitution is incorrect, and supports his interpretation – the synthesis view – with an appeal to Congar's article. But for Congar and Schmaus, the issue does not arise out of the history of *Lumen Gentium* or out of the inconsistencies between the two streams present in the text: they defend the synthesis view on grounds of principle. Congar criticizes *Lumen Gentium* for not utilizing the biblical notion fully, but his arguments show that even if this had been done, the most important points would still have been missing.

Schmaus starts from the difference in central term between *Mystici Corporis* and *Lumen Gentium*. He assumes that 'people of God' functions as the leading image of Vatican II. *Lumen Gentium* devotes a whole chapter to 'people of God' while 'body of Christ' is only an image among other images, albeit an important one. This leads to a conflict with, and at first sight a repudiation of, *Mystici Corporis*, which contains the solemn declaration that 'to describe and to define the church of Christ . . . there is no name more noble, none more excellent, none more divine than "the mystical body of Jesus Christ".'[18] On the basis of the synthesis in which 'people of God' is the wider notion which embraces 'body of Christ' and in which 'body of Christ' is the concept which presents the content, Schmaus concludes that there is no question of a repudiation since 'body of Christ' is still the most profound explanation of the church. To this he adds that 'body of Christ' is subordinate to 'people of God' as the Son is subordinate to the Father.[19] Given this argument it is clear that Schmaus too defends the synthesis view on grounds of principle.

It is not surprising to find both Congar and Schmaus defending this synthesis before the council.[20] This aspect reveals an important point for the evaluation: the synthesis view is not to be evaluated in the light of the analysis of *Lumen Gentium* alone, but also in the light of the arguments for a necessary complementarity of 'people of God' with 'body of Christ' – or, as Beumer puts it, for the necessary occurrence of 'body of Christ' in the description of the church.[21] If this last point could be established, it would carry much weight in support of the claim that this synthesis is the only possible way of resolving the problems discovered in the analysis of *Lumen Gentium*. If not, the synthesis view would lose much of its appeal. How convincing are the arguments for a necessary complementarity?

The basic presupposition in this type of argument is that 'people of God' remains basically an Old Testament notion. But this presupposition is brought into question by the occurrence of 'people of God' as a fundamental concept in the

New Testament. Or, as Keller remarks: 'It remains obscure why the church of the New Testament should have selected a description of its nature which only secured its relationship to past history without at the same time including the demarcation and the newness'. And he adds that 'body of Christ' cannot fulfil this function since it is not the concept of the church of the New Testament: it is used only by Paul, and Paul uses other concepts as well.[22] This general point of criticism can be used against Congar's line of argument, for he mentions some of the ideas related to 'people of God' but not the concept itself in its New Testament setting. Another point of criticism can be raised as well: he prejudges the issue by his formulations, for the introduction of 'body of Christ' in his formulations of the shortcomings is not necessary or even obvious. The theme of heir and heritage is a central connotation of 'people of God', as Congar acknowledges, and the transposition in the understanding of heritage and heir, apparent in the New Testament, is also present in the Old Testament, as Congar admits.[23] So there is no need to appeal to another notion. And even if this change is so fundamental that 'people of God' cannot be used any longer, it is not clear why 'family of God', another related concept, could not have been emphasized, or why this change could not have been marked by the addition of 'new' or 'true'. 'Adoption' does not necessarily suggest 'incorporation', and these two concepts cannot be connected that easily either.

The theme of God dwelling among his people is not exclusively related to the notion of 'the body of Christ', as Congar himself indicates: God dwells among Christians, who through the action of the Spirit form the temple of God.[24] Congar does not appeal to Scripture for calling the Holy Spirit the soul of the church-body, but to Augustine and *Mystici Corporis*. The quotation from Joel in Acts shows, though, that the sending of the Spirit can be articulated in a different way as well. Even the emphasis on the group as distinct from individuals, which Congar thinks important, can be expressed by 'people of God'.[25] The final argument about this new spiritual people appeals also to non-scriptural sources. Apart from not developing the qualification *tertium genus,* which indicates a third kind of people next to the Jews and the

Gentiles, the use of *corpus* and *corporatio* assumes a straight line between the religious and the legal or juridical use of *corpus* which is far from obvious.[26] Moreover, if the people of God is called into existence by God and consists of those who respond to his call, faith seems to be a central feature, with the consequence that the people of Israel and the people of God do not automatically coincide. But if faith is from the beginning a central feature of the people of God, the insistence upon the difference between the people of God of the Old Testament and that of the New Testament in terms of blood *versus* faith is incorrect.[27] Finally, if Congar's argument about the spiritual character of this new people is taken seriously, one of the positive points mentioned by him no longer seems to apply – the point, namely, that 'people' implies organization, functions, and structures.[28]

Related to Congar's final argument is Schmaus' emphasis on the correct way of understanding 'people of God' if used for the church. By insisting that 'people of God' should not be contrasted and compared with 'people' in its ordinary sense, but with the people of God of the Old Testament, Schmaus makes the complement of 'body of Christ' superfluous. It is enough to specify the role of Jesus. Schmaus does this by calling him the Messiah, which does not necessarily call for 'body of Christ', and by calling him the way to the Father, which does not call for 'body of Christ' either, as Schmaus himself reveals when he writes that on this way the people of God becomes and remains the people of God.[29] As in the case of Congar, this way of fixing the meaning of 'people of God' undermines the positive evaluation of 'people of God' in the light of present democratic culture. Schmaus also presents his synthesis as the solution to the discrepancy between the choice of the central term in *Mystici Corporis* and the choice of the central term in *Lumen Gentium*; but this solution cannot be accepted as a real one, and the reason for this negative judgement is not just the previous argument. Schmaus proceeds by arguing that *Mystici Corporis* and *Lumen Gentium* are complementary on this point, since 'body of Christ' and 'people of God' are complementary in Paul's writings, but such a procedure yields results only if the understanding of these terms is the same in all cases. Schmaus's own outline of Paul's understanding of 'body of Christ' contains two elements: the relationship to Christ and the relationship of the members to each other, to which Schmaus adds that the basic equality of all members is implied and that no hierarchical order is entailed. But this outline is not the same as the understanding of 'mystical body of Christ' in *Mystici Corporis*.[30] Moreover, the statement that 'body of Christ' expresses the most profound explanation, which is the basis for saving the pronouncement in *Mystici Corporis*, is contradicted by Schmaus' other statement that 'body of Christ' is subordinate to 'people of God' as Christ is subordinate to the Father. If Christ is not the aim, but, as Schmaus puts it, the pilgrim pointing to the Father, 'body of Christ' can in no ordinary sense of 'profound' be the most profound explanation of the church.[31] Ratzinger qualifies 'body of Christ' as the *differentia specifica* indicating the fundamentally different way the new people of God is a people and by which it is distinguished from the way other peoples, including Israel, are people.[32] But if the difference is so fundamental it raises the question whether *differentia specifica* is a qualification that should be used, since it presupposes the same genus: people. Moreover, Ratzinger defines this difference in terms of a cultic community (the people become people in the cult) and in terms of ties of faith and service. But all these aspects are basic to the Old Testament concept of people of God. Here, too, there is no need to introduce 'body of Christ' as a necessary complement. Küng, who regards 'people of God' as fundamental and all the other notions as secondary, faces the problem of clarifying why and how a fundamental concept has to be complemented by a secondary one. An additional problem is that Küng also raises baptism and eucharist – the two aspects of the church which he uses to introduce 'body of Christ', and which apparently are to be taken as the basis of the necessary complementarity – in the context of his discussion of 'people of God'.[33]

This leads to the conclusions that, on the basis of the presuppositions of the theologians and on the basis of very general data, the synthesis view does not appear to be coherent, and that there is no decisive argument in favour of the thesis that 'people of God' necessarily has to be complemented by 'body of Christ'. Since the analysis in the previous section has shown that *Lumen Gentium* does not integrate the notions 'people of God' and 'body of Christ' but leaves them juxtaposed in an uncertain and far from clear relationship, the synthesis view cannot be said to be a correct interpretation of *Lumen Gentium*. And, given the conclusion that 'people of God' is not necessarily to be complemented, the usefulness of the synthesis view in the further development of the insights of *Lumen Gentium* towards an ecclesiology is highly questionable.

2.1.2 *'People of God' as the central term*

Koster's best known and debated contribution to the field of ecclesiology, 'Ekklesiologie im Werden', dates from 1940. Given his attack on the mystical-body theology of that period and his own plea in favour of 'people of God', it is not surprising to find him during the council period arguing again that the council should take 'people of God' as its leading image.[1] Such a leading image needs to be one that captures the whole of the church as intended by Christ, and needs therefore to be based upon Scripture and upon New Testament cult. The church can have only one leading image of this kind, since more than one overall leading image results in a contradiction. This means that 'body of Christ' and 'people of God' cannot at the same time function as such an image. Koster therefore rejects the attempts to synthesize the two. He argues for 'people of God' as the leading image on the following ground: in the New Testament the total image of the church is expressed by means of three terms, *ekklesia*, *laos theou*, and *soma Christou*. These terms have the same meaning and content, which is not so difficult to show in the cases of *ekklesia* and *laos theou*, and, *ekklesia* and *soma Christou*. The problem is whether *laos theou* and *soma Christou*, 'people of God' and 'body of Christ', express the same leading image. Many theologians give a negative answer, but, according to Koster, these two terms express the same image. He gives two main arguments in support of his positive answer. First, in the letter to the Ephesians, 'body' is used for the unity of the church consisting of Jews and Gentiles, while in Romans 'people' is used with the same reference (Rom 9–11) and the phrase 'you are all one in Christ Jesus' (Gal 3:28) can only refer to 'people'. The second argument is that the Greek *soma Christou* is the material translation of the Hebrew *goi Elohim*.

Koster holds this on the following grounds: Paul could not use 'people of God' for his missionary activities, and therefore chose 'body of Christ'. Although there is no direct link between *laos theou* and *soma Christou*, there is such a link between *goi Elohim* and *soma Christou*. *Goi* cannot be connected with JHWH or *soma* with *theou*. Moreover, *soma* and *goi* do not conceive of people as an undifferentiated mass of men, but of people as men with the same origin, and both express the idea that men belong to their origin.[2] This explanation leads Koster to say that those who maintain that the relationship to Christ is lacking in 'people of God' are mistaken, for the relationship to Christ does not fundamentally change the structure and essence of the church as the congregation of Christ's and God's men and women, i.e., as the people of God. 'You are Christ's and Christ is God's' (1 Cor 3:23) indicates that the church belongs to Christ and that Christ belongs to the Father. 'Body of Christ' underlines only that the church is the people of God. Koster finds a similar remark in *Mystici Corporis* where 'mystical body of Christ' is called a transferral expression (metaphor), implying – although not explicitly saying – that it refers to the people of God and of Christ.[3] Having established 'people of God' as the leading image, Koster proceeds to develop it in three steps: first, he mentions the order that can be discerned in the people of God right from the beginning, and via two analyses of 'bride of Christ' and 'family of God' the elements of service to God and to the world and of leadership are introduced. His conclusion is the following description of the church: the church is the faithful and sacramental people of God and of Christ which as maid-servant serves God and men each in a different way, and which is guided internally by the Holy Spirit and externally by the Pope and, with and under him, by the bishops as Christ's vicars.[4]

These arguments in favour of 'people of God' as the central term or leading image are not convincing, since they contain some basic mistakes and show some puzzling features. In his argument that the term 'body of Christ' is the material translation of 'people of God', Koster refers to the Hebrew *goi Elohim,* but this combination does not occur in the Old Testament, which means that his first argument *(goi* is not connected with JHWH and *soma* cannot be connected with *theou)* fails even on its premises. The two terms used to refer to the people of Israel are *am* and *goi*, and although it is impossible to treat them as two completely separate concepts each has different connotations. *Goi* carries connotations of race, government, and territory, though the relationship to God and to origins are not entirely absent. These last aspects are more prominent in *am*, however, which connotes primarily family relationships, internal relationships (help), and the relationship to God.[5] Given this distinction, the choice of *goi* in the other arguments is not an obvious one. Moreover, in the argument about origins Koster changes from the concept of 'people of God' to that of 'the people of Abraham', but in terms of the type of origin, 'people of God' and 'people of Christ' are closer than 'people of Abraham' and 'people of Christ'. In the third argument he changes back to 'people of God', but *goi* does not express service to its origin.

Apart from these mistakes with regard to general biblical data Koster makes the strange claims that 'body' means simply 'people' and that 'body of . . .' refers to the origin of the body.[6] As a whole this argument is puzzling, since Koster starts it after saying that there does not exist a direct material relation between *soma Christou* and *laos theou*. But *laos theou* is the translation of the Hebrew *Am JHWH*, people of God. It is therefore far from clear why there should exist a material relation between the two in the one case and not in the other.[7] Another puzzling feature is that the attempt to show that 'body of Christ' and 'people of Christ' mean the same undermines the whole argument that 'people of God', and precisely this term, should be the leading image. In Koster's article there are two series of remarks, one about 'people of God' as the leading image expressed in the whole argument which tries to show that 'body of Christ' is the material translation of 'people of God', and the other about the interchangeability of 'body of Christ' and 'people of God', related to remarks that he is not so much concerned with the linguistic expressions of the leading image, although they are relevant, and that either 'people of God' or 'body of Christ' can be chosen for pastoral or ecumenical reasons.[8] The roots of this combination lie in the thesis that the terms *ekklesia*, *laos theou*, and *soma Christou* must have the same meaning and content. If this only means that they refer to the same reality, or, as Koster formulates it, 'the reality of faith that according to God's and Christ's intention exists in the church',[9] this would not lead to any particular problem. It is common that different names or descriptions refer to the same person, place, or event. But it leads to problems if attempts are made to show that since these names and descriptions refer to the same person, place, or event, they mean the same as well. 'The medieval university city on the Isis' and 'the city where Newman preached his university sermons' both refer to Oxford, but are by no means synonymous and do not have the same 'content'.[10] The thesis itself implies a difference between the leading image and the expressions of that image. The fact that Koster selects one of these biblical expressions as the formulation of that leading image, namely 'people of God', conceals the difference, and with it the problem of how to conceive of this difference. Koster also sometimes uses 'the people of God and of Christ' to express this leading image, but this formulation calls into question the link with the Old Testament concept which is presupposed in the arguments.[11]

While Koster wrote his article during the council period, Luneau published his book *Eglise ou troupeau?* several years after the council closed.[12] The thesis he sets out to defend is that the church is not a flock because it is the people of God.[13] When the church uses 'people of God' to describe itself, it implies a return to the purity of its origins, to the early Christian community where more attention was given to the whole and the poor than to privileged groups and the rich. Moreover, it enables the church to make itself understood in the modern world, for in the all-pervading changes in church and society a new awareness breaks through: the people want a greater democracy and participation, the people want to be heard. By using 'people of God' the church appeals to these feelings as well. Luneau supports this thesis via analyses of 'people', 'people of God', and *Lumen Gentium*.[14]

Luneau discerns in the concept 'people' certain constant elements which become clear when 'people' is contrasted with concepts like 'multitude', 'mass', and 'nation'; these elements are: number, awareness of the same values and destination, organization, responsibility, equality, and history – and history is understood here as the history of the unimportant and the oppressed. The word 'people' is thus rich and evocative, but for that very reason imprecise. This explains the appeal and the ambiguity of 'people of God'.[15] Luneau sees three major positive points in the use of 'people of God' for the church. He follows Congar here, but makes some different emphases. First, 'people of God' underlines the human nature of the church. It is God's people since he calls it together, but it is also a 'people' indicating the importance of the collective aspect of the human contribution, i.e., the role of mankind in God's plan and the importance of the response by man. This feature prevents attempts to hypostatize the church and to place it outside the human situation. Secondly, it indicates the historical continuity with Israel: the church is a messianic and pilgrim people. This implies that it is open to failure and sin and that it is not absolutely perfect, although it will never err completely. Thirdly, it gives the first place to the community of faith and baptism, i.e., to the people and not to the hierarchy. This implies a basic equality of brothers, which does not exclude structure, etc., since 'people' connotes also structure and authority.[16]

These elements are highly valued at the present time, since they take into account elements such as personal responsibility, decision, liberty, and equality. The use of 'people of God' for the church therefore has appeal, while 'church' evokes too much a history of mistakes and clerical dominance, and 'body of Christ' remains a strange and obscure term. The Second Vatican Council set out to be a pastoral council and therefore chose 'people of God' and attached great value to it, as is apparent from *Lumen Gentium*.[17] Nevertheless, Luneau observes, *Lumen Gentium* uses 'church' more often than 'people of God'. The reason for this is not just habit: 'people of God' presents Christ's work in its historical and human dimension, while 'church of God' expresses better the mystery of the church.[18] 'People of God' is, moreover, too short and remains ambivalent. It does not specify sufficiently the new features of the New Testament message: hope partly realized instead of mere promises, the role of Jesus, and the crossing of the limits set by territory and race. Basically, 'people of God' remains an Old Testament formula. It is a dangerous term, too, for with its present connotations, 'people of God' can suggest that the church is a democracy in which people decide by majority vote upon laws, structure, etc.; these connotations do not disappear by the addition 'of God'.[19]

Luneau concludes that 'people of God' is not a bad term, but one that leads easily to misunderstanding. It is therefore not the first term and stands in need of correctives, namely 'church' and 'body of Christ'. 'Church' is a term that is preferred by Vatican II and that occurs frequently in Scripture. 'Church', *ekklesia, qahal JHWH* refer to the assembly or congregation called together by God, while 'people' refers to a group formed by its own initiative, but 'church' does not express the importance of Christ. 'Body of Christ', which receives ample attention in the documents of Vatican II, is not a substitute for 'people of God' and 'church', but states what these are: 'body of Christ' gives these other terms a New Testament face. It expresses, moreover, the unity among members and growth – a concept that belongs to 'body'.[20] These reflections lead Luneau to say that, since one image cannot exhaust the reality of the church, one cannot build an ecclesiology upon one image only: one must, like Vatican II and like the Scriptures, use many images. Not all images are equally important: 'people of God' occupies one of the most important places among them. He remarks, too, that since the church must use an intelligible language, the church must at the present time use 'people of God'.[21]

This conclusion and the preceding arguments reveal several tensions. Luneau sets out to establish the thesis that the church is the people of God, and supports this with a major line of argument concerned with the content of 'people of God' and with a minor one concerned with the evocative power of the term 'people' in our contemporary culture. The major line exhibits a declining importance of 'people of God', though. Luneau starts by saying that the church is able to rediscover the purity of its origins if it uses 'people of God' and that *Lumen Gentium* does not see 'people of God' as one image among others but as reality. He continues by saying that the council prefers 'church' because it expresses the mystery better and that 'people of God' is in need of correctives, and he concludes by listing 'people of God' among other images. This drastic change in the course of the argument shows that the initial thesis is not supported by this argument.

Apart from this, the argument contains contradictory remarks which shows that the change is not just a question of a weakening of the argument. The claim of the purity of the origins and the remark that 'people of God' expresses the work of Jesus, in its historical and human dimension cannot be reconciled with the remark that 'people of God' remains an Old Testament concept and that it does not express Jesus's role. And there are further points on which Luneau contradicts himself: to invoke 'church' as a corrective, because 'church' connotes God's initiative in calling together men, while 'people' connotes men's own initiative, involves refuting the earlier positive evaluation of 'people of God'. That Luneau invokes 'church' is especially strange, since it does not specify Jesus's role, as he remarks himself, and since it has the undesirable connotations he mentions. What remains is the other, minor line of argument. But this line is not without ambiguities either, since he cites the current appeal which 'people' has as an argument for using 'people of God', and yet mentions rather fundamental differences between 'people' and 'people of God', which seems to destroy at least part of the power of 'people'. If the positive points Luneau mentions at the beginning are sufficient to turn 'people of God' into a term with appeal, it means that the decisive factors for using 'people of God' as the central term is a practical one.

So, in the end, both Koster and Luneau are left with arguments stressing practical points. The question arises whether this is all that can or need to be said about the central term in ecclesiology.

2.1.3 Another term
Apart from the synthesis view and the thesis that 'people of God' should be the central term, there is a third type of argument that can be found in the literature related to Vatican II and discussing this issue of the central term explicitly. This argument proposes a term different from either 'people of God' or 'body of Christ'. It is not the case that theologians are led to this proposal only by their analysis of 'people of God' and 'mystical body of Christ': their views about the nature of

theology and of theological language also play a role, and a decisive one in certain versions of this argument. Relevant at this point, though, are the remarks made about the content of 'people of God' and of 'body of Christ', and, where they exist, the comments on *Lumen Gentium*. These remarks taken in isolation reveal the presence of important elements of the synthesis view.

Aymans as a canon lawyer is not so much concerned with the inquiry into the relationship between the two 'image-concepts', but is mainly interested in what the council says about the juridical structure of the church when it uses 'people of God' or 'body of Christ'.[1] Nevertheless, remarks about the relationship can be found. Despite the fact that 'people of God' is the leading image, in Aymans' judgement *Lumen Gentium* avoids a one-sided emphasis by using 'people of God' and 'body of Christ' equally often.[2] The relation between the two is not indicated in the text of *Lumen Gentium* but the theologians tend to take 'people of God' as the more encompassing and more general concept.[3] But his main attention is directed to the consequences for juridical structure that are implied in 'body of Christ' and 'people of God'. 'People of God', as used for Israel, has a religious meaning which is not the same as the normal meaning: God constitutes the people by his will and directs them towards his aim. The addition of 'new' indicating the role of Jesus does not change this fundamental perspective. Although the community-character of people does not exclude a juridical structure beforehand, such a structure cannot be deduced from 'people of God' via the rule *ubi societas ibi jus* since the people of God is not just a people. God's lordship, not human power, determines the basic structure of the church. 'People of God' cannot be used as a justification for either the concrete form of the hierarchical structure or a political-democratic structure.[4] 'Mystical body' has profoundly influenced the development and the place of canon law since it was understood juridically. Because of this interpretation, the relationship between the church-body and the eucharistic body was severed, and consequently the relationship between the structure of the church and its sacramental basis. The church, though, does not have an order because it is the mystical body in the juridical sense, i.e., a corporation, but because it celebrates the eucharist. It is in the eucharist that a difference in role emerges, and this is the basis of hierarchical structure.[5] Aymans thinks that *communio* is a concept that is best able to accommodate the central elements of both 'people of God' and 'body of Christ' and to develop the juridical aspects contained in those: it expresses the community-character of 'people of God' and the sacramental character of 'body of Christ' (hierarchy).[6]

A concept similar to Aymans's choice is 'communion', which King prefers above 'sacrament' in restating Paul's synthetic view of the church.[7] In his article on an adequate concept of the church, written during the council period, King sets out to establish an 'antecedent necessity' of such a concept, i.e., 'a synthesis of the juridical and spiritual viewpoints', a synthesis that can be found in Paul's letters.[8] Among the many images Paul uses 'people of God' and 'body of Christ' occupy the most prominent places. 'People of God' expresses the societal, visible aspect: 'This notion of the people of God is without doubt an institutional and juridical one'.[9] The difference between the people of the Old Testament and the people of the New is that the latter has an exclusively religious character and that it is purchased with Christ's blood.[10] 'Body of Christ' expresses the life, the spiritual aspect.[11] In both cases the influence of Paul's realized eschatology is noticeable: the church is, and has to become, the people of God, and the church's life must grow. The identification of these two notions is central to Paul's thinking about the church. 'There is only one reality which is at once visible and spiritual. *Body* thus qualifies, complements *people*'.[12] 'The people of God is not only an identifiable corporeity but also an organism alive with the life of Christ. The body of Christ . . . is not just an individual invisible sharing but one which possesses a corporate aspect'.[13] 'Communion' is the term adequate to restate this synthesis, for it indicates that the church is a 'solidarity' growing out of the common possession of the life in Christ and giving rise to the common activity, the life, of the new people of God.[14]

Unlike King, who rejects it, the concept of 'sacrament' is taken as the central category in the systematic part of the *Mysterium Salutis* volume on the church. It is not the only possible choice, it is claimed, but it is a meaningful and good choice on several grounds: it expresses the same view as *Lumen Gentium*; it is adequate for a salvation-historical approach, for it relates the church to Christ and the eschaton; it links the visible and the invisible elements of the church; it exhibits the salvation-historical relationship between Christ, the sacrament, and the church, the root-sacrament; it shows the church as the salvation of the church; and it connects the biblical images.[15] How this last point is envisaged is made clear by Semmelroth in an article on the unity of the church concept written before the council.[16] In it he argues that the concept 'primordial sacrament' indicates the relation between the inner and the outer aspect of the church; these two aspects are expressed, as in King's vision, by means of 'people of God' and 'body of Christ'.[17] In a later article commenting on *Lumen Gentium*, he remains within this formal frame of a synthesis, but develops 'people of God' in a somewhat different way around two main points: the unity and fundamental equality within the hierarchical church, and the salvation-historical character.[18]

'Communion' or 'mystical communion' again plays a role in the way Dulles understands 'people of God' and 'body of Christ', and in his interpretation of *Lumen Gentium*. With regard to the understanding of 'mystical body of Christ', Dulles notes a difference between *Mystici Corporis* and *Lumen Gentium*, which has, moreover, 'people of God' as its 'principal paradigm'. 'People of God' and 'mystical body of Christ' have many features in common: they are co-extensive. They are both more democratic than 'the church as society or institution' and they both emphasize the relation between believers and the Holy Spirit, the mutual service of the members, and the subordination to the whole.[19] Dulles mentions, apart from these common elements, the strong and weak points of each notion. In the case of 'people of God', the distance between church and Christ, the faithful as responsible persons, and the need of reform are its strong points; while its weak points consist in its failure to express the newness and uniqueness and its presumptuous, egoistical, and monopolistic claims. 'Body of Christ' expresses the uniqueness better, but it can lead to the divinisation of the church; moreover, it is not clear in the modern understanding whether it refers to a communion of grace or to an essentially visible communion.[20] 'In sum, the two models of Body of Christ and People of God both illuminate from different angles the notion of the Church as communion or community. The Church, from this point of view, is not in the first instance an institution or visible organized society. Rather it is a communion of men, primarily interior but also expressed by external bonds of creed, worship and ecclesiastical fellowship'.[21]

As Dulles draws attention to 'communion' as the common background of 'people of God' and 'mystical body of Christ', so Mühlen sets out to show that both are based upon the same idea of the *Gross-Ich*, his translation of 'corporate personality'.[22] The two metaphors both highlight one aspect of the reality of this *'Gross-Ich'*.[23] Mühlen sees a difference between 'people of God' in the Old Testament and in the New Testament. In the Old Testament it contains ethnic, cultural, and similar components and a religious component, while in the New Testament 'people of God' is understood purely in the religious sense: in the New Testament 'people' is thus used analogically. While in the Old Testament the *punctum tertium comparationis* is formed by the *'Gross-Ich'* consisting of biological, historical and religious elements, in the New Testament the coherence of the *'Gross-Ich'* is only determined by faith and grace.[24] In a commentary on the council he notes the difference between *Mystici Corporis* and *Lumen Gentium* and locates the introduction of 'people of God' in the desire to accentuate the salvation-historical dimension of the church. This cannot be done by means of 'body of Christ'.[25] With regard to the section on the mystical body in the first chapter of *Lumen Gentium*, he remarks that this attempts to connect 'people of God' and 'body of Christ': the church is the new people of God in such a way that it exists as body of Christ.[26]

As is the case with the defenders of the synthesis view, these theologians understand 'people of God' and 'body of Christ' in conflicting ways. While Mühlen, Semmelroth, and King understand 'people of God' in institutional and societal terms, Dulles sees a difference between the church as people of God and the church as society and institution, and Aymans does not want to use 'people of God' to justify either a hierarchical or a democratic structure. There are also internal tensions, as, for example, on the one hand the insistence upon the special meaning of 'people of God', and on the other the appeal to 'people' for the structure. (King, Mühlen). The interpretation of 'people of God' makes it either superfluous or results in an interpretation of 'mystical body of Christ' expressing the inner side only. But given the organizational interpretation of 'mystical body of Christ' in *Mystici Corporis*, this limited interpretation is forbidden, as Semmelroth and King acknowledge, with the consequence that 'people of God' understood in the limited sense becomes superfluous. King shows this last point when in his conclusion he does not mention 'people of God', but writes that 'in order to restate the Pauline synthesis in our day, we must first recognize the Church as a complex reality which is at once visible and invisible. We must recognize that the Mystical Body and the Roman Catholic Church are one and the same reality'.[27] This all means that as far as content is concerned there is, on these presuppositions with regard to the understanding of 'people of God' and 'body of Christ', no need for another concept. So, in this type of argument, even if it is not recognized by the theologians, the decisive argument must be the one about the 'linguistic status' of 'body of Christ' and 'people of God'.

2.2 *The linguistic status of the terms*

Most theologians do not explicitly discuss the nature of terms like 'body of Christ' and 'people of God' when applied to the church, do not argue for any qualification but simply call them 'metaphor', 'concept' or something else, and do not develop systematically their ideas about what can and what cannot be done with these terms. They make remarks in passing, and these remarks, taken together, present rather a chaotic picture.

Some see a difference in the status of 'body of Christ' and 'people of God', while others consider them to be of the same kind. Koster, for instance, introduces a sharp distinction between the two: 'body of Christ' is a metaphor and belongs to the pre-theological level, 'people of God' is an imageless material name and belongs to the theological level. In his later article he uses 'leading image' to qualify 'people of God' and 'people of God and of Christ'. This leading image is also expressed in 'people of God' and 'body of Christ', and equally well; these expressions belong presumably to the same pre-theological level.[1] Luneau and Philips also introduce a distinction between the two terms with regard to their linguistic status by saying that 'people of God' is not just an image among other images, or a comparison, but reality. Both use this formulation to capture the difference in treatment that can be found in the text of *Lumen Gentium* between 'field' and 'vine' on the one hand and 'people of God' on the other hand. The church is not strictly speaking a vine or a field, but it is truly the people of God, as Luneau puts it;[2] or, according to Philips, the church is not similar to the people of God, it is the people of God.[3] Philips uses several terms for 'the body of Christ' or 'the mystical body of Christ': allegory, image, figure of speech, comparison or simile, representation. Luneau uses, apart from 'image', neutral terms like 'formula' and 'expression' to qualify 'body of Christ'.[4]

Koster's opposition between the mere metaphor 'body of Christ' and the imageless material name 'people of God' is rejected by Beumer, Ratzinger, and Mühlen. Ratzinger argues that 'people' is used in an analogical sense, as do Congar and Schmaus.[5] Beumer concludes from this analogical use that 'people of God' is a metaphor like 'body of Christ'.[6] Mühlen reports a consensus about the metaphorical character of 'body of Christ' and argues like the other theologians: the original biological, linguistic, and cultural relations characteristic for 'people of God' in the Old Testament are disturbed when 'people of God' is applied to the church. The only important relation is that of faith; 'people' is therefore used analogically, and so 'people of God' is a metaphor when used of the church. Mühlen also calls both terms 'concepts'. Metaphors are contrasted by him with real definitions and essence-descriptions, and also with dogmatic formulae that are formal summaries of what is essential. Such a formula does not contain an image and expresses the mystery as such – expresses the mystery itself directly.[7]

Schmaus, too, sees 'people of God' and 'body of Christ' as one of a kind, but instead of using one qualification, he uses several: image, image-representation, image-concept, concept, leading-image are used for both, while people-concept and body-concept is used for each respectively. 'Body of Christ' and 'people of God' together form the full concept, or the

Scripture-concept.[8] Dulles qualifies both as 'images', 'metaphors', and 'models'. 'People of God' is a metaphor since it is based upon a type of military and political treaty.[9] Semmelroth considers both to have an equal linguistic status (metaphor and image) and also uses 'concept', despite his own misgivings about a conceptual, rational approach and a definition.[10] Aymans calls both 'graphic descriptions' and specifies them further as 'theological images'. Theological images occupy a middle position between pure metaphors or analogies and concepts that identify something directly. What is expressed in an image connects with something in the world, but does not stay on this level of analogical use. The image is transformed to a new level where it names and refers to a new reality: the church is like a people and is like a body, and really is a people and really is a body.[11]

Related to this classification is an evaluation on the point of suitability and adequacy of these terms for theology. Mühlen and Koster both judge that metaphors or images cannot be used on the level of theology. According to Mühlen, an image illuminates one aspect but does not present completely the reality referred to. An image presents something graphically, but that always implies onesidedness, and this has important consequences, especially in the case of the mysteries of faith. The mystery cannot in the end be presented graphically, for more must always remain to be said, precisely because the mystery exceeds all human imagination. An image of such a mystery is only an aid to elucidation by way of analogy – as, for instance, Paul indicates when he first tells about the different gifts of the Spirit and of the one Spirit, and then as an elucidation refers to the many members and the one body (1 Cor 12). The danger of metaphors is that people remain on the level of images, overlook the differences, and forget to pay attention to the *punctum tertium comparationis*.[12] Koster concludes that (German) ecclesiology of that period (1940) still belongs to the pre-theological level. One of the symptoms of this is the use of metaphors, especially that of 'body of Christ', and one of the factors that impede the move towards the truly theological level is the view that theologians should be satisfied with using rhetorical devices that really belong to the level of preaching. Preaching and proclaiming have the aim to please and to persuade, for which purposes metaphors are more apt than abstract concepts. But it is incorrect to think that metaphors should be used in theology as well, that they should be terminal points of reflection, for this presupposes that theology and preaching are the same.[13] Koster argues further that it is impossible to start reflections from images only, for images, despite their greater appeal, mean less than material descriptions: figurative language remains unintelligible without these descriptions.[14]

But Beumer, who does not agree with Koster's distinction between metaphors and material names or essential descriptions, asks whether it is not an unbiblical and untheological distinction, and whether we cannot in fact express the supranatural reality, but necessarily analogically and therefore graphically.[15] Philips also differs from Koster and Mühlen. He remarks that theologians prefer a clear and abstract conceptual language as opposed to the evocative language of the parables and he acknowledges that theology cannot do without concepts. Nevertheless, it is clear that Philips evaluates metaphors higher than concepts. Since concepts do not have evocative power they are not really adequate to express the message of the gospel: this message is concerned with man's relationship with God and with man's life, and has therefore to be articulated in a way that touches people. For this purpose figurative language, although vague and difficult to understand, is more effective than conceptual language. Moreover, concepts are more dangerous, since people are tempted to forget the analogical character of concepts, while in the case of metaphors the contradictions are so obvious that people do not make this fatal mistake. And, apart from this, man reaches the divine domain more easily via material (i.e., metaphorical) language than via the abstract level of concepts. Philips quotes Thomas in support of this positive evaluation of metaphors.[16] And Semmelroth argues that since one cannot capture the essence of the church in one concept or in one image, several are required. The theologian must be aware, moreover, that he cannot understand or express supranatural reality by means of natural concepts.[17] Aymans thinks image-concepts especially apt to refer to the mysterious reality of (for example) the essence of the church.[18] Dulles, also referring to the mystery of the church, maintains that clear, univocal concepts are impossible. This does not mean, though, that we can only be silent about the church, for there are other positive possibilities like models.[19] A definition of the church is, on this line of argument, ruled out, while Koster among others thinks it possible.[20]

In the face of such a variety of qualifications and evaluations, the question arises which one is correct, especially since some contradict others, while certain views appear on reflection to be incoherent. Beumer (cf Congar and Schmaus) implies by his argument that the difference between biblical and theological language is not one of image or metaphor and concept, while Mühlen, Koster, Philips and Aymans stress the difference, especially as one between metaphor and concept; but Philips does not evaluate this difference in the way Mühlen and Koster evaluate it. Some argue (e.g., Semmelroth and Dulles) that to express and to safeguard the mystery a number of metaphors are required, while Mühlen thinks that a concept performs this task better. The issue of definition is related to this: some think the mystery of the church cannot be defined, while others think it is possible, and Mühlen prefers yet another type of description, the theological formula.

The incoherence in (e.g.) Philips's and Luneau's views appear when their qualification of 'people of God' as reality is taken seriously. They use this qualification to explain the difference between 'people of God' and 'body of Christ' in *Lumen Gentium*. In Philips's view this leads to another type of language, which is not conceptual or figurative. For, given his positive evaluation of 'people of God' and his rather negative remarks about theological concepts, it is unlikely that 'people of God' is a concept. But how does this new type of language relate to the other two? Does it express the mystery even better than metaphors do? Does one need only one term like 'people of God'? Given his views, an affirmative answer to the last question seems probable, but that results in a contradiction with the synthesis-view which he also defends. A more subtle sign of incoherence is the wide variety of terms, ranging from metaphor to concept, which are all used indiscriminately. Intuitively, there is a difference between the two extremes, and the use of both for the same term at the same time seems *prima facie* incorrect and in need of explanation. Even the simple juxtaposition of metaphors and similes or comparisons seems to be wrong. And the bewildering appeal to analogy does not improve the confusing situation.[21] Strange word combinations like 'image-concept' reveal a dissatisfaction with both image and concept and suggest, like the incoherences and the contradictions, a fundamental uncertainty about the linguistic status of 'people of God' and 'body of Christ' – about what kind of terms these are and for what use they can be employed – which must have repercussions for the overall argument presented by the theologians.

2.3 Conclusion
The analysis of the reactions of various theologians to *Lumen Gentium* and of the arguments presented by these theologians with regard to the content and status of 'people of God' and 'body of Christ', to the relation between these two notions, and to their usefulness as central terms in ecclesiology or for a definition or description of the church, reveals a number of incorrect, incoherent, and mutually exclusive views on these matters. First, the interpretation of *Lumen Gentium* as having 'people of God' as its leading image or as exhibiting a synthesis between 'people of God' and 'body of Christ' appears to be incorrect in the light of the analyses of the previous section. There it is shown that *Lumen Gentium* does not have *one* leading image and that *Lumen Gentium* does not indicate the relation between 'people of God' and 'body of Christ'. Secondly, among the defenders of the synthesis thesis (see also the other theologians) there are points of difference in the interpretation of both 'people of God' and 'body of Christ' which do not seem to be mere differences in emphasis (equality, the salvation-history dimension, organization and structure) and which suggest that certain interests or theories influence those interpretations.[1] Thirdly, the comments on the linguistic status of 'people of God' and 'body of Christ' show a chaotic disparity. The analysis shows that theologians relate their qualifications to remarks and arguments about the relation or difference between biblical and theological language, about the way the mystery of the church can or should be expressed. Some argue that no definition can be given, but that only a number of

metaphors or models can be used, and that there is no sharp distinction between biblical and theological language, so calling into question the very possibility of theology.

The comments on metaphor reveal a certain view which has been under attack for some time. Over the last fifty years one cannot only discern a growing interest in metaphor, but also the emergence of an approach which differs considerably from the traditional rhetorical metaphor-theory. Remarks like 'metaphors are used to please people', 'metaphors are just aids for elucidation', 'it is only a metaphor' and 'it is not a metaphor but reality', which can be found in the writings of theologians and which reveal shared presuppositions despite their different arguments, are all expressions of this criticized rhetorical view. Because of the link between these remarks and those made about the possibility of a definition of the church, and about the possibility of theology, because the removal of uncertainty about the linguistic status of the central term seems a necessary preliminary to any systematic treatment, and because of the prominent use of metaphors and images in *Lumen Gentium*, a reflection upon metaphors and their possible function in theology is necessary before decisions can be taken as to whether a metaphor, a combination of metaphors, or some other kind of term should be the central term in the development of the insights of Vatican II, and therefore necessary to that development.

Some of the differences in interpretation might be removed by accepting the biblical understanding of 'people of God' and 'body of Christ' as a common point of departure, but such a move would, apart from the questionable presupposition of *the* biblical understanding, still fail to solve the methodological problems. The points concerned with the central term in ecclesiology have to be clarified if the whole enterprise of developing the insights of Vatican II into an ecclesiology is not to be doomed to failure. The arguments of the following chapters aim at such a clarification. The next chapter concentrates upon metaphor and the theory explaining the structure and function of metaphors; the third chapter presents three types of argument about the role of metaphor in theology. The final chapter relates the results to the problems encountered in this first chapter.

Chapter II

Metaphor

This chapter, the first step in solving the problems we have discovered in our analyses of *Lumen Gentium* and of the arguments presented by various theologians, contains the development of a theory of metaphor. After stating the requirements of such a theory, we offer an outline and a further development of central notions and categories. A contrast with other theories and a discussion of two problems form a continuation of the search for appropriate notions in the theory of metaphor. The overall argument is summarized in the final section.

1. *Preliminary remarks*

1.1 *The requirements*
Before a theory of metaphor can be developed, the requirements such a theory must fulfil have to be clear. There are two main points that will direct the formulation of these requirements: first, the theory must explain metaphors; and secondly, the theory must explain metaphors in such a way that the theory can be used to clarify the problems discovered in the previous chapter. This last point means that the theory must deal with two main questions: 'what is the structure or mechanism of a metaphor?' and, 'what is the function of a metaphor?', and that the discussion must focus on the semantic aspects involved in these two questions.[1] This implies some limitations and restrictions: although the theory that will be proposed gives an explanation of the important features of metaphor in general, it neither discusses aesthetic aspects like rhyme, rhythm, and sound which are of importance in the case of poetic metaphor, nor considers the emotional qualities of metaphor. A second

requirement is implied in this first point. A 'semantic' theory of metaphor should not just explain the formal structure of metaphors, but should explain how meaning in metaphors comes about, what the mechanisms are that make metaphors part of communication, and how people are able to understand metaphors that they have not encountered before. Such a theory should also give criteria for distinguishing between metaphors on the one hand and mistakes, nonsense, and falsities on the other hand. Related to this requirement is another. A semantic theory for natural languages that claims to explain how people use and understand language must also be able to explain metaphors, since metaphors are a normal part of natural languages. So the third requirement is that a theory of metaphor should be part of a more general semantic theory. This means that the same central notions and the same basic presuppositions should be used in both cases, although a qualification of these notions may be necessary. A general semantic theory that is not able to accommodate a theory of metaphor, or a theory of metaphor that does not fit into a more general theory, cannot be considered to be adequate.

The first point – that a theory of metaphor must explain metaphors – may seem too obvious to be mentioned, but a determination of the phenomena that are to be explained is not so easy. There is not a generally accepted modern definition or theory that can be used as a starting-point, and the ordinary use of 'metaphor' is not helpful either since it reveals the traces of a wide variety of descriptions employed in the course of history.[2] The best solution seems to be to start with some examples of what most, if not all, writers would call metaphors,[3] and to look for those features that should play a prominent part in an adequate theory of metaphor:[4]

(a) I'll yet follow
the wounded chance of Anthony, though my reason
sits in the wind against me
(b) life's but a walking shadow; a poor player,
that struts and frets his hour upon the stage,
and then is heard no more: it is a tale
told by an idiot, full of sound and fury,
signifying nothing

(c) especially when the October wind
    with frosty finges punishes my hair
(d) The yellow fog that rubs it back upon the window-panes
    the yellow smoke that rubs its muzzle on the window-panes
    licked its tongue into the corners of the evening . . .
(e) Time and bell have buried the day
    the black cloud carries the sun away
(f) I am aware of the damp souls of the housemaids
    sprouting despondently at area gates

A first feature that should be noticed is that a metaphor is not a word but a combination of (at least) two words: it is an expression or a sentence. This is a purely formal description that suffices as a starting-point, but that needs further development in the theory. A decisive step towards such a development is set when the second important feature is recognised: the words in these sentences have retained their normal, usual meaning, but are used in a special way, and form an extraordinary combination. The crucial distinction here is the one between 'metaphorical sense' and 'metaphorical use'.[5] A word can have normal sense or normal senses and metaphorical sense or metaphorical senses and both are listed in dictionaries. To use a word in its metaphorical sense is to use that word literally. The metaphorical use of a word cannot be found in dictionaries, however, simply because there is not such thing as *the* metaphorical use of a word: metaphorical uses cannot be found in dictionaries for the same reason that sentences cannot be found there. Words with a metaphorical sense are often called 'dead metaphors' and are contrasted with 'living metaphors', i.e., with words used metaphorically. But there is a danger in this terminology: it suggests that both belong to the same category, while in fact they describe two different phenomena from two different angles. 'Dead metaphor' refers to the extended sense of a word and says something about the history of that extension; 'living metaphors' says something about an expression or a sentence, and about the actual use of words in that expression or sentence. The same caution should be applied to a term like 'ex-metaphor' (Weinrich) or a classification like 'extinct-dormant-active' metaphors (Black).

These two features are connected: only on the level of a

sentence can one talk about the use of words, and only on the level of a sentence can one talk about the metaphorical use of words. The strangeness of a metaphor arises precisely from its metaphorical use, from the extra-ordinary combination of words that retain their ordinary meaning: it is this strangeness that leads to the recognition of a metaphor, and it is this that needs explanation in a semantic theory. So a fourth requirement can be formulated as follows: a theory of metaphor should explain the metaphorical use of language, and not the metaphorical sense of words. Of these four requirements, the last is in a sense the most important, for a theory of metaphor that ignores the point about metaphors being sentences and the distinction between metaphorical sense and metaphorical use is doomed to failure. This is shown by linguistic theories about metaphor, and can be illustrated by a discussion among some linguists about the question as to what a linguistic theory of metaphor should be like.

1.2 *A discussion among linguists*

The discussion about the theory of metaphor centres around the distinction between competence and performance, which is introduced by Chomsky as a corrective of the Saussurian distinction between *langue* and *parole*. F. de Saussure can be called the father of modern linguistics in two senses: he circumscribed the task of linguistics as being to define the units of language, their relation and their combination-rules. This view has influenced linguistics so much that 'someone who wishes to take issue with Saussure's view of the task of linguistics would not do so by attacking Saussure but by challenging the idea of linguistics itself'.[1] Moreover, linguistics can be seen as an inquiry into the concepts and distinctions that de Saussure used or introduced. One of the crucial distinctions he made is the one between *langue* and *parole*. *Langue* is the system of forms, the underlying social system, *parole* is the individual realization of that potential system in speech-acts.[2] *Langue* is the proper subject of linguistic investigations. Chomsky replaces this distinction with another one: competence (the speaker-hearer's knowledge of his or her language) and performance (the actual use of language in concrete situations). He does so, since de Saussure sees language 'as merely a systematic inventory of items',[3] as 'a store of signs with their grammatical properties, that is a store of word-like elements, fixed phrases and, perhaps, certain limited phrase types.'[4] Chomsky sets out to include the 'rule-governed creativity' that occurs in sentence-formation on the side of *langue*. But he does not question the distinction as such; on the contrary, he calls the distinction 'fundamental' and says that if linguistics is to be 'a serious' discipline, the use of language cannot constitute the subject-matter of linguistics. 'A grammar of language purports to be a description of the ideal speaker-hearer's intrinsic competence.'[5] So both de Saussure and Chomsky insist that a linguistic theory should be a theory about *langue* or competence.

The instructive debate about metaphor and metaphor-theory among linguists was opened by Bickerton in 1969.[6] He begins his article with the argument that a new theory of metaphor is necessary and that such a theory should be a linguistic one. Other approaches have only obscured the issue and have failed because they were not linguistic theories. But even within the linguistic approach, within generative grammar, those notions that seem to be helpful in constructing a theory of metaphor are, in fact, of no use. He has in mind notions like the violation of specific rules. The reason why these notions are of no use is that generative grammar is not able to distinguish between metaphor and non-metaphor: all metaphors can be viewed as rule-violations, but not all rule-violations are metaphors.[7] Bickerton quotes the following examples to support this claim: 'hearts that spaniel'd me at heels' and 'scientists truth the universe' (both instances of major category rule violations), 'misery loves company' and 'ability gripped the town' (sub-category rule violations), 'the flinty and steel couch of war' and 'short hats' (projection rule violation). The first sentences of these couples are metaphors, while the second sentences are meaningless.[8]

Bickerton uses in his own proposal the notion of 'specific attribution assignment', and this notion provides the criterion for distinguishing between metaphors and deviance or nonsense. Taking the words 'iron' and 'steel' and using examples like 'iron determination' – 'steel determination', 'iron will' – 'steel will', 'iron discipline' – 'steel discipline', he remarks that in English the attribute 'hardness' is attached to 'iron' and not to 'steel'.

Lexemes like 'iron' Bickerton calls 'marked signs' and words like 'steel' 'unmarked signs'. The fact that certain attributes are attached to certain signs makes it 'possible for those signs to combine with, or stand in the place of, other signs held to share the same attributes'.[9] This is the reason why the 'iron'-combinations make sense and the 'steel'-combinations do not. To distinguish between metaphors and nonsense is now possible: one has to look for the marked signs. In the final stage of his argument Bickerton turns to what he calls 'true' metaphors ('original and near-unique creations') and maintains that 'these . . . may be best regarded as merely an extension of the system of attribute assignment . . .'[10]

Matthews' contribution to the discussion consists partly in a criticism of Bickerton and partly in his own proposal. According to Matthews, a theory of metaphor should fulfil two minimal requirements. The first one is: 'the theory of metaphor would have to be such that it establishes necessary and sufficient conditions for the distinguishing of metaphor from non-metaphor'. The second requirement is: 'the theory of metaphor would have to be such that it accounts for how, in terms of linguistic competence, the speaker understands or interprets metaphors'.[11] Bickerton fails to meet these two requirements, and since Bickerton hardly comments on the speaker's competence, most of Matthews' criticism centres around the first requirement. He argues that the notion of marked signs begs the question: '. . . the question as to whether or not a particular sign is in fact "marked" will presupposed our being able to determine that it is potentially metaphorical, and not simly deviant, *even before* we have ascertained its "marking".'[12] Moreover, it does not give the necessary condition mentioned in the first requirement. Almost all of Bickerton's examples which he indicates as unmarked signs, deviant and meaningless, can be taken as metaphors given an appropriate (linguistic or extra-linguistic) context. Matthews refers then to 'green ears' but as Bickerton remarks 'the main colour-terms are usually marked',[13] i.e., usually have a metaphorical sense. There are other examples in Bickerton's text that show the point Matthews wants to make in a clearer way; e.g., 'she stabbed my self-respect', 'quit donkeying with my car . . .', 'the house faced the car', 'the sea faced the house'.

Matthews also has doubts as to whether Bickerton's theory meets the sufficiency condition, since it fails to deal with 'true' metaphors, those metaphors 'which do (and could) not involve a "marking" simply because they have not been previously constructed'.[14]

Matthews summarizes his criticism as follows: '. . . Bickerton's fundamental error in his notion of "marked signs" was the presumption that the performance distinction between metaphor and non-metaphor was equivalent to the competence distinction between potential metaphor and simple deviance, rather than between deviant and non-deviant sentences'.[15] Since a linguistic theory should deal with phenomena on the competence level (Matthews' second requirement), a theory of metaphor should explain 'deviance'. Matthews argues that the violation of selectional restrictions[16] causes the deviance. These restrictions are specified in terms of lexical features and these 'characterise the *common use* of the lexical entry'.[17] This notion of selectional restriction violation fulfils the first requirement. With regard to the second requirement, Matthews claims that metaphors are understood in the same way that normal sentences are understood, with the difference that the features connected with the violation are not important. In 'man is a wolf', for example, the features 'human' and 'non-human' are less important than the features 'vicious', 'predatory', and 'nocturnal' which are not involved in the violation.

So Bickerton's explanation is, according to Matthews, inadequate because he confuses the competence and the performance level. Since a linguistic theory should only deal with the competence level, Bickerton does not in fact provide a linguistic theory of metaphor. But Matthews' own proposal involves those notions which Bickerton rejects as central notions of a theory of metaphor. When Bickerton finishes his short discussion of a Chomsky-inspired approach — and Matthews' theory falls into this category – his conclusion is that 'there is no level of rule violation at which metaphor and non-metaphor cannot coexist, and no means within the theory for distinguishing between them at any level'.[18] This may at first sight not cover Matthews' proposal, but if 'metaphor' and 'non-metaphor' are replaced by 'deviant (= metaphor)' and 'deviant (= non-metaphor)', it becomes apparent that this criticism is also directed against Matthews' proposal. So, Matthews criticizes Bickerton and Bickerton in fact criticizes Matthews. This is a puzzling but at the same time a revealing situation. Matthews' criticism, that Bickerton confuses performance and competence, implies that he thinks that Bickerton gives a competence theory, i.e., a synchronic analysis, of metaphors – but is this the case? Matthews, who fits into the category of the generative grammarians criticized by Bickerton, sets out to give a competence theory of metaphors – but does he provide an explanation of metaphors? The answer in both cases is 'no', for Bickerton provides a diachronic analysis, and Matthews only an explanation of deviant sentences.

That Bickerton really is talking about how metaphorical meaning originates is made obvious by the following indications. He begins his article by quoting Bolinger's remark that 'a semantic theory must account for the *process* of metaphorical invention . . .'.[19] This remark can be found in a section of Bolinger's paper which bears the subheading 'the problem of metaphor', and in that section Bolinger makes remarks like 'A complete semantic theory must not only map the markers of all senses but show how markers are added and subtracted to alter the sense of words', '. . . one corroboration of a marker theory would be its ability to predict semantic shifts . . .', and '. . . the radical shifts effected by metaphor . . .'.[20] All these quotations show that Bolinger is concerned with the process of meaning-change. Bickerton shares this concern. This is the reason why he criticizes the generative grammarians for being too much fascinated by logic and too much inclined to think in rigid semantic categories: due to this, they do not ask the relevant question about the transfer of signs from one category to another.[21] Consequently, he explains how words acquire metaphorical meaning, and his examples are, not surprisingly, examples of metaphorical sense. It is quite understandable why he is not able to cope with 'true' metaphors, and why the examples which he qualifies as meaningless and which Matthews correctly sees as examples of metaphor, have an asterisk attached to them: they are not examples of metaphorical sense.[22]

Matthews, on the other hand, gives a synchronic analysis,

but he is not able to explain metaphors – that is to say, he is able to give a formal analysis of metaphors, but nothing more. He can give the necessary conditions, but not the sufficient conditions: he cannot explain the metaphor-mechanism. All he can say is that metaphors are deviant sentences, and that is clearly not enough, for, as Bickerton correctly remarks, not all deviant sentences are metaphors. Bickerton saw the problem of a synchronic approach to metaphors and correctly concluded that this approach would not do. But in his own proposal he gives a diachronic explanation, and that is even worse, for not only does it explain metaphors in terms of meaning-change, it also shifts the focus from sentence to words. These two aspects are of course connected: one can only talk about *words* acquiring metaphorical sense. The only way to escape this dilemma is to maintain that the explanation has to be found on the level of sentences and to reject the self-imposed limitation to the competence-aspect: that is to say, metaphors have to be treated in terms of speech-acts. This means, given the definition of linguistics as exclusively dealing with competence, that linguistics cannot deal adequately with metaphors.

The problematic insistence on competence in metaphor theory is taken up by Price and Loewenberg in their criticism of Matthews, and their comments elucidate further the conclusion reached about the linguistic approach to metaphors. Price argues that Matthews fails to keep the distinction between competence and performance himself, since he uses the performance-concept of 'intention'; he argues further that Matthews, within his competence theory, is able to distinguish between non-deviance and deviance, but not between metaphor-deviance and nonsense-deviance. Price is correct: Matthews adds in his conclusion 'excepting of course those cases where utterances are not intended to be meaningful'.[23] Having made these points, Price asks the fundamental question 'whether Matthews' failure to construct a linguistic theory of metaphor is an isolated case or whether there is some consideration which, in principle, would preclude an understanding of metaphor on the language competence model alone'.[24] Price thinks that it is not an isolated case, and suggests that a further exploration of the role of creativity in language might be helpful. Chomsky makes a distinction between the creativity that leaves the rules unchanged and that manifests itself in the production and understanding of new sentences, and the creativity that changes the rules. Do metaphors change the language rules, or do they fall under the first type of creativity, with the consequence that it should be possible to explain them on the competence model? Price thinks that metaphors belong to the rule-changing creativity and recommends the development of linguistics of that kind of creativity as an important step towards an adequate theory of metaphor. But Price here makes the same mistake as Bickerton: he thinks that the explanation of metaphor is an explanation of a change of meaning. To think that a linguistics of rule-changing creativity can help the construction of an adequate theory of metaphor is to think that a change of meaning occurs in the words used in a metaphor. But there is a further problem here, for by introducing 'change of rule' Price does not introduce a synchronic concept. So, although his attempt might at first sight seem an improvement on Bickerton's word-centred approach, the focus on change of rule makes it impossible for him to explain metaphorical use.

Loewenberg's comments on Matthews' article are part of a more general criticism. Her article is concerned with the identification of metaphors and she argues that formal linguistics are not able to make this identification. The reason for this is the important influence of two distinctions that shape the linguistic theory. The first is the distinction between linguistic knowledge and extra-linguistic knowledge, and the second is the distinction between knowledge of language (competence) and the use of language (performance). A linguistic theory must deal with the knowledge of language understood as linguistic knowledge. Both distinctions can be made, but not in the way that formal linguistics make and use them, namely, as separated, isolated parts for which a theory can be devised. With regard to the performance-competence distinction, she remarks that they are interdependent, not only on the level of discovery ('... regular patterns in my speech *do* reflect my competence, and regular patterns discernible in the speech of speakers of a language determine what counts as competence in that language'), but also on the level of theory-formation ('performance data suggest the form and the content of a theory of competence; the predictions of the competence theory . . . test the theory's adequacy').[25] She agrees, in fact, with Price that a competence theory of metaphor is impossible, but while Price adheres to the distinction between competence and performance, she questions it. But how radical her position is becomes clear when she also questions the other distinction between linguistic and extra-linguistic knowledge. Loewenberg argues correctly that without taking into account extra-linguistic knowledge metaphors cannot be distinguished or identified as such. 'I was a morsel for a monarch' implies the claim that 'humans are (in most places at the present time) not used as food', a claim which cannot be classified as linguistic knowledge. But this claim is 'crucial' to the conflict between the meaning of words.[26] She does not just question the competence-approach, she questions the whole linguistic programme.[27] This change in perspective from 'words' or 'sentences' to 'utterances' – to use Loewenberg's terminology[28] – is a change from a purely linguistic interest to an interest in how language is used to make speech-acts (statements and questions about states of affairs, promises, etc.), how this process is related to the speaker and the hearer, and how the context contributes to communication.

The result of this discussion is not only that the importance of considering metaphors as sentences is shown, but also that some of the implications of this starting-point have become clear. It is not enough to start with 'a metaphor is a sentence', for if a sentence is understood as an extra-long word, nothing is changed. Only if the function of sentences, their role in communication, is considered can the two mistakes or deficiencies of the linguistic approach – i.e., explaining metaphors in terms of change of meaning, or describing them as deviant sentences – be avoided. A further result is a clarification about the usefulness of certain notions for a theory of metaphor. Two notions should not be used: the first is 'change of meaning', for it directs the attention to a diachronic explanation; and the second is the notion central to Matthews' theory, 'violation of rules'. Even apart from the question whether it should be used in a theory of metaphor, this is a strange notion, for, on its own, it can only explain nonsense and not meaningful language. Since it requires an additional notion, like 'change of rule' or 'change of meaning', and since these further notions are not adequate, 'violation of rule' should be dropped as well.

The conclusion of this exploration of the requirements of a theory of metaphor can be summarized as follows: a theory of metaphor must be able to explain, in terms of a general theory of language, how meaning is produced and understood when language is used metaphorically, and what function such use fulfils. This requires that metaphors are understood as sentences functioning in a communication process. The discussion among linguists shows that another approach ends up either explaining the change of meaning of a word over a certain period of time, or 'explaining' nonsense as well, without being able to distinguish between metaphor and nonsense.

2. *A theory of metaphor*

2.1. *The general outline*

A basic presupposition in the study of language and in the theories about the communicative function of language is the thesis that all language is rule-governed behaviour. In a sentence like 'the beautiful house on the corner was destroyed by fire' one can distinguish several aspects, if one considers it as a speech-act:[1]

(a) The utterance aspect: the noise that is produced during the uttering or the signs that are written down, and the uttering of vocables or writing down of combinations of signs, as belonging to a certain vocabulary, according to a certain grammar.[2]

(b) the content aspect: this aspect is concerned with reference and predication. To use the example above: reference is made to a house, which is further specified by 'on the corner' and 'beautiful'; this house is said to be 'destroyed by fire'. Searle calls this the propositional act.[3]

(c) the frame aspect: the content aspect is always presented in a certain frame. In the case of the example the frame is that of an assertion. But the content could easily be presented in a question frame, a promise frame, a

command frame, etc. This aspect is normally called the illocutionary aspect, or the illocutionary force.[4]
(d) the effect aspect: this aspect refers to the effect of the speech-act and is commonly called the perlocutionary force. In the case of the example this might be pity.

To all these aspects rules and criteria correspond, and the precise rules differ from level to level. To the first aspect correspond rules about pronunciation and spelling, and rules about the construction of grammatical expressions and sentences. The rules concerning the second aspect deal with how to refer and to predicate; the rules of the third aspect state what counts as an assertion, question, promise, etc.; and the conventions and rules of the final aspect make effects possible or prevent them – a promise becomes a marriage-vow because of certain conventions.

Meaning and understanding and communication depend on the correct employment of these rules. And although not all the rules seem equally important for these purposes – a pronunciation error or spelling mistake may not prevent understanding, or may have less consequences than a promise made under insufficient circumstances – the general link between meaning, understanding, and communication on the one hand and rules and conventions on the other is of great importance. If one wants to give a theory of metaphor which explains the meaning-mechanism and how it is possible that people can understand these types of sentences, it seems obvious that one has to look at the rules used in language and see whether something special happens to them when language is used metaphorically. It is clear that not all the rules are important in this respect. Sentences are neither metaphors because they are spelled or pronounced in a certain way nor are they metaphors because their grammar differs from that of ordinary sentences. A metaphor is not distinguished by form. And since metaphors can occur in all kinds of illocutionary frames – they can be questions, promises, etc. – it seems that the illocutionary rules are not affected by the metaphorical use of language.

But Warner argues that living metaphors should be treated as a distinct class of utterances and that their metaphorical force should be considered a special type of illocutionary force, namely 'hortatory' or 'suggestive': '. . . the force of the utterance is to encourage one to try to see something as something else, and the point of doing so may well be illumination'.[5] It is difficult to maintain this position, however, since there are several problems attached to it. First, if all metaphors have a suggestive force, does that imply that all sentences with a suggestive force are metaphors? 'Think of p as q and you will notice aspects of p brought together which you had not noticed before'[6] is of course not an advice that only 'the coiner of a powerful and fertile metaphor' is giving.[7] So, one needs at least an additional criterion.

Secondly, if metaphors become a special class of utterance with a distinct metaphorical force, they should be contrasted with other illocutionary forces and they should belong to the same level – one cannot make an assertion and a question at the same time. Warner suggests the contrast when he writes that 'the key here is to cease treating such metaphors as assertions with unusual properties'.[8] But that means that one cannot consider a question in which a metaphor occurs as a question. But what to do then with 'In what furnace was thy brain?'? with 'I promise to be aware of the damp souls of the housemaids'? or with 'I warn you that the yellow fog that rubs it back upon the window-panes may attack you!'?[9] The conclusion must be that 'hortatory' or 'suggestive' is not of the same type and does not belong to the same category as assertion, question, promise, etc.

The third problem arises when is assumed that hortatory belongs to the same category as assertion. In Searle's scheme there are several different rules that play a part on the level of illocutions, and of all the illocutions mentioned – request, assertion, question, thanks, advice, warning, congratulation, greeting – only greeting does not have a specification of rules concerning its propositional content. In the case of a request this specification is related to the future act of the hearer, in the case of a warning to a future event or state of affairs, etc. Would 'suggestion' have such a propositional content rule? It seems very likely.[10] But what kind of specification is needed? Would the proposition be limited to future events, to past acts, or would any proposition do? An affirmative answer to the last question would be inconsistent with Warner's position, since it would mean that 'suggestions' would then have the same rules as assertions (and questions). Moreover, it would beg the question: why should they be suggestive? So a special kind of propositional act is required. Which one? To pursue this line, or even the idea that every proposition will do, is in fact to cease to explain metaphors on the illocutionary level: the discussion has moved to the locutionary level.

Warner, though, suggests something else as well: 'and the point of doing so may well be illumination'. Could metaphors perhaps be explained sufficiently in terms of effect, that is, with regard to rules concerning the perlocutionary aspect? No. 'Illumination' or a similar concept would be too broad, since a lot of other sentences would be covered as well, and, moreover, this explanation does not answer the question about the production of meaning and understanding. For such an answer, an appeal to an extra-linguistic convention is not very helpful; and that means that only the propositional content is left.

So, the whole discussion of Warner's suggestions points to the content aspect and the rules concerned with that aspect as the place to look for an explanation of the special character of metaphors. The metaphor is basically a predication. And 'basically' is added to accommodate those expressions which do not have the explicit structure of 'x is y', but that can be reconstructed in this way.[11] But what is the special character of metaphorical predication? Earlier it was remarked that the strangeness of the metaphor, the reason why it is conspicuous, lies in the fact that the words in it retain their normal, usual meaning. This striking aspect can only be produced if the combination of the words is not just unexpected, but also extraordinary. The strangeness of the examples quoted at the beginning is thus based upon the extraordinary combinations of words, concepts like 'life' and 'talc', 'clouds' and 'carry away', 'fog' and 'back', etc.

At this stage a distinction is needed between concepts and sets of concepts or conceptual realms, between, e.g., 'blue' and 'red' or 'pain' and 'love' on the one hand and 'colour' or 'feeling' on the other.[12] This distinction makes explicit what is normally implicit in a predication, but is not meant to suggest that a predication is normally a two-step process. The purpose of introducing the distinction is to explain the difference between falsity and metaphor and to explain, partially at least, the intelligibility of the metaphor despite its extraordinary combination. The combination that causes the strangeness occurs on the level of sets of concepts, involves conceptual realms, and does not occur on the level of concepts. If an extraordinary combination is made on the level of concepts, i.e., within a normal combination of realms, the result is a mistake or a falsity. If, though, in an extraordinary combination the concepts that are used clash on the level of concepts the metaphor can be incoherent. An example can illustrate these points using the earlier quoted 'when the October wind with frosty fingers punishes my hair'. If 'frosty fingers' is replaced by 'balmy arms' and 'punishes' by 'caresses', it is still a metaphor, although a rather different one from the original. If 'October wind' is replaced by the name of a person, 'frosty' by 'long' and 'punishes' by 'touches' the result is a normal sentence, and if the person in question has long fingers and touches my hair the sentence is true. If 'October wind' were replaced by 'July wind', the clash between 'July' and 'frosty' would render the metaphor incoherent and unintelligible. A variation on this general pattern is formed by those metaphorical predications in which one of the concepts involved is so highly determined that it can be considered almost as a realm of its own and that the extraordinariness typical for the metaphor arises from its being used outside its customary combination. Examples are the names of historical personages or names of figures from fiction. In these cases cultural influences will be even stronger than in the other cases.

If the specific character of metaphors has to be explained on the level of realms or sets of concepts and in terms of rules concerning those realms or sets, the question arises as to how exactly this explanation should be phrased. 'To follow' those rules would not give an explanation of the apparent difference between normally and metaphorically used language, but neither would 'to break' or 'to violate' those rules do as an explanation. As mentioned earlier, if meaning is connected with obedience to rules, violation of rules must result in nonsense or in meaningless language whether the rules concerned are those governing concepts or sets of concepts. The solution to take the violation as a first step to which a second step – the change of rules – is added, is also inadequate, since a change of rules implies a change of meaning. To put this point in a somewhat different way: the notion 'change of rule' (and, for that matter, 'addition to rules' or 'extension of rules') is not helpful, since it presupposes a frequency of use which does not refer to a repetition of the same sentence, but to a similar use in other sentences by a community of speakers. 'Change', 'addition', and 'extension' can only be used if there is a different pattern that shows some consistency. So 'change', 'addition', and 'extension' seem to be too strong, too drastic, and too permanent. 'Relaxing the rules' seems to be the notion that captures best the metaphorical use of language: the rules remain active and influential, and they are being used, but they are being used in a somewhat different way than they are used normally. But this 'relaxing the rules' is not enough, since, as it stands, the distinction between 'relaxing' and 'changing' is not clear. 'Relaxing' needs a further qualification: the rules are relaxed for the time being, or, for this particular occasion. This qualification is not so strange if one realizes that a metaphor is a sentence and that the meaning of a sentence can be called 'occasional'.[13]

The basic answer to the question about the mechanism of the metaphor can now be put as follows: in using and understanding language metaphorically, the rules governing the use of the sets of concepts or the conceptual realms involved are relaxed for this particular occasion, and on that level a combination is allowed which under normal circumstances would not be permitted.

With this outline in mind, the second main question can be approached – the question about the function of metaphor. Why do people want to make an extraordinary combination between conceptual realms? The way we normally combine sets of concepts reflects how we see reality, and a change on that level results in a change in our view about what reality looks like. For example, if we should decide to talk about colourless phenomena in terms of colour, about inanimate things in terms of feelings, our organization of reality would be quite different from our present one, with all kinds of consequences – what would happen to road-construction and mining if land and rock had feelings? But if we decided to use 'orange' instead of 'blue', or 'disappointment' instead of 'pleasure', our outlook on reality would not change that much, and we would continue to live the way we live now. To allow for an extraordinary combination of sets of concepts, of conceptual realms, is therefore to allow for another organization of reality – for a 'redescription of reality', to use Ricoeur's phrase. But since a metaphor does not involve a change of rules, it cannot be said that a metaphor constitutes a redescription of reality *tout court*: it is, more precisely, a proposal or suggestion of such a redescription.[14]

In the most general, though heavy, terms, this seems to be the function of metaphor. There can be all kinds of reasons for such a proposal and the various answers that have been given in the course of history can be repeated here. On the one hand, language can be used metaphorically to talk about known situations and states of affairs with the purpose of creating insight, or to propose an alternative to the dissatisfying flat descriptions of reality, or to avoid a particular terminology. On the other hand, language can be used metaphorically to talk about new phenomena and situations: the reason can be that the available conceptual structure is not adequate to place the new phenomena, or that the unknown can only be known and explored via the known, i.e., in relation to the accepted situation, or because the situation is not clearly surveyable and needs organization, internally or externally. Depending on the further specification of these reasons, the description of the function of metaphors as suggesting or proposing a redescription of reality can and should be qualified, for this rather ponderous terminology may seem to correspond to the purpose of religion and poetry but to sound overstated in the case of everyday language metaphors.

The outline of the required theory of metaphor can now be summarized: in a metaphor the rules governing the sets of concepts or conceptual realms involved are relaxed for this occasion in function of a proposed redescription of reality.

2.2 *The background*
The outline of the theory is stated in terms of relaxing rules.

'Rules' and its related notions like 'following rules', 'changing rules', 'relaxing rules' have to be explored further. How are rules in language to be understood? Is language thoroughly rule-governed? What is involved in following a rule? How easily are rules changed? The answers to these and similar questions will help to provide the background for the theory.

When the notion 'rule' is used, it has normally two aspects: a descriptive aspect which states the regularity in behaviour, and a regulative aspect which makes it a criterion for correctness. These two aspects are not always present at the same time. Sometimes 'rule' is used only to describe a regularity, e.g., the daily routine, but in the majority of cases the two aspects can be discerned, as in the case of language rules: dictionaries and books on grammar and syntax describe the usage of a particular period and at the same time state the criterion for correct use. In view of this, two extreme accounts of language-rules have to be rejected. First, the account that construes rules and rule-following too liberally, and does not give enough emphasis to the prescriptive aspect. If this aspect is underestimated, mistakes are no longer possible, for there is no criterion for correctness. The consequence of a too liberal construction is that the process of communication and understanding becomes inexplicable and impossible. Only by sharing and obeying common rules can communication and understanding take place. Another consequence is that there is no longer a difference between metaphorically used and non-metaphorically used language. But the opposite account that emphasizes the prescriptive aspect too much runs into other problems. It is quite a normal feature of language that words change their meaning, that constructions and phrases become old-fashioned, that new concepts and notions are introduced. If rules are seen as laying down in advance all applications, if rule-following is seen as following a fixed pattern, these changes cannot be explained – certainly not if one realizes that these changes are often slow processes involving a substantial part of the language-speaking community. On too strict an account metaphors become nonsense. How can we avoid these two extremes? What is the basis of the prescriptive aspect? Reality? Are some rules more prescriptive than others? Can all rules be changed? A discussion of the conventional character of language, of the relation between language and reality, can provide an answer to these questions.[1]

To call language 'conventional' is to oppose a certain view on the relation between language and reality, namely that there is a domain of facts – an objective world 'out there' – completely separated from the domain of concepts and language. The relation between these domains is, in this view, such that the concepts are 'read off' from the objective world and that the structure of reality necessitates the system of concepts. There are several problems with this view. It holds that there is a necessary connection between changes in one domain and changes in the the other. In a number of cases – e.g., in the discovery of a new physical element, the emergence of a new fashion, etc. – the change in one domain corresponds to the change in the other, but there is not always such a necessary connection. Changes in psychological or sociological terminology or differences in philosophical theories do not necessarily imply a change in the domain of facts.[2] A more important point of criticism is that it is incoherent to hold this view. Imagine a term t and an object x and suppose that t denotes x. In order to understand this we must understand the meaning of t, the meaning of the expression x, and the denotation-relation. But the expression x belongs also to the language used, and in order to understand that expression, it is necessary to understand or know another statement like 'the expression x denotes object y', etc. On this division between language and reality it becomes impossible to explain how an object can be named.[3] Furthermore, no explanation can be given of the fact that different peoples and cultures have different concepts and structures of concepts. Anthropologists and comparative linguists have shown the existence of differences in vocabulary – e.g. in the number of colour-terms – have pointed to the problems surrounding the translation of typical terms (fair, *überhaupt, ennui*), and have given evidence of differences in grammar and syntax, e.g. the lack of tense in verbs.[4] If one accepts this view of language mirroring reality, and if one does not want to allow that there are different realities, one has to argue that one, and only one, of these structures of concepts is correct. But which one? And how can one be sure that it is this one and not that one which is correct?

The main mistake of this view is that not enough attention is paid to the role of language and of language-users in structuring reality. The information given by anthropologists and comparative linguists has led to another view in which language determines reality. This view advocates a relativism that is, in fact, based upon the same division between language and reality present in the first view, but with a difference of direction. In this view language is primary and language creates and constructs reality. One of the problems here is that any form of translation becomes impossible, and what is more important, that the identification of the differences between various cultures is out of the question. It rejects what it presupposes, and that makes this view as incoherent as the first one.

This suggests that there is something wrong with the picture of the two completely separated domains which underlies these two views. Wittgenstein in his later work takes a different starting-point which enables him to combine the correct points of both views without falling into one of the two extremes. His starting-point is that language-use is a human activity and that it is one element in life, and like other elements supported by a form of life, and that it is determined by who and what people are and by the purpose for which they use it. Because of this starting-point he can maintain at the same time the arbitrariness or the conventionality of language and the non-arbitrariness of language and of the conceptual structure and locate their precise place and mutual relation.

To describe a concept – that is, to describe its relation to other concepts, to indicate what kind of questions are appropriate, what kind of experience counts as understanding it, etc. – is summarized in the grammar of that concept.[5] The grammar of 'chair' consists, among other things, in the relation of 'chair' to 'sofa', 'stool', 'throne', 'table', 'bed', 'carpet', 'picture', 'music-stand', etc.; in what counts as 'to own a chair', 'to make a chair', 'to upholster a chair'; in what constitutes 'to sit in a chair', 'to sit on a chair'. 'It is part of the grammar of the word "chair" that *this* is what we call "to sit on a chair"'.[6] In Wittgenstein's view grammar thus understood is autonomous, since concepts and conceptual systems are not justified or justifiable by facts.[7] 'One is tempted to justify rules of grammar by sentences like "But there really are four primary colours". And the saying that the rules of grammar are arbitrary is directed against the possibility of this justification, which is constructed on the model of justifying a sentence by pointing to what verifies it'.[8] This justification is impossible because it presupposes what it attempts to justify. 'Grammatical conventions cannot be justified by describing what is presented: any such description already presupposes the grammatical rules'.[9] There is simply no position where an observer can oversee and compare the domain of facts and the domain of language: language is necessary to describe the domain of facts, and with the description, with language, that conceptual structure is introduced. It is possible to justify a system from the point of view of another system: one can talk about the different ways of measurement, of dividing colours, of looking at the past, etc. But such justification does not show that the one is correct because it corresponds to reality: it shows that the one is more fruitful, more economical, more illuminating.[10] The conventional character of language Wittgenstein is talking about is not the type of conventionality that is the result of the decisions of certain legislative bodies (decisions on spelling or on the occurrence of foreign words): the argument for the autonomy of grammar aims at showing that the current system is not absolute and not the only correct one. That is the reason why Wittgenstein gives examples of different conceptual systems, narrates alternative, and fictitious natural histories: '. . . if anyone believes that certain concepts are absolutely the correct ones, and that having different ones would mean not realizing something that we realize – then let him imagine certain very general facts of nature to be different from what we are used to, and the formation of concepts different from the usual ones will become intelligible to him'.[11]

This method shows the other aspect: the role of nature.[12] The facts of nature are central in Wittgenstein's view on the non-arbitrariness of concepts and their structure. Although nature does not necessitate concepts and the conceptual system, there is nevertheless a relation between the two: the concepts are related to us living in the world, to the natural history of men, to 'very general facts', to 'observations which no one has doubted but which have escaped remark only because they are always before our eyes'.[13] Examples of these very general facts are features of constancy in external nature and in human nature. 'We say we know that water boils and does not freeze under such-and-such circumstances. Is it conceivable that we are wrong? Wouldn't a mistake topple all judgement with it? More: what could stand if that were to fall? Might someone discover something that made us say "It was a mistake"? Whatever may happen in the future, however water may behave in the future, – we *know* that up to now it has behaved *thus* in innumerable instances. This fact is fused into the foundations of our language-game'.[14] There is a similarity in people's reaction to certain situations, e.g., pain, and in their judgements: 'the common behaviour of mankind is the system of reference by means of which we interpret an unknown language'.[15] Another factual feature of human nature is that we use language and that we think and that both are combined, creating a specific human form of life. 'One can imagine an animal angry, frightened, unhappy, happy startled. But hopeful? And why not? . . . Can only those hope who can talk? Only those who have mastered the use of a language. That is to say, the phenomena of hope are modes of this complicated form of life. . . .'[16] All these features are based upon the way we are and behave, upon our action: 'it is our *acting* which lies at the bottom of the language-game'.[17]

There are other features as well which limit the otherwise sheer arbitrariness of the conceptual structure. First, the individual user cannot whimsically change the meaning of a word every time he uses it: he is committed to a certain constancy and regularity. Furthermore, the sound or sign for a concept may be arbitrary, but its meaning is not in the sense that it is part of a whole structure. Change of meaning of a concept implies a change in the conceptual system. And there is also the non-linguistic behaviour the speaker is committed to. If he or she changes the meaning of 'chair', he or she can not go on to behave with regard to chairs as if nothing has happened. Secondly, the social aspects of language also prevent a view of sheer arbitrariness. The whole structure is given in the process of learning and education.[18] It is because of these individual and social commitments that language can function as a means of communication.

But we can imagine those very general facts to be different.

We can imagine people who experience pain only if they are in contact with some surface or in a certain region; those surfaces would be called 'painful' and one could say 'it is painful here' or 'it is painful today'.[19] Or we can imagine people who fix the price of wood with regard to the surface covered by it, but without taking into account the height of the pile; if a high pile covering a small area were spread out over a big area, it would cost more and would be considered to be a lot of wood.[20] Or we can imagine people who are educated not to express their feelings and in the process of education complaints were punished. 'Shamming' these people might say, 'what a ridiculous concept!' (as if one were to distinguish between a murder with one shot and one with three)'.[21] 'I want to say: an education quite different from ours might also be the foundation for quite different concepts. For here life would run on differently. – What interests us would not interest *them*. Here different concepts would no longer be unimaginable. In fact, this is the only way in which *essentially* different concepts are imaginable'.[22] But there is something strange in these examples: all of them are initially intelligible, but while some of them, when developed, could be incorporated into our way of life with more or less important changes as a consequence (e.g., the abandonment of property), others would imply such a different way of life that we have to say 'These men would have nothing human about them. Why? – We could not possibly make ourselves understood to them. Not even as we can do to a dog. We could not find our feet with them'.[23] Those examples in particular which imply a completely different form of life show two things: first, that there are alternative systems, and secondly, that we cannot understand these systems completely because they are so different from our system.

So, the arbitrariness of language is linked with the possibilities of alternative systems and with the impossibility of justifying a system by an appeal to reality, while the non-arbitrariness is linked with our natural history and with the commitment of the speakers.

Within this overall picture of the arbitrariness and non-arbitrariness of language, the function and the nature of rules is determined. An example used by Wittgenstein can clarify what is meant by 'following a rule', 'breaking a rule', etc. A pupil is taught to continue a series by adding '2'; he writes down 2, 4, 6, 8, . . . 996, 998, 1000, 1004, 1008, 1012. In the discussion of this example Wittgenstein opposes a view which understands linguistic rules as rules of a calculus; his choice of a mathematical example is based on the argument that even in mathematics, let alone in language, this calculus-view does not work.[24] The calculus-view maintains that the consequences are contained in the rule and that the only thing that has to be done is to trace them.[25] What is a correct use and what is not, is all contained, comprised, in the rule. Wittgenstein discredits the connection between rule and necessity by imagining a genuine discussion about the application of the rule. If the pupil continues the series in the way he does not because of stupidity or misunderstanding but because he thinks this is the way the series should be continued, the teacher cannot appeal to an argument like 'he did not do the same as before' or 'he did not do what I meant',[26] for what determines 'sameness' except using the same term?[27] And how is 'what I meant' to be understood? As an infinite number of propositions like writing 1868 after 1866 and 100036 after 100034?[28] An appeal to reality is not possible and an appeal to past usage insufficient, because every action can be made out to accord with a rule. But that leads to a paradox: 'no course of action could be determined by a rule, because every course of action can be made out to accord with the rule. The answer was: if everything can be made out to accord with the rule, then it can also be made out to conflict with it. And so there would be neither accord nor conflict here'.[29] And that would mean: no understanding, no communication.

This does not mean that the concept of rule has to be abandoned: it only means that following a rule cannot be understood as being compelled by some objective pattern. If there is a necessity or compulsion, it is a psychological one: it is not the rule which compels us, but we compel ourselves to use the term in a certain way. Rules have a function: they are criteria and they give guidance. That everything can be interpreted as following a rule does not imply that everything whatsoever counts as following a rule: '. . . there is a way of grasping a rule which is *not* an interpretation, but which is exhibited in what we call "obeying a rule" and "going against it" in actual cases'.³⁰ That is to say, one cannot go on adding interpretation to interpretation: there are no rules for applying rules.³¹ In the end one has to refer to common practice.³² The infinite number of causes, of possible interpretations, should not be confused with the reasons, the finite chain of actual reasons.³³ The chain of reasons has an end.³⁴ 'But the end is not an ungrounded presupposition: it is an ungrounded way of acting'.³⁵ This is all related to being brought up in a certain tradition, and being taught the agreements of the community; because of this training it becomes natural to us to use a term in a certain way. 'If we teach a human being such-and-such a technique by means of examples – that he then proceeds like *this* and not like *that* in a particular new case, or that in this case he gets stuck, and that this and not that is the "natural" continuation for him: this of itself is an extremely important fact of nature'.³⁶ To apply a rule correctly is to apply it like the other members of the community, is to conform to an agreed and shared practice, and is not to follow a pre-fixed pattern.

Against this background, the remarks about rules and metaphors can be understood. Because there is a prescriptive side to rules and because not everything counts as following a rule, metaphorically-used language is different from non-metaphorically-used language; because rules are not fixed, divergence is possible without the creation of nonsense as a necessary consequence. Furthermore, this view of language can clarify three features in the use of metaphors. First, certain metaphors change rather easily into metaphorical meaning, while other remain metaphors. The time of origin, or the frequency of use is not decisive here, as the Shakespearian metaphors quoted in the beginning of this chapter show. It seems that the place the concepts involved occupy in the whole structure and their relation to our natural history play a decisive role: the more consequences that would follow from the acceptance of a change of a rule, the more resistance there is in the process from metaphor to metaphorical meaning.³⁷ Secondly, because of the interwovenness of language and life, the way people live and behave plays a role in what counts and what does not count as a metaphor. In other words, metaphors are culturally determined, and as such parasitical. Thirdly, the function of the metaphor as proposing a redescription of reality appears to be a possible and coherent aim. And given the structure of metaphors, their usefulness for this purpose is clear. Wittgenstein makes a remark about what to do when one meets somebody with a different picture of reality. 'I can imagine a man who had grown up in quite special circumstances and been taught that the earth came into being 50 years ago, and therefore believed this. We might instruct him: the earth has long ... etc. – We would be trying to give him our picture of the world. This would happen through a kind of *persuasion*'.[38] Metaphors have always been important tools for persuasion. This very fact has been the ground for both praise and condemnation.[39]

3. *Theories of metaphor*
In this section several theories of metaphor will be discussed under three headings: the word approach, the sentence approach and the category-mistake approach. This discussion has a double aim which also functions as the selection criterion: first, to contribute to the argumentation of the theory proposed in the previous section, be it in a somewhat negative way, since the examination will bring out the inadequacies and incoherent features of these theories; and secondly, to facilitate the discussion in the next chapter, for these theories are used by theologians and philosophers of religion in their discussions of metaphors and models.[1]

3.1 *The word approach*
There is a long tradition, starting with Aristotle, of defining the metaphor as a word.[1] Aristotle describes the metaphor as follows: 'Metaphor consists in giving the thing a name that belongs to something else; the transference being either from genus to species, or from species to genus, or from species to species, or on grounds of analogy'.[2] Aristotle uses this definition from the *Poetics* in his *Rhetoric* also. In this definition at least three features can be distinguished: the metaphor is described as something that happens to a word *(onoma)*, what happens to that word is specified in terms of movement *(epiphora)*, and the word concerned is further qualified as 'strange' *(allotrios)*.

That the metaphor is defined as a word is not surprising, since the definition and the discussion that follows it are part of a broad analysis and discussion of *lexis* (style), which covers the whole process of combining words into an intelligible sequence.[3] Aristotle divides *lexis* into several elements: the letter or element *(stoicheion)*, syllable *(syllabe)*, conjunction or connection *(sundesmos)*, article or joint *(arthron)*,[4] noun *(onoma)*, verb *(rhema)*, case or inflection *(ptoosis)*, and speech or discourse *(logos)*. *Onoma* is the key-term in this list. The four elements mentioned before *onoma* are all non-significant elements and are described in such a way that they are directed towards the first significant element: word, noun.[5] And in the description of verb, case and speech, Aristotle uses the *onoma*-definition as the basis and adds to it or modifies it. The whole treatment of *lexis* centres around the word, and the sentence does not occupy a privileged place.[6]

The more immediate context of the metaphor definition is formed by a list in which Aristotle brings together the different ways in which words can be qualified: ordinary, foreign, metaphor, ornament, coined, lengthened, curtailed, and altered. The first term of this list, 'ordinary' *(kurion)* refers to 'our' current usage, while the second one, 'foreign' *(glootta)* refers to the current usage in other countries or in other times.[7] This means that metaphor is contrasted with current usage, which is brought out by the reference to *allotrios* in the definition.[8] In the passages that follow, *allotrios* is connected with 'deviant'.[9] Ricoeur points out that apart from this negative aspect – deviant – *allotrios* implies also the positive notion of borrowing: it is always possible to mention the domain of origin.[10] There is a third element which Aristotle on most occasions connects with *allotrios* and which is implied in the contrast with *kurion*, namely, that of substitution: the metaphor can be replaced by an ordinary word except in those cases where there is no such word available.[11]

The later tradition takes over this focus on the word as the central unit of meaning and develops Aristotle's view on metaphors in a certain, narrower way.[12] The theories of argumentation and composition no longer belong to the field of rhetoric, as they did in Aristotle's conception: rhetoric is limited to the theory of style and becomes an elaborate classification of tropes. Ricoeur lists a series of postulates which exhibits the model of the tropology and which shows how the primacy of the word and the view that a metaphor is only an ornament are connected.[13] Certain words belong properly to certain things, and in the case of style-figures (e.g., metaphors) the words are used improperly. The reason for using an improper word is the lack of a proper word and this can be either a stylistic gap or a real gap. This gap is filled by borrowing a strange word, which constitutes a deviance. The borrowed term can be replaced by a word with a proper sense. There is a relation between the improper term and the absent term, and in the case of metaphor this relation is one of resemblance. Understanding a trope is finding, guided by the appropriate type of relation, the absent word, and this restitution is in fact an exhaustive paraphrase. This means that the metaphor conveys no special information and has only an ornamental function.

According to Ricoeur the contemporary 'Nouvelle Rhétorique' stays within this word-centred framework in its discussion of metaphors.[14] And within linguistics Ullmann's work is an example of a theory that takes the word as the central unit of meaning, which has consequences for his theory of metaphor.[15] Ullmann distinguishes between the name (phonetic shape) of a word and the sense of that word, i.e., 'the information which the name conveys to the hearer'.[16] He makes further the familiar distinction between descriptive (synchronic) analysis and historical (diachronic) analysis. Descriptive analysis is concerned among other things with the relations between the sense and the name of a word, and polysemy – the phenomenon that one name has several different senses – is an important type of such a relation. Related to polysemy is the semantic change with which historical analysis deals. Metaphor is discussed in this context: it is a change of meaning. So, the study of metaphor is limited to diachronic analysis and all that can be said about metaphor on the synchronic level is that it is a word with more than one sense, a case of polysemy.[17] Other writers, too, use Aristotle's definition as their starting-point, or approach the metaphor basically as a word.[18]

There are two stages in the criticism of this type of metaphor theories: the first is concerned with the underlying theory of meaning, and the second with the theory of metaphor proper. These stages are connected, for one cannot criticize the rhetorical theory of metaphor fundamentally without calling into question the word-centred theory of meaning. In this theory, the meaning of a word is not distinguished from the meaning of a sentence: a sentence is an extra-long word. In modern theories of meaning, though, the difference between word and sentence, between word-meaning and sentence-meaning, is fundamental. One cannot communicate or understand, one cannot perform speech-acts like stating, questioning, promising on the level of a word but only on the level of a sentence. Or, as Ryle puts it: 'Sentences are things we say. Words and phrases are what we say things *with*', and, 'Sentences and clauses make sense or no sense, where words neither do nor do not make sense but only have meanings'.[19] A theory of meaning that attempts to explain how people communicate and understand language has to take the sentence as the central unit of meaning.

Frege's remark 'we ought always to keep before our eyes a complete proposition. Only in a proposition do the words really have meaning'[20] became so influential because he was able to explain this truism.[21] Dummett expresses this explanation in the slogan: 'in the order of *explanation* the sense of a sentence is primary, but in the order of *recognition* the sense of the word is primary'.[22] The word is primary since we 'derive our knowledge of the sense of any given sentence from our previous knowledge of the senses of the words that compose it, together with our observation of the way in which they are combined in that sentence'.[23] But the sentence is primary if we want to explain 'what it is for sentences and words to have a sense, that is, what it is for us to grasp their sense'.[24] The sense of a word consists in the contribution it makes to the determination of the sense of the sentence. But that means that the sense of the sentence must be explained without reference to the words used, otherwise the explanation would be circular.[25] The fact that in the order of explanation – the order to which questions about the structure of the metaphor belong – the sentence is primary does not imply that word meaning is not important or a totally wrong concept. But the thesis that 'only in the context of the sentence do words have meaning' states that word meaning cannot be the starting-point for a theory of meaning. And how central the sentence is, is even noticeable in the order of recognition. Words are classified on a grammatical basis, that is, on the basis of their use in a sentence. And, more important, the senses of a word – and most words have more than one sense – are derived, distilled from past uses in actual sentences and actual contexts, and indicate possible future uses.[26] If used, the actual context or the actual sentence selects the meaning that is appropriate and required.[27]

The second stage of criticism is concerned with the theory of metaphor proper. To define a metaphor as 'a word that . . .' is in a certain sense obviously wrong: one needs more than one word to make a metaphor. But given the definition of metaphor as a word, the explanation must invoke notions like 'strange' or 'change of meaning'. How could one otherwise explain, within this framework, the difference between a normal sentence and a metaphor? But it is here that problems arise. The assumption that a word receives a new meaning or acquires a special meaning in these cases is contrary to the observation that words retain their standard meaning when used in a metaphor. This observation corresponds to the points already mentioned with regard to the order of recognition: the ordinary senses of words, distilled from past use, are the only ones available. The assumption is also incoherent: a word does not lose its ordinary, dictionary sense(s), nor does it exchange its sense(s) for another sense just for one occasion. This is not possible because a change of meaning is, as argued before in the context of rules, a process that is stretched out over a certain period of time involving at least a substantial part of the language-speaking community. And although an individual speaker can change the meanings of certain words, he or she has to be consistent and has to draw the consequences of this change, if he or she wants to communicate. Both conditions are such that individual stipulation is much more difficult than may appear at first sight. It is also not possible to use the notion 'rule', for rule, obeying a rule, etc., imply that there is more than one application.[28] If the notion 'change of meaning' is taken seriously, the result is that metaphors can only be discovered and explained in a historical or diachronic analysis. And the consequence of this is that the actual use and actual understanding of metaphors becomes inexplicable. Finally, 'change of meaning for just one occasion' is also incoherent for another reason: terms like 'occasion' cannot be used in connection with word meanings. 'Occasion' and 'event' are terms that belong to sentence meaning. A word has meanings or meanings in general, a sentence has meaning on a particular occasion.[29] Ricoeur rightly lists as the first special feature of the sentence that it is an 'event'.[30] Here, as in the previous points, it is clear how the two stages in this criticism of the rhetorical theory of metaphor are connected.

3.2 *The sentence approach*

In recent decades several books and articles have been published in which the traditional rhetorical treatment of metaphor is criticized and in which another theory of metaphor is presented. The feature these theories have in common is that they do not limit the metaphor to a word, but that they consider it, more or less explicitly, as a sentence. That these theories in the end are not successful is due to the fact that the shift of attention is not radical enough and that residues of the traditional theory still function in them.

I. A. Richards is commonly considered to be the first author in the English-speaking world to propose a theory of metaphor that differs on main points from the traditional one.[1] His view forms the basis of other theories.[2] His short book *The Philosophy of Rhetoric* contains a series of lectures in which he aims at a revitalization of 'rhetoric', 'the study of verbal understanding and misunderstanding'.[3] He reflects on the workings of language and submits a theory of metaphor as part of that reflection. In his general theory of language he objects to two related views of language: the first one is 'the common belief... that a word has a meaning of its own (ideally, only one) independent of and controlling its use and the purpose for which it should be uttered': the 'Proper Meaning Superstition'.[4] The second view is the 'Doctrine of Usage' that holds 'that there is a right or good use for every word'.[5] What Richards does in these lectures is not only attack the view that words have fixed meanings which they carry as such into a sentence,[6] but also the primacy of the word in the theory of language: 'we have to renounce, for a while, the view that words just have their meanings and that what discourse does is to be explained as a composition of these meanings . . .'.[7] The correct approach is not from words to discourse, but from discourse to words. The common way of stating the problem is to ask 'what happens when we put words together', but we should ask 'what happens when out of the integral utterance which is the sentence, we try to isolate the discrete meanings of the words of which it is composed'.[8] Instead of a fixed word-meaning view, Richards proposes a 'context theorem of meaning': 'what a word means is the missing parts of the context from which it draws its delegated efficacy'.[9] Words exert 'mutual control and interanimation' and this includes even the words that are not uttered but are only in the background.[10] The meanings of the words 'are the resultants which we arrive at only through the interplay of interpretative possibilities of the whole utterance'.[11]

Richards' simplest formulation of his theory of metaphor is: 'when we use a metaphor we have two thoughts of different things active together and supported by a single word, or phrase, whose meaning is the resultant of their interaction'.[12] He introduces further the terms 'tenor' and 'vehicle': 'tenor' is 'the underlying idea or principal subject which the vehicle or figure means'.[13] And he stresses that 'the co-presence of the vehicle and tenor results in a meaning (to be clearly distinguished from the tenor) which is not attainable without their interaction',[14] that the vehicle is not just an embellishment, and that the respective contributions of tenor and vehicle differ from case to case.[15] His argument, therefore, is that a metaphor is not just an ornament, and the basis for this argument is a theory of metaphor in terms of 'tenor' and 'vehicle' interacting.

This theory of metaphor is not given simply against the background of a general theory of language: metaphor theory and language theory are really the same. Richards acknowledges this when he says that the context theorem of meaning is a 'summary account of the principle of metaphor'.[14] The interchangeability of the two is possible because 'metaphor is the omnipresent principle of language'.[15] It is rather difficult to accept this without qualifications. If Richards understands it as a commentary on the diachronic structure of language it might be correct, but it is irrelevant for the present discussion; if he intends it to be taken as a synchronic observation, it is incorrect and insufficient, for it denies the difference between metaphorically-used language and non-metaphorically-used language, and between metaphorical use and metaphorical sense. One can agree with Richards that 'this favourite old distinction between dead and living metaphors . . . is, indeed, a device which is very often a hindrance to the play of sagacity and discernment throughout the subject. For serious purposes it needs drastic re-examination',[18] but one has to disagree with him about the result of his re-examination: he abolishes the distinction, while it would have been better to locate the problem in the suggestion that both refer to the same or to a similar language phenomenon, and to reject that suggestion. The remarks about metaphor show, moreover, traces of the traditional rhetorical theory, namely, the focus on the word and its change of meaning. Richards recommends starting with discourse, with the sentence, and going from there to words, but the only consequence he draws from this shift in perspective is a rival theory of word meaning: words do not have fixed meanings, but the meanings they have are the result of interanimation.[19] In his theory of metaphor this results in the view that 'two thoughts of different things are supported by a single word, or phrase, whose meaning is the result of their interaction'. And apart from the problems with the broadness of 'different', the resultant meaning can only refer to a change of meaning of that single word or phrase. The remark that this resultant meaning must be clearly distinguished from the tenor points in the same direction.[20] This explains, too, why 'tenor' and 'vehicle' sometimes refer to words in the text, sometimes to objects or ideas not explicitly mentioned.[21]

Richards' theory is further developed and refined by M. Black, who criticizes the rhetorical substitution and comparison views and presents his own interaction-theory.[22] His starting-point is that metaphors are sentences or expressions 'in which *some* words are used metaphorically while the remainder are used non-metaphorically'.[23] His version of the interaction-theory runs as follows: in a metaphor, e.g., 'man is a wolf', the subsidiary subject (wolf) acts like a filter and 'the system of associated common-places' that is connected with that subsidiary subject organizes the view of the principal subject (man): in this case, man is seen through wolf, through the metaphorical expression.[24]

At first sight this version is an improvement: metaphors are explicitly called sentences and are treated as predications (principal and subsidiary subjects), but further reflection shows that the main weaknesses of Richards' theory are still present in this refined version. First, the distinction between metaphorical and non-metaphorical language. The interaction is now formulated by means of 'filtering' and 'organizing'. This explains the working of metaphorical and non-metaphorical language alike, but not the specific character of the metaphor: 'filtering', 'organizing' describes the process that occurs in all kinds of predications. 'That man is a wolf' comes close enough to Black's own example 'man is a wolf' to be helpful for the discussion. If 'that man is a wolf' is compared to 'that man is a gentleman', 'that man is a fascist', and 'that man is a father', it is clear that in all four cases 'that man' is seen through the subsidiary subject and that our view of 'that man' is organized by the various systems of commonplace associations. One might argue now that despite a superficial likeness there are really two different processes: in the case of the last three examples, all the defining properties are attributed to 'that man', while in the case of 'that man is a wolf' not all the defining properties are attributed. In the case of a metaphor those properties that cause an 'undue strain' are suppressed: in the case of metaphors, 'filtering' refers to that process of suppression.[25]

This argument locates the difference in a complete and a non-complete attribution of properties. The non-complete attribution one can understand in two ways: as a suppression of all defining properties or as a suppression of some of the defining properties. Here it is understood in the last sense.[26] The question then is in which of the two subjects the selection-criterion lies. Black's formulation suggests that the subsidiary subject exerts the greatest influence, but he maintains also that the other subject determines the process.[27] And that means that only those properties that are common to both subjects are selected, with the result that a metaphor states the resemblance between the two subjects with regard to certain properties.[28] But this conclusion seems to be contrary to Black's intention to liberate the metaphor from the comparison view. A more fundamental question is whether the selection of defining properties is typical for a metaphorical predication. In sentences like 'I love my wife', 'I love my son', 'I love music', 'I love my country', 'I love God' such a selection occurs. The flexibility or broadness of verbs like 'to love', 'to do', 'to make', 'to feel', of words like 'war', 'peace', 'struggle', 'hope', 'game', 'movement' – the feature of language to which Wittgenstein refers with his 'concepts with blurred edges', which make selection both possible and necessary, is not limited to metaphorically-used language.

The second problematic point is that there are residues of the traditional theory left in the general description of metaphor. Black distinguishes between some words that are used metaphorically, while the rest are used non-metaphorically.[29] The metaphorically-used words Black calls 'the focus', the rest of the sentence 'the frame'. The terms 'focus' and 'frame' are introduced to improve Richards' terminology. The focal word 'obtains a new meaning which is not quite its meaning in literal uses, not quite the meaning which any literal substitute would have', it undergoes 'an extension of meaning, a change of meaning. The reader must attend to both the old and the new meaning together'.[30] The interaction is thus located in the focal word and this interaction is further qualified as 'change of meaning'. This is of course compatible, for 'change of meaning' is a notion that belongs to the level of words, more precisely to the diachronic structure of words. But, as argued before, in the context of a theory of metaphor this notion is misplaced. This residue of the traditional theory makes it impossible for Black to develop fully the perspective he gained by calling the metaphor a sentence and a predication.

In a recent article Black elaborates and defends his interaction view. Some of the differences between this article and the earlier one are related to the topics discussed: instead of talking about metaphors as sentences, he now uses 'statements' and places the metaphor within the speaker-hearer situation. In the outline of his interaction view some changes occur also: the set of associated implications are now said to be comprised in the 'implicative complex'. 'The making of metaphorical statements selects, emphasises, suppresses and organizes features of the primary subject by applying to it statements isomorphic with the members of the secondary subject's implicative complex'. 'In the context of a particular metaphorical statement the two subjects "interact" in the following ways: (i) the presence of the primary subjects incites the hearer to select some of the secondary subject's properties; and (ii) invites him to construct a parallel "implicative complex" that can fit the primary subject; and (iii) reciprocally induces parallel changes in the secondary subject'.[31]

But these differences do not fundamentally change the interaction view, and the criticism of the earlier article can be directed against this one as well: it is a view that explains the general features of the meaning process but not the particular features of metaphorically-used language. Remarks that a metaphor is 'an instrument for drawing implications grounded in perceived analogies of structure between two subjects belonging to different domains'[32] is not sufficient as long as the difference is not further determined. Black's remark that the interaction view is 'an attempted application of Richards' striking image of the "interanimation of words"'[33] is a revealing comment in this context. The other point of criticism – the appeal to the notion 'change of meaning' – can be maintained also, for that notion is still central: 'that the use of the relevant concepts employed should *change* (so that "game" is *made* to apply to marriage; "information" to life; "reed" to man; and so on) seems essential to the operation'.[34]

In the course of discussing Black's first article the suggestion that metaphors could be sufficiently explained in terms of the selection of defining properties was developed in a certain way. Beardsley's contribution to the theory of metaphor consists in a different development of that suggestion: in his original theory and in subsequent revisions 'defining properties' play a central role, for he explains the mechanism of the metaphor with reference to extension and intension.[35] And there is another reason why his theory is of interest for the present discussion: the theory he rejects can be understood as the theory we proposed in the previous section.

Like Richards and Black, Beardsley rejects the traditional

rhetorical theory and proposes his own theory against the background of a non-referential theory about the status of a literary work. These two elements return in the titles he gives to his own theory and to the rival theory: 'verbal-opposition theory' and 'object-comparison theory'. He criticizes the object-comparison theory not only for treating metaphors as comparisons or similes, but also for using a 'thing-approach'. The 'thing-approach' maintains that 'the modifier . . . in the metaphor . . . retains its standard designative role when it enters into the metaphor and therefore continues in that context to denote the same object it denotes in literal contexts'.[36] The three arguments Beardsley gives for rejecting this approach are: first, the properties an object is believed to have are important for a metaphor, and these believed properties are not considered if one looks for an object; secondly, the search for an object often results in 'that flow of idiosyncratic imagery that is a serious barrier between the reader and the poem';[37] and lastly, this theory tends to lead to 'the unfortunate theory of appropriateness'.[38] The last two arguments are not very strong, because they point only to possible or actual abuses, which are not necessarily connected with this approach.[39] The first argument has more force, but could be accommodated for by including in the theory the way objects are perceived by a community of speakers. This rival theory can also be formulated without reference to objects, but with reference to the meaning of words that remain the same. This means that Beardsley's theory can be understood as a criticism of the theory proposed earlier. Is Beardsley's theory a genuine alternative?

Beardsley's starting-point is that a metaphor is a kind of attribution, i.e., 'a linguistic expression containing at least two words, one of which denotes a class and also characterises it in some way, and the other of which qualifies or modifies the characterization'.[40] The possibility of metaphorical language depends upon the difference between two sets of properties in the intension of a general term: the difference between defining properties, whose presence is a necessary condition for the correct use of the term and the accidental properties, or, the difference between 'central meaning' and 'marginal meaning'. In the metaphor theory this distinction is used as follows:

'when a term is combined with others in such a way that there would be a logical opposition between its central meaning and that of the other terms, there occurs that shift from central to marginal meaning which shows the word is to be taken in a metaphorical way'.[41] This shift implies that 'the predicate loses its ordinary extension, because it acquires a new intension, perhaps one that it has in no other context'.[42]

So there are three elements in Beardsley's theory: a logical opposition, or, as he puts it sometimes, an absurdity; a difference between two levels of meaning within a term, and, a shift within the modifier from one level to another, from central meaning (designation) to marginal meaning (connotation in the literary sense).[43] These elements do not lead to an adequate theory of metaphor, though, as a closer examination reveals. The central place is occupied by the notion of marginal meaning, and Beardsley has apparently sensed the problematic aspects of this notion, for in his two revisions he makes changes on this point. In his first revision, he adds a further distinction inside the marginal meaning, inside the 'potential range of connotations': staple connotations and connotations that 'wait so to say, lurking in the nature of things for actualization'.[44] But this refinement inside the marginal meaning does not solve the main problem that surrounds this notion and the shift to marginal meaning. These suggest that the central meanings can be separated from the marginal ones and can be put out of order, so to say, but the link between the two cannot so easily be severed. For example, 'quietness' can belong to the connotations of a ghost-town, a medieval church, a forest, and the adagio of Schubert's string quintet, but it makes a difference to which of these 'quietness' belongs. The shift further suggests that in the case of metaphors the level of marginal meanings is the really important one and this leads to a reductionist, rhetorical theory of metaphor, for it is not clear why the level of the central meaning is necessary: the speaker could have chosen a shorter way and could have expressed himself more directly.

Beardsley cannot, strictly speaking, appeal to the central meanings as a continuous source for new implications.[45] The formulation of the shift in terms of extension-intension does not make the situation much clearer. 'The predication loses its ordinary extension, because it acquires a new intension, perhaps one that it has in no other context'.[46] The extension of a term consists of the class of objects to which the term is applicable and this class can consist of many (human being), of one (sun), or none (unicorn). 'Losing its extension' means, then, that the term is no longer applied or applicable to its usual class, but since a term has by definition an extension (which may or may not be empty), 'losing its extension' cannot be understood as saying that this term, which once had an extension, does not have one now. The question now is how this new extension is related to the ordinary one. If the central meaning of a term – i.e. the defining characteristics – is dropped, completely, as Beardsley suggests, the marginal meanings are presumably the defining characteristics of this new extension. The reason the term loses its ordinary extension is the acquisition of a new intension. How is the marginal meaning related to the intension of a term? The intension of a term consists of the attributes or characteristics an object must have in order to qualify for the application of a term. The intension is commonly divided into 'objective intension' – all the attributes that the objects in the denotation of the term have in common – 'subjective intension' – the attributes that come to a person's mind when he or she uses the term – and 'conventional intension' – the necessary and sufficient conditions for regarding an object as qualifying for the term. Marginal meaning comes, at first sight, closest to subjective intension, but subjective intension normally includes defining characteristics. Marginal meanings, or accidental properties, seem therefore to point to personal associations.[47] If that is the case, the presuppositions of a communication structure are destroyed, and the 'meaning' of a metaphor becomes something personal and individual.

These problems attached to the distinction between the two levels of meaning cast doubt upon that distinction. Beardsley may be correct in pointing to 'a *felt* difference between sets of properties',[48] but he is incorrect in interpreting this difference as a difference of meaning. Mackie, who qualifies Beardsley's theory as 'the most adequate account of the semantic structure of metaphor', says, nevertheless, referring to marginal meaning, that he is 'of course wrong to call this "meaning".'[49] The explanation in terms of a shift to marginal 'meanings' does therefore not constitute an explanation of metaphors functioning in a communication process.

In his second revision, Beardsley returns again to this central notion of marginal meaning. Compared with the previous version, it contains some terminological differences: a metaphorical sequence, or metaphor, is now divided into a metaphorical segment and a non-metaphorical segment; the intension of a term, understood as a set of properties, is now formulated in terms of 'sense'; each distinguishable intension is a sense, and a standard sense is the sense that stays unchanged in various similar contexts. For the outline of the theory of metaphor this results in, a metaphorical segment 'acquires a sense different from any of its standard senses'.[50] The properties that are of importance in the case of a metaphor are the believed properties – 'credence properties' – that include 'the undenied defining properties of the members of the extension of the metaphorical segment'.[51] The inclusion of the 'undenied properties' is due to the acceptance of a point of criticism made by Mackie.[52] But this revision of 'the marginal meaning' notion is more drastic than the previous one which concerned a refinement inside the marginal meaning: here Beardsley allows the defining properties to continue to determine the meaning of a term. This means that the original shift from one level to another is replaced by the denial of some defining properties, and the result is a theory very much like the one Black proposes.[53]

So Beardsley's possible alternative to the theory proposed in the previous section does not turn out to be a genuine one. His theory, based upon the suggestion that in a metaphor a non-complete attribution of defining properties occurs, develops this suggestion originally in the most radical way and maintains that all defining properties are suppressed. But this development does not prove to be coherent. In his latest revision Beardsley presents a less radical interpretation of that suggestion by claiming that only some of the defining properties are suppressed, but this way of solving the problems, which is similar to Black's theory, does not give a sufficient explanation of metaphorical predication.

3.3 *The category-mistake approach*

In the literature on metaphors one can find a few attempts to link metaphors with category-mistakes or type-crossings. At first sight these theories resemble the one proposed in the previous section, but there are major differences with regard to identification and explanation, which call the helpfulness of this approach into question.

'Category mistake' is a concept used by Ryle.[1] Ryle lists two kinds of sentences as specimens of category mistakes, i.e. mistakes in the use of concepts. First, sentences like 'I am now lying' and 'heterological is heterological'; and, secondly, 'Saturday is in bed'.[2] Both kinds are 'absurd', and their absurdity is the result of 'type-trespassing', 'type-rule breaking', and 'improper coupling'. But since the two kinds are rather different, the relation of the metaphor with regard to these two has to be established. Do metaphors belong to the first kind? This is the kind Ryle is mainly interested in. The important feature of this type is that people who make this kind of mistake do not fully know the use of the concepts involved, and that is precisely the reason why they are 'theoretically interesting' and 'insidious'.[3] But insufficient knowledge of the concepts involved does not result in metaphors, nor does it play a role in understanding them. So one has to locate metaphors among the sentences of the second kind. Ryle makes only a few remarks about this type of sentences: they are formulated only with 'the deliberate intention to produce balderdash' and they are 'obviously absurd'.[4] These two points might be correct for the description and qualification of sentences like 'the concept of real numbers is drowning between the morning star and poverty', but are they also correct in the case of metaphors? Can metaphors be identified by means of these two characteristics? No, for metaphors are produced with the intention to make sense and are not obviously absurd. 'Absurdity' seems to suggest and to indicate that one cannot make sense, that one cannot give a context to the sentence, and 'obviously' points to clear evidence of the nonsense. But absurdity is often a qualification that is applied after a search for meaning. Very few grammatically well-formed sentences are 'obviously absurd', more sentences appear to be absurd after some inquiry, but even Ryle's example 'Saturday is in bed' does not belong to that category. And apart from the problem of how to identify metaphors with the help of Ryle's remarks, there is also the problem how to explain them in terms of Ryle's analysis. Ryle talks about 'rule-breaking' which is a correct explanation for mistakes, absurdity, and meaninglessness, but, as argued earlier, this notion is distinctly unhelpful in explaining metaphors. How then do writers, who use this notion of category mistake in their theory of metaphor, solve these problems?

Turbayne is one of these authors and he uses Ryle's notion to improve certain facets of the Aristotelian definition of metaphor which he thinks basically correct.[5] Two phrases from Ryle's *The Concept of Mind* – 'the presentation of the facts of one category in the idiom of the other', and 'it represents the facts of mental life as if they belonged to another' – help him to state the necessary and the sufficient conditions for a metaphor: it is a sort-crossing and it has an as-if character. But he does not adopt Ryle's analysis completely: in order to facilitate the link between category mistake and metaphor Turbayne tries to soften the mistake aspect. 'But it seems altogether unlikely that Ryle regards metaphors as mistakes, for such category mistakes may have great value. It is not necessarily a mistake to cross sorts'.[6] Turbayne's solution is then to introduce a distinction between sort-crossing or category-fusion on the one hand, and sort-trespassing or category-confusion on the other. The distinction is connected with a duality of sense. The last word of the sentence 'timberwolves and men are wolves' does not refer to different sorts of wolves as in 'timberwolves and Tasmanian wolves are wolves', because in the first sentence 'wolves' is used in two different senses, even though it looks as if it is being used only in one sense. The two senses are called the literal and the metaphorical sense of 'wolf'.[7] Metaphor is a category fusion if the users are aware of the duality of sense and pretend that the two senses, literal and metaphorical, are one.[8] Metaphor is a category confusion and a mistake when it is taken literally, i.e., when the metaphorical sense is taken for the literal one.[9] And this leads Turbayne to the statement that 'since a metaphor is not a metaphor *per se*, but only for someone, from one point of view it is better to say that sometimes the metaphor is not noticed; it is hidden. That is, if X is aware of the metaphor while Y is not, X says that Y is being taken in by the metaphor, or being used by it, or taking it literally. But for Y it is not the case of taking the metaphor literally at all, because for him there is no metaphor'.[10]

Turbayne's way of applying Ryle's notion does not solve the problems that arise when 'category mistake' is employed in metaphor theory. On the contrary, the introduction of the distinction between category fusion and category confusion adds some more problems. The distinction presupposes that a metaphor is a word with a metaphorical sense. The distinction changes the original concept almost completely, moreover. The result is that whether a sentence is a metaphor or not depends on the personal understanding of the user, and that no metaphor can be taken literally, for if it is taken literally it is not a metaphor. The first point destroys the communication structure, while the second undermines Turbayne's argument. The strangeness of the appeal to 'interpretation', which underlies this argument (cf Beardsley) is hidden by the presupposition of the duality of sense; it is much clearer in a book about the basis of meaningless sentences, which also mentions metaphors briefly and which belongs to this type of approach, namely, Drange's *Typecrossing*.[11]

Drange defines a typecrossing as a sentence 'which ascribes in a positive manner to a thing (or set of things) x, a property, the type associated with which is a class to which x does not belong'.[12] Some of his examples can elucidate this definition: 'chemistry is a greater ordinal than the concept of truth', 'the number 5 weighs more than the number 6' and 'the theory of relativity is blue'. These sentences are meaningless, and their meaninglessness cannot be explained in terms of the violation of rules, or type-rules, or linguistic conventions (so, e.g., Ryle), but must be explained in terms of 'unthinkability'. Typecrossings designate unthinkable propositions, i.e., 'combinations of concepts which cannot be put together in thought'.[13] Interpretation plays a crucial role in this argument and it links metaphors and type-crossings. 'All typecrossings then are meaningless and this is so by virtue of the interpretation given to them . . . what distinguishes a metaphorical sentence from a typecrossing composed of the same words in the same order is the meaning or interpretation to be given to some of the words.

No doubt most metaphorical sentences would be typecrossings, if they were taken literally'.[14] And Drange returns to this theme at the end of the book: 'Actually, a metaphorical sentence, taken literally, is invariably a typecrossing . . . Since it cannot be taken literally, the reader or listener is forced to reinterpret what is presented to him'.[15]

The problem here is not just that there is an inconsistency between the two quotations (most-invariably), nor that the metaphor is seen as a word with a special non-literal sense: the main problem lies in the use of 'interpretation' in connection with meaninglessness and metaphors. Drange's use of 'interpretation' is similar to that of Turbayne and Beardsley.[16] How is 'interpretation' to be understood? That a sentence is meaningless in virtue of the interpretation given to the words used is correct, if 'interpretation' is understood and used in the sense of 'understanding these words in their normal senses'. For if this is not the case, everything is allowed and possible. An absurd and meaningless sentence like 'the square root of $-5¼$ sits on the mat' become a meaningful sentence if 'the square root of $-5¼$' is interpreted as 'cat'. This absurd conclusion can only be avoided by recognizing that the words used determine, guide and limit the interpretation. An interpretation without this type of control undermines the communication function of language and questions the need of using precisely these words. But if understood in this way, the thesis is also correct in the case of meaningful sentences: it is trivially true. 'Interpretation', refers, then to what was earlier called the interanimation or interaction of words in a sentence, and so refers to the selection procedure that takes place in every sentence. 'Interpretation' can also be understood as a 'second move' in the process of understanding a sentence. Interpretation furthers understanding by correcting or developing the initial understanding via specifying the precise meaning of a technical term or via referring to the appropriate context or theory, etc. In this sense events, objects, words, texts, etc. are interpreted in an everyday way or in a more systematic way in the sciences. This 'reflective interpretation' cannot be used to distinguish the understanding of metaphors from the understanding of other sentences since such a process can be called for in both cases.[17]

So, although 'interpretation' in either sense can be used within a metaphor-theory, it cannot fulfil the task some think it can: it cannot mark the difference between metaphors on the one hand and other sentences, meaningful or meaningless, on the other, and it cannot explain the meaning mechanism of the metaphor sufficiently. 'Interpretation' can only give the suggestion of being an explanatory term if metaphorical sense is thought to be the explanandum. The conclusion, therefore, is that the notion of category mistake as used by Ryle is not very helpful for metaphor theory, and the changes made by Turbayne (to soften the mistake aspect) and Drange (to drop rule violation) change the notion rather drastically. But even with these changes the proposed theories are not satisfactory, because of their concentration on metaphorical sense and because of their peculiar use of 'interpretation'.[18]

4. Two problems

The discussion of two issues with a somewhat different focus concludes the exposition of our theory of metaphor. The first issue is the need to introduce 'true' and 'false' into metaphor theory, the second is the paraphrase of metaphors. While the discussion of these issues can be seen as the continuation of the search for appropriate notions in metaphor theory, the second is more concerned with some consequences of the proposed theory and as such also forms a link with the following chapters.

4.1 *True and false*

Are the notions 'true' and 'false', or one of these, indispensable to a coherent theory of metaphor? Do both, or does one of, these notions have to be introduced into the theory to explain the typical, characteristic features of metaphor? Some authors employ these notions, but what are their reasons for doing so?

When Berggren explains the point which constitutes the new insight of interaction theory, or tension theory as he calls it, he notices two related dimensions in the tension: 'On the one hand, a logical or empirical absurdity stands in apparent conflict with a possible truth. On the other hand, this possible truth may itself depend upon a creative interaction between diverse perspectives which cannot be literalized or disentangled without destroying the kind of insight, truth, or reality which the metaphor provides'.[1] As this quotation indicates, and as Berggren again stresses when he says that the truth of a metaphor 'can survive only at the intersection of the diverse perspectives whose interaction made it possible',[2] the truth of a metaphor is related to the interaction. These sayings imply also that every metaphor, or every 'vital metaphor',[3] is true. There are three problematic features to this and similar positions (cf Beardsley).

First, the appeal to the special meaning, to the 'creative interaction between diverse perspectives', is an appeal to a 'stereoscopic vision', in which 'the perspectives prior to and subsequent to the transformation of the metaphor's principle and subsidiary subjects must both be conjointly maintained',[4] – an appeal to both the normal meanings and the metaphorical meanings. But this interpretation and explanation of metaphor is not an adequate one, and cannot therefore function as the ground for introducing 'true'. Secondly, the argument leads Berggren to maintain that a metaphor is false or absurd *and* true. This is the consequence of his appeal to both the normal and the metaphorical meanings. But, as the previous section has shown, the view that an absurd sentence becomes a metaphor via an additional interpretation (metaphorical meaning) is not coherent. The same criticism can be used against 'intention', another possible addition. 'Intention' is not an element exclusive to metaphorical language and is not a decisive element in it: the words used in it do not change their meaning by mere intention.

Even if we only wanted to keep one of these notions, there is still the third problematic feature, viz., that the metaphor is called 'true' in a special way (the metaphor is not true, but 'true') or that the notion 'metaphorical truth' is introduced. This provokes a 'suspicion of equivocation',[5] especially when, as in Berggren, all 'vital metaphors' are true. That implies a departure from the normal use of 'true', for it is not customary to claim that every statement is true. One can decide 'to take metaphors as true merely by stipulative definition, when novel and as no longer metaphorical, but rather literally true or false when deceased', as Loewenberg prefers. But, as she acknowledges, 'truth by stipulation is, of course, too trivial to be helpful'.[6] Ricoeur uses 'metaphorical truth' to indicate the final consequences of the tension or interaction theory.[7] He asks whether the tension that affects the relational function of the copula also affect the existential function of the copula. He proceeds in a dialectical way and reaches in the end an affirmative answer. He points to the inadequacies of the non-critical insistence upon the logical commitment implied in metaphor, as (e.g.) Wheelwright does, and to the inadequacies of the critical interpretation of metaphor that stresses the need to expose and demythologize metaphors, as Turbayne does. In the first case the 'is-not' is neglected, in the second case the 'is', but both elements have to be maintained. Ricoeur thinks the concept 'metaphorical truth' apt to express both elements, for it 'includes the point of criticism of the "is not" (literally) in the ontological impetuosity of the "is" (metaphorically).'[8] Or in other words, 'metaphorical truth' expresses the same as the notion 'proposal to redescribe reality', which is the refinement of another notion used by Ricoeur. This makes clear that it is a notion explaining the function of the metaphor, as also is indicated by Berggren when he juxtaposes 'insight' and 'truth'. But apart from this, 'proposal to redescribe reality' seems to be more apt to capture and express the tensive relation with reality than 'metaphorical truth', without the suspicion of equivocation. That the relation with reality does not necessarily have to be expressed by means of 'true' is shown by hypotheses, which reveal a somewhat similar tensive relation with reality.[9]

So, the arguments for introducing 'true' and 'false', or 'true' alone, as indispensable concepts in metaphor theory are not convincing. What is problematic about metaphors is not that they are true or false, or neither true nor false (cf hypotheses), but that they present an extraordinary combination of concepts.

4.2 *Paraphrase*

It is a common agreement among modern writers that a paraphrase of a metaphor lacks the evocative power of the original. But the question whether a paraphrase necessarily causes a difference in 'cognitive content' does not receive such a unanimous answer. The interaction theorists argue for a strong thesis: a paraphrase is inadequate with regard to both the evocative power and the cognitive content. Others argue for a weaker thesis and maintain that there is only a difference in evocative power.[1]

Black formulates the stronger thesis like this: 'But the set of literal statements so obtained will not have the same power to inform and enlighten as the original... The literal paraphrase inevitably says too much – and with the wrong emphasis. One of the points I most wish to stress is that the loss in such cases is a loss in cognitive content; the relevant weakness of the literal paraphrase is not that it may be tiresomely prolix or boringly explicit (or deficient in qualities of style); it fails to give the insight that the metaphor did'.[2] And Berggren argues: 'It is precisely this transformation of both referents, moreover, interacting with their normal meanings, which makes it ultimately impossible to reduce completely the cognitive import of any vital metaphor to any set of univocal, literal or non-tensional statements. For a special meaning and in some cases even a new sort of reality, is achieved which cannot survive except at the intersection of the two perspectives which produce it'.[3] There are several claims in these quotations: there is a special meaning due to the interaction which is lost in a paraphrase,[4] there is a difference of cognitive content between the metaphor and its paraphrase,[5] and the paraphrase does not have the same effect, i.e., does not give the same insight that the metaphor gives. Although the elements are interconnected, the first two are different from the third: the former concern the mechanism of metaphor, the latter concerns the effect of metaphor, and the two should not be confused. This strong thesis seems to be robbed of its basic argument by the discussion in the previous section about the inappropriateness for metaphor theory of the notion 'change of meaning' or 'special meaning localized in the focal word'. Is this the only argument in favour of the strong thesis? Are other arguments possible? What are the criticisms and arguments of those who defend the weaker thesis?

Warner concerns himself with Black's article only and he concentrates his criticism on the notion 'cognitive content' and the way Black employs it. Warner defines cognitive content in terms of truth conditions: 'The content of an utterance is presumably cognitive ... in so far as it is capable of being asserted to make a truth claim'.[6] If sentences have the same cognitive content, they have also the same truth conditions; if they have a different cognitive content, they have different truth conditions. Thus, when Black says that there is a difference in cognitive content between a metaphor and its paraphrase, it implies that there are different truth conditions in both cases. Warner selects two phrases from Black and develops these. The first one is 'the literal paraphrase says too much'; this implies that 'there are logically possible conditions in which the metaphor will hold and the paraphrase be false'.[7] But this does not amount to the claim that a metaphor has some inexpressible truth; it only means a refusal to specify the truth conditions of the metaphor. The second remark Warner develops is the one about 'the loss of cognitive content', and this remark implies the opposite: 'in certain circumstances the metaphor will fail to hold while the paraphrase is true'.[8] If this is the case we can adjust the paraphrase. So, this only says that one cannot be sure that one has given all possible implications and paraphrases, but it does not mean that, when one sees that an implication is missing, one cannot put it into a paraphrase.[9] Manns has argued that Warner, by connecting 'cognitive content' with truth conditions, gives it an interpretation which is narrower than Black's and narrower than the term itself suggests.[10] Manns is correct. Furthermore, Warner places too much emphasis on the remark he develops first: Black's main point is the second remark; moreover, Black adds to the first remark 'with the wrong emphasis', for a paraphrase presents the implications 'explicitly as though having equal weight'.[11] What is left of Warner's argument is that 'loss of content' refers to the fact that due to the 'open texture' metaphors may imply more implications than one has realized.[12]

Paul's criticism of the strong thesis centres around the way 'meaning' is used in defence of that thesis, namely, that meanings or parts of meaning are not accessible to translation or explication.[13] According to Paul, a string of words has meaning 'if and only if it is intelligible (understandable, comprehensible) to suitable informed speakers of the language . . . if and only if there would be consensus among the speakers of the language as to its meaning'.[14] If there is no consensus about the string, it is a nonsense-string.[15] An indication of the difference between sense- and nonsense-string is that the first is paraphrasable, that is to say, that the meaning of the sentence as a whole is paraphrasable, and not just the individual words that are used in it. What a sentence means can be determined by looking at how speakers paraphrase, explicate, use the sentence: '. . . meaning in a language is a public matter for which paraphrase, explication and use are the only plausible public criteria'.[16] The strong thesis maintains now that there remains some residue of meaning that cannot be captured by a paraphrase, but can this 'more' be called 'meaning'? No, 'since there is no reliable indicator that different speakers attribute the same residue of inaccessible meaning to the metaphor, there is no reason to suppose that it actually does mean anything more than is brought out in the analysis'.[17] Meaning is not a matter of 'idiosyncratic feelings individual speakers may have'.[18] Paul adds further that 'semantic indeterminacy', i.e., 'the uncertainty as to what we really take the metaphor to mean'[19] causes this idea that the paraphrase is inadequate. But what this indeterminacy really amounts to is not that 'we perceive in the metaphor some aspect of its meaning that defies specification, but that we are not sure *what* we take it to mean'.[20] Paul's argument about the public character of meaning is correct.[21] It is therefore surprising that Paul fails to see that the thesis would not follow if the claim that the meaning of the focal word changes is taken seriously, and that he fails to question that claim. His final comment is surprising, too, since 'we are not sure exactly what we take it to mean' seems to contradict his previous argument and to be inadmissible on his own description of meaning. But he is certainly correct to point to the semantic indeterminacy of the metaphor.

So, both Warner's remaining, valid point and Paul's semantic indeterminacy imply that there is an uncertainty as to whether the given paraphrases cover all the elements and implication of the metaphor, and as to whether the balance is correct. This is an important point and it gives the metaphor a special function on the level of heuristics. This is acknowledged by the interaction theorists, and it seems that this is the point that remains valid when the appeal to the change of meaning is removed. This reconciliation between the two parties seems a little too easy, though, for there is another element in the whole discussion that colours the views on both sides and that prevents them from seeing this common point: the shared view of what 'paraphrase' stands for.

With regard to paraphrase there is first a point that concerns the paraphrase of literal and metaphorical sentences alike. Apart from the problem of synonymity, the possibility of an adequate paraphrase on the interanimation view does not seem to be so great: other words exert another controlling influence. Even if one does not accept this argument, one has to deal with the following point. Equivalence in paraphrase, covering everything (including personal, psychological associations) has been given up since it is an impossible ideal. But this has turned equivalence in cognitive meaning into a 'chimera' as well. 'For, if cognitive meaning is that meaning which remains constant between two sentences which are mutual paraphrases, we are begging the question we wanted to answer. And no better definition of cognitive meaning has been offered'.[22] We are in fact satisfied with less than equivalent paraphrases in the case of normal sentences; why should we require equivalent paraphrases in the case of metaphors?

But there is another point that is more important for this discussion. The parties involved share the presupposition that in the case of a normal sentence and in the case of a metaphorical sentence 'paraphrase' amounts to the same. But is that presupposition correct? Manns points to a remarkable feature of the paraphrase discussion: the participants come up with their own attempts at paraphrasing, while they use poetical metaphors as their examples. Hardly anybody refers to 'the genuine source of the great majority of paraphrase': literary criticism. If one looks at the practice of literary critics one sees that they are *'making no attempt whatever* at delineating in full the sense of any metaphor. What they are doing is directing with words our intellectual gaze in a manner which, it is hoped, will enable us to trace out for ourselves the myriad of implications, associations, and images that diffuse themselves behind the concentrated focus that is the metaphor'.[23] This is not special to literary critics, or to poetical metaphors. Stewart argues that to paraphrase a non-metaphorical expression is something different from paraphrasing any metaphor. If one paraphrases a non-metaphorical sentence, the relation between the original and the paraphrase is symmetrical. 'If we are to say that one expression means the same thing as another expression, then we must say that the second expression means the same thing as the first'.[24] Paraphrases of metaphors, including those of 'moribund' metaphors like 'Richard is a lion', do not achieve this kind of symmetry. A symmetrical paraphrase is possible in the case of normal sentences, since they have an accepted meaning; in the case of metaphors there are several interpretations possible.[25] This point can be put in terms used earlier: in the case of a normal expression the rules are followed, and that is the reason why there is an accepted, established meaning; it can be paraphrased in a 'symmetrical way' because it remains within the accepted structure of concepts. In the case of metaphorically-used language, the rules are relaxed for the time being and the paraphrase attempts to bring out the implications, possible connections, eventual revisions in the structure that would form the consequence if this metaphorical connection was accepted as a normal one. The semantic indeterminacy of the metaphor, the openness of the metaphor, requires a type of paraphrase all its own. One may wish to give some explication of the words used in a metaphor, but if one remains satisfied with this phase, one is not only incapable of doing justice to the richness and complexity of the metaphor, but one is also in danger of treating the metaphor as a word. Precisely what this special type of paraphrase will look like will depend on the purpose for which it is given, but it will be some variation on the general pattern of revealing and showing 'the myriad of implications' of the extraordinary combination.

5. *Conclusion*

The starting-point determining the whole discussion about metaphor theory is the observation that a metaphor is a sentence. This rather formal beginning leads to the discovery of two crucial elements: the need to concentrate upon the metaphorical use of words, and the recognition that the characteristic features of metaphors have to be located on the level of propositional content. In the development of this recognition, it appears that the typical features of metaphors, which accounts for their strangeness, is caused by their extraordinary combination between ranges or realms of concepts which are normally not combined. The need to concentrate upon metaphorical use bars any explanation in terms that suggest or indicate some kind of permanency. The solution, then, is to explain the meaning mechanism of the metaphor in terms of a temporary relaxation of the rules governing those realms of concept. And since the way these concepts are structured and can be combined is related to the way we see reality and the way we live, the function of such an extraordinary combination, the function of metaphor, can be formulated as a proposal to redescribe reality. The exploration of the question of how the relation between language and reality has to be seen constitutes a coherence test for this solution. Reflections upon the conventional character of language, the function of rules in language, and the interweaving of language and life show that it is possible to explain the meaning mechanism of the metaphor in these terms.

In the course of the discussion elements and notions also emerge that turn out to be inappropriate, misleading or incorrect for a theory of metaphor. The other side of the concentration upon metaphorical use is that metaphorical sense – the metaphorical meaning a word has acquired in the past – is not an issue in a theory of metaphor. Consequently, explanations suggesting a change of meaning or a change of rules are beside the point. Moreover, the focus on metaphorical meaning implies a focus on a 'metaphorical word'. These elements return in a more systematic discussion of other theories. The analysis of the word approach shows that this type of theory can only give a diachronic analysis, i.e., an analysis of how words receive a metaphorical extension. Given the starting-point this is understandable, and also the only possible explanation.

As the discussion among linguists shows, broadening the view to metaphors as a phrase or sentence is not enough if one remains within the sphere of linguistic competence. The self-imposed limitation to the study of linguistic competence only results either in an incapacity to distinguish between metaphor and deviant sentences or in a diachronic explanation of meaning acquisition. Only if the metaphor is treated as a speech-act can the special kind of predication that it is be discovered. The account given in the interaction theories is insufficient insofar as the selection and interaction procedure which occurs in every sentence or predication is presented as the explanation of the typical features of the metaphor, and correct insofar as a preoccupation with metaphorical sense and change of meaning still determines the theories.

Other inappropriate notions or misleading concepts and presuppositions are discovered as well in the course of a systematic discussion. Use of the term 'category mistake' itself suggests that the distinction between metaphor and mistake has disappeared. The appeal, made in this context but also in others, to interpretation or intention as a second phase does not solve the problem, and leads in the end to the destruction of the communicative function of language. 'Truth' (or 'metaphorical truth', which is a problematic notion in itself) is not a necessary category in a theory of metaphor: the problematic aspect of metaphors does not lie in the fact that they are true or false or neither true nor false, but that they express an extraordinary combination. It is this which requires a type of paraphrase that differs from what is presupposed in most of the discussion about the possibility of paraphrasing a metaphor.

So, the notion of 'relaxing the rules for the time being', and the further specification of the rules as those rules that govern the use of ranges of concepts, is central and sufficient to the explanation of the meaning mechanism, of the metaphorical use of words, while the notion 'proposal to redescribe reality' captures the variety of purposes such a use has.

Chapter III

Three Answers

A discussion of the relation between metaphor and theology is the second step in solving the problems brought to light by the analyses of Chapter I. Against the background of the theory proposed in Chapter II, the following questions have to be answered: Do metaphors play a crucial role in theology? Can they? Should they? Some answers have been indicated, albeit rather sketchily, by some theologians in their discussion of the central term of *Lumen Gentium*. The negative answers of traditional systematic theology can be discovered in, e.g., Mühlen's and Koster's arguments, while Dulles, by using models, and Philips, by stressing the evocative power of parables, reflect a positive answer which has been developed in recent years. The more elaborate answers have to be examined. But since the presuppositions about metaphor in these theoretical discussions are not always correct, the various arguments have to be restated and reconstrued in order to make a proper evaluation possible. A first positive answer can be found in narrative theology, although both a radical and a moderate version can be discerned. (Section 1.) A second positive answer is presented by some philosophers of religion, who stress the similarity between the use of models in science and in theology. In this context a closer look at one particular theory in the philosophy of science is necessary in order to evaluate the transition from metaphor to model. (Section 2) A negative answer is given in traditional systematic theology. An exponent who is mentioned and criticized by some narrative theologians, and who stands at the head of the process which has led to the division between exegesis and systematic theology, is Thomas Aquinas. He discusses the issue explicitly in his first and last systematic theological works, and his views provide material for the negative answer. (Section 3.)

1. *Narrative theology*

In recent literature on narrative theology one can distinguish different sources or emphases.[1] A first important source is the analysis of scriptural language, especially the language of the New Testament. 'Story' appears as a central category, referring either to the gospel genre or to the parable genre. Gospel or parable are considered the most characteristic formulations and expressions of Christian faith.[2] A second source is formed by autobiography and biography. The starting-point here is the understanding of life as a story and the influence of religion in that life, the changes it causes, and the developments it brings about. In the case of biography contemporary religious men or women are often selected and presented as examples.[3] A third source is concerned with the link between experience and story or narrative. All experience takes place in time, which means that it occurs in one of the modalities of time: past, present, or future. These modalities are not separated but united in every experience. This unity exhibits the beginning of a narrative form: 'the formal quality of experience through time is inherently narrative'.[4] Related to this is a criticism of academic or argumentative theology: this type of theology fails to relate to people's experiences and is distinctly unhelpful in education, counselling, and preaching, for its language does not appeal to people.[5]

These elements, albeit with differences of emphasis and approach, can be discerned in a book by S. TeSelle, which deals explicitly with the main question of this chapter, and in the view of narrative theology developed over the recent years by J.-B. Metz. These views will be presented in the next two subsections, while in a third the questions provoked by a construction of a 'metaphorical theology' on the basis of these arguments will be discussed.

1.1 *Intermediary theology*

TeSelle's *Speaking in Parables: A Study in Metaphor and Theology* is divided into a foundational and a constructive part.[1] In the first part TeSelle argues for a kind of theology that she calls 'parabolic' or 'intermediary', i.e., a theology that uses metaphors and parables as basic forms of reflection. In the second part the sources of this type of theology are discussed: poem, story, and autobiography. For the present discussion the first part is the more interesting.

In the introduction TeSelle states that theology could better fulfil its function of making the gospel credible or possible in our secular and disbelieving time if theology were 'to attend to Jesus' parables as models of theological reflection, for parables keep "in solution" the language, belief and life we are called to, and hence they address people totally'.[2] In this quotation two different arguments can be distinguished – one about the function of theology and one about metaphor – which are both developed in the following chapters.

The argument about metaphor is connected with the overall argument by means of an identification between metaphor and parable: parables are extended metaphors. A metaphor is 'a word used in an unfamiliar context to give us new insight . . . metaphor is a way of *knowing*, not just a way of communicating'.[3] This connection between metaphor and knowledge is discussed in a chapter entitled 'Metaphor: the heart of the matter', together with two other connections: first, the connection between metaphor and the creation of new meaning – metaphors create new meanings, which are only available in metaphors; and secondly, the connection between metaphor and the constitution of language – metaphor is the foundation of language, since 'language, all language is ultimately traceable to metaphors'.[4] These two connections lead to the most important one: metaphor is basic 'to all human thought of whatever sort',[5] and 'all thought is metaphorical'.[6] In exploring this connection TeSelle uses the notion 'move' ('Metaphor as Human Movement' is the title of a section): 'Metaphorical thinking . . . is the way human beings, selves (not mere minds), *move* in all areas of discovery, whether these be scientific, religious, poetic, social, political or personal'.[7] and 'our movement, of whatever sort, is always metaphorical, with ourselves as one term of the metaphor',[8] i.e., human beings understand the unknown in terms of themselves. This implies an epistemological position; 'human knowing, at its most profound, is not disembodied, abstract or conceptual; the analogy for human knowing is not the Cartesian machine but the evolutionary organism – the stretching of the whole creature beyond itself into the unknown';[9] 'Metaphor . . . is *the* way of human knowing'.[10] Abstract thought and abstract language seem the natural completion of metaphorical language, but it is 'unfortunate' to consider this completion as the 'highest' development: it is more appropriate to see it as a degeneration. 'Discursive language, then, the language which relates, communicates, designates, measures, enumerates, dissects, analyzes, systematizes, depends on metaphorical language – it is, in fact the old age of such language'.[11]

In the light of the previous chapter the inadequacies of this view of metaphor will be apparent. The definition ('a word used in an unfamiliar context') is a word-centred definition and the discussion of the connection between metaphor on the one hand and the change of meaning and the constitution of language on the other, reveal that the crucial distinction between metaphorical sense and metaphorical use is not made. The central connection between metaphor and knowledge and the claims made concerning this connection are only possible because of the vagueness and the imprecision of the definition. 'Unfamiliar' is a subjective and temporal term. Something can be unfamiliar to one person but not to another, and something can be unfamiliar to someone up to a certain time, till he becomes acquainted with it. If this is applied to metaphor, it means that a metaphor ceases to be metaphor after one has encountered it, or used it a few times, and that whether a sentence is a metaphor or not depends on personal experience. 'Context', too, is problematic, since, if it is understood linguistically, all new information, even all new sentences, are covered by this definition of metaphor. For the same reason, the addition of 'novel connection'[12] does not go far enough. The use of 'move' and 'movement' show the same vagueness. In the Aristotelian definition 'movement' is used to point to the transference of the meaning of a word, which normally refers to one thing, to another thing, but TeSelle goes further by interpreting 'movement' as 'getting from here to there'. If this were taken seriously, every syllogism would be a metaphor. Apart from the vagueness of the definition, the account confuses two rather different claims: first, that metaphors are basic to thought, and secondly, that thought-processes or persons ('Jesus is the metaphor *par excellence*') are metaphors or metaphorical. TeSelle can only maintain the first point because of her vague and insufficient definition of metaphor. With regard to the second point, it is necessary to say that a metaphor is a qualification of a certain use of language, and that, if this qualification is used for non-linguistic entities, it is not used literally. What is explained by calling non-linguistic entities 'metaphors' depends on the theory and definition of metaphor, but if they are inadequate hardly anything is explained.[13]

The second argument of the central claim is concerned with the function of theology. The purpose and function of theology is, according to TeSelle, to make the gospel 'possible' and 'credible', to help 'people to be encountered by the word of God',[14] to make it possible for people to respond and to come to a moment of insight,[15] to renovate the basic Christian language so that it will again be 'authoritative', 'revelatory', 'meaningful',[16] to translate the gospel in such a way that people of a certain place and time are addressed totally.[17] Theology is not primarily concerned with 'formulations or systems', but with how people 'get from unbelief to believing'[18] – with '"believing", a process which is more like a story than it is like a doctrine'.[19] To fulfil this task the theologian must use a language that keeps 'in solution' language, belief, and life, and must unite form and content, as parables do. Theologians must be metaphorical in language, i.e., utilize common language to evoke the uncommon; they must be metaphorical in belief, i.e., concerned with the 'narrative quality of believing', with 'the loves and fears and hopes that move one'; they must be metaphorical in life, i.e., they must be 'unabashedly autobiographical'.[20] 'Is the theologian like an aesthetician and philosopher or more like the literary critic? Is it his or her job to create a system which explains, interprets and organizes the primary data, or is it to help the preacher, to help the people to help the word of God today? I think it is the latter . . .'[21]

It is clear that TeSelle's proposal for an 'intermediary' theology implies a criticism of existing theological language and the prevalent way of thinking, but it is not clear how fundamental her criticism is meant to be. On the one hand she seems to propose parabolic or intermediary theology as an addition to the existing tradition or systematic theology, or, more precisely, as a reinforcement of a way of doing theology which has always been present but which should be emphasized in our time because of its special needs. Parabolic theology does not deny the necessity of systematic theology.[22] TeSelle calls intermediary theology 'a way from religious experience to systematic theology'.[23] On the other hand, though, she seems to reject traditional systematic theology: she talks about a radical correction of form and content that is needed and about a systematic theology that makes it 'more difficult, if not impossible for one to believe . . .'.[24] This ambivalence can be readily removed by looking at her remarks about metaphor and thinking, and by looking at her description of the task of theology. If these are taken seriously – and that seems necessary, for the whole argument would otherwise collapse – TeSelle must hold the latter view, and must be proposing a radical narrative or radical parabolic theology to replace traditional argumentative theology.

TeSelle's argument for a narrative and metaphorical theology in the strong sense is thus supported by two arguments: one concerning the task of theology, and one concerning metaphors. The second argument cannot be maintained, since it rests on an inadequate theory of metaphor. Does this mean that the case for narrative and metaphorical theology collapses? One could hold that the first argument is still sufficient to support the claim, and one could even argue that a theory of metaphor as proposed in Chapter II above could be used for further support. One of the functions of metaphor is to give insight, to influence people, to change, to persuade, and to affect them, and it is exactly this which – according to TeSelle – theology should do. The coherence of such a radical metaphorical theology will be discussed after a closer look at a somewhat different approach to narrative theology.

1.2 *Apologia for narrative theology*
J.-B. Metz's arguments for a narrative theology are intended to show that stories, narratives, are not just aids in the field of applied theology, but essential parts of theology. 'The distinction "proclamation tells stories, theology argues", seems to be

too quick and too superficial and to eclipse the fundamentally narrative structure of theology'.[1] His arguments did not originally arise from analyses of parables, but constitute a phase in the development of his understanding of theology as political theology; in a more systematic presentation, however, an appeal to scriptural language does play a role.[2]

Metz's starting-point is that the justification of hope (1 Pet 3:15) forms a fundamental feature of every Christian theology. For such a project of justification to make sense, it has to take into account the ideas and processes that determine the culture and the situation in which it takes place. At the present time the context of theology is formed by the ideas of the Enlightenment, embodying important changes and crises in the traditional western understanding of man, nature, and society, and provoking processes of liberation and emancipation. 'The principle of exchange' has become crucial in the organization of society: those values determined by it constitute the public sphere and are not considered to be necessary or primary (so, for example, religion). Tradition loses its power to determine and guide actions and becomes a topic for research instead; authority is questioned, because it implies a relation of inequality and guardianship. Since being enlightened is related to using one's reason in all areas publicly, the practical and political dimensions of the use of reason come to the fore and the need to create situations in which free use can be made of reason is felt. These points have a bearing upon revealed religion, which is consequently criticized for being ideological – i.e. a function of social processes and a support of a political fabric – and in opposition to revealed religion a 'religio naturalis' is put forward.[3] Theology has to take these ideas seriously and to use them critically. But neither their rejection by the traditionalists and neo-scholastic apologetics, nor their acceptance by contemporary theology, are examples of such critical and serious use, for the former do not want to accept the changed situation or the new questions, while the latter accepts them too easily and does not 'enlighten the Enlightenment'. This last point is only possible, according to Metz, if the subject of these processes, the bourgeoisie, is considered and criticized. It is a fatal mistake of theology to identify this bourgeois subject with the subject in the religious sense, or to identify bourgeois practice with truly Christian practice.[4] In his outline of a theology that responds adequately to the task of providing a justification of hope in these times, Metz uses 'subject' and 'practice' or 'praxis' as key concepts and relates both concepts to that of 'narrative'.[5]

His insistence on attention to the subject is part of a criticism of the Enlightenment and of conceptions of emancipation and history derived from the Enlightenment. In these conceptions, the concrete subject more and more tends to disappear, and 'development', 'progress', 'freedom', and 'future' are discussed in abstract terms. The dangers of uncontrolled technology and purely economic planning are examples of the consequences of such abstract approaches to freedom and development. The subject of history is, for example, the 'Weltgeist' or 'the proletariat', and its history is seen solely in terms of success and victory, while failure and suffering are not related to that subject of history.[6]

The importance of praxis in the understanding of theology is not just, or even primarily, due to the insistence of the Enlightenment on practical reason, but has its foundation in the biblical concept of God. Thinking about God is practical, for it takes place as a revision of immediate needs and self-interest: 'metanoia' and 'exodus' are noetical categories.[7] Similar remarks can be made about Christology, which has 'imitation' as its central category. 'Only in imitating him (i.e., Christ) can Christians know with whom they have associated themselves and who has saved them'.[8] The biblical stories narrating the imitation of Christ (and those narrating exodus and metanoia) set out to change their hearers and to bring them to imitation (or metanoia). This means that Christological knowledge is not in the first place transmitted by concepts, but by stories. The practical constitution of theology is in this way the basis for the narrative features of theological language.[9]

The stories of Scripture, moreover, do not present faith as something that is added to an already existing personality or people, but show that faith – the relationship to God – constitutes the subject, forms the identity of a person or people, and is essential to the maintenance of that identity. The central categories in these processes are 'memory' and 'narrative'. Memory is not to be understood here as a nostalgic and escapist remembrance of the past, but as a 'dangerous memory', recalling failure and suffering and expectations that were and are not fulfilled. This type of memory is dangerous, for it undermines the obvious character of the present and leads to rebellion and liberation. Emphasis on the subject, therefore, although not unrelated to the enlightening of the Enlightenment, has – like the primacy of praxis – its basis in the Christian understanding of faith and religion.

These views determine the way Metz approaches and criticizes other treatments of what he considers to be the main problem of contemporary theology: the relation between salvation (or the history of salvation) and the experience of suffering and failure. Here again 'narrative' plays a central role. This main problem appears, for example, in his discussion of the diminishing influence of Christianity and the problems this creates for its own self-understanding.[10] All solutions employ, according to Metz, an idealistic conception of history, be it a universal or a transcendental conception. As a clarification Metz cites and explains the tale of the race between the hare and the hedgehog. The hedgehog wins the match without having to run by using a trick: he places himself and his wife who looks like him, at either end of the course. Every time the hare approaches an end, he or his wife appears and is seen to be already there. The hare runs from one end to the other until he collapses. The criticized solutions embody aspects of this hedgehog trick. The universal view embodies the trick in the sense that one oversees the whole course of history, and the meaning of history is there without interruption by danger. The transcendental view expresses another element: the threatened identity of Christianity is saved by a tautology, for beginning and end are identical, and the meantime – history – is not relevant. A plausible rejoinder to this criticism is that Christian theology cannot but depart from the assumption that history makes universal sense, for is the sense of history not determined by God's eschatological act in Jesus?[12] The common solution to this dilemma – either not taking the history of suffering fully seriously, or futurizing salvation to such an extent that it is exchanged for utopia – is to locate the experience of failure in the individual. The individual can then either apply or refuse to apply the history of salvation to his own history.[13] But this can only be done in narrative if there is no distortion of the individual history and the universal history of salvation.[14] For a story is 'on a small scale and without pretence' and 'it does not contain the dialectical key – not even from the hand of God – by which light could be brought in all dark corridors of history before one has entered and passed through them. But it is not without light'.[15]

Metz acknowledges his dependence on Weinrich for his understanding of narrative.[16] Weinrich gives criteria for determining what belongs to the category 'narrative'.[17] The criteria are syntactical signals – like verbs in the imperfect tense, temporal adverbs, or adverbs and conjunctions that appear in large parts of the text – and metalinguistic signals as indications ('novel'). Concepts like 'past' and 'truth', though, are irrelevant as criteria.[18] The criteria Weinrich gives are developed in the context of his work in the field of literary criticism, but in his application some confusion is caused, for he seems to refer to narrative in an ordinary sense and to narrative understood as literature. Metz, too, refers to literature.[19] But despite the apparent resemblance between Weinrich and Metz, Metz applies 'narrrative' to a less restricted category than either narrative in the ordinary sense or narrative in the sense of literature. For him, 'narrative' appears to be connected with 'original experience', 'new', 'beginning and end' and 'never been before', and his thesis is that these experiences disrupt argumentative language and can only be expressed in narrative language.[20] Narrative language is thus opposed to argumentative, conceptual language that describes normal, regular, customary, and unexceptional situations. Narrative language thus becomes identical with an open and open-ended language.[21] His conception of narrative language makes Metz's arguments relevant to the discussion about the role of metaphor in theology. It is these disruptive features which are characteristic for metaphor; and it is the expression of the new and the exceptional, the redescription of reality, which are the functions we have ascribed to metaphor.

An important question in the context of the present discussion is whether he proposes a radical narrative theology or whether he argues for a 'mixed discourse'. As in the case of TeSelle, one can find quotations supporting either answer.

The link between narrative language and original, new experience leads to the radical version ('can only'). Similar exclusive remarks can be found when Metz discusses the way the history of salvation is related to the history of suffering: only narrative language can give an adequate solution. 'A conceptual-argumentative mediation and reconciliation between, on the one hand, the effective salvation that has taken place and, on the other, the human history of suffering seems to me impossible . . . The dilemma can, in my opinion, not be solved by any subtle speculative reasoning, but only by another way of expressing in language the effective salvation that has taken place in the non-identity of the suffering . . .', 'soteriology . . . cannot be purely argumentative; it has to explain narratively; it is a fundamentally memorative-narrative soteriology'.[22] Or again, in the context of an analysis of the biblical concept of God: the practical constitution of the concept of God is also the basis for 'the essential and unalterably memorative and narrative nature of the fundamental structure' of the language about God.[23] Religion and the process of becoming and remaining a subject belong inseparably together, and for these processes, memory and narrative are fundamental categories.[24]

But there are also remarks that point towards a 'mixed discourse'. Metz stresses that he wants to show the inseparability of argument and narrative, and that his arguments are not directed against argument in theology as such: narrative versus argumentation implies a regressive standpoint.[24] He aims to relativize argument, not to reject it, for it has a task of its own: 'to safeguard the narrative memory of salvation in our scientific world, to interrupt it critically, and to lead us back time and again to narrative . . .'[25] The relation indicated here, Metz elsewhere describes as follows: '. . . the linguistic content of Christianity is to be understood primarily as an inclusive story *(Grosserzählung)*, which also contains and originates argumentative elements and structures . . .'[26] So, the narrative acts as a kind of frame which is and remains primary and fundamental.[27] Although on the basis of the first series of statements it seems difficult to come to any other than the radical view, his acceptance of a mixed discourse at the same time does not result in an incoherent position. And the reason for this lies in the way Metz envisages this mixed discourse: it does not consist of two equal parts, for argument plays only a minor and secondary role.[28] But can this position be maintained?

1.3 *Metaphorical theology: reconstruction and coherence*

The arguments put forward by the narrative theologians are explicitly or implicitly relevant to the central question of this chapter. Although TeSelle's metaphor theory is clearly inadequate, and although Metz does not mention metaphors, the function they allocate to metaphors or narrative can be assigned to metaphors understood by means of the theory proposed in Chapter II. On the basis of these arguments for either an exclusive narrative theology or a mixed discourse, one can reconstruct a radical metaphorical theology or one in which metaphors dominate the discourse, while concepts or arguments play only a minor and auxiliary role. The coherence of such a reconstruction depends on the arguments used for narrative theology. How coherent are these arguments? Can some of the basic presuppositions that determine the line of argument be maintained seriously? What are the consequences of a radical and exclusively metaphorical theology?

Three groups of remarks are relevant in view of these questions. The first group is concerned with the role of narrative in the past and the present. Although not immediately relevant for the reconstruction of a metaphorical theology, these views have some bearing upon the evaluation of concepts. If narrative theologians are correct on this point, and if conceptual language constitutes a deterioration, this could be used as an argument against a conceptual theology and in favour of metaphorical theology. TeSelle suggests such an argument.[1] The second group of remarks is related to the appeal or the effect stories have. The same can be said of metaphors: like stories, they provoke a response. The possibility of abuse is clear in both cases. Do narrative theologians allow for procedures that decide whether such abuses occur? In the third group of remarks 'history' occupies a central place, and these have an immediate bearing upon the reconstruction. If it is correct that conceptual refinement cannot solve the central problems of contemporary theology – i.e., the relation between the history of salvation and the history of suffering – then a criticism of metaphorical theology and a plea in favour of conceptual theology are open to the same objection. But how is this objection to be understood? Is the suggestion that the arguments found in the philosophy of history are helpful a correct suggestion?[2] A closer look at these remarks will reveal how coherent a reconstruction of a metaphorical theology on the basis of the arguments put forward by TeSelle and Metz is.

1.3.1 'Narrative innocence'?

Both types of narrative theology presuppose an understanding of story-telling that is based upon historical evaluation and upon an assessment of the role of narrative in contemporary culture. But this double basis is highly questionable. The historical evaluation is expressed in claims like 'originally, the Christian community was a story-telling community, not an argumentative community' (Metz and Weinrich). The early church is then pictured as a community in which the stories of Jesus and about Jesus are told and retold. 'We can imagine a Christianity which transmits itself from generation to generation in an endless chain of retelling of stories: "faith comes by hearing".'[1] But Christianity did not remain that story-telling community: it lost its narrative innocence when it entered the Hellenistic world. But this black-and-white picture is clearly wrong and oversimplistic. The Christian community did not exist apart from its Jewish background, where discussions about the interpretation of the Law, about the resurrection, about the question which commandment is the most important played an important role, as is clear from the gospels. Moreover, the New Testament does not consist of stories alone, and Jesus is portrayed as interspersing stories with arguments. Furthermore, myth and story are characteristic of the Hellenistic world as well, as Weinrich elsewhere points out.[2] To say Plato's attempt to give new brilliance to myth failed and that philosophers have ever since refused to tell stories might be correct, but is certainly not enough to support the claim that the Hellenistic world was a predominantly argumentative culture.[3]

Most writers on narrative theology are aware of the problems surrounding story-telling in contemporary culture. Weinrich points to the fact that fiction has lost its narrative innocence – that contemporary writers 'subject the process of story-telling itself to critical examination' when they tell a story.[4]

TeSelle acknowledges the fact that even those among modern writers who are considered to be the best do not seem to tell stories.[5] But the reaction to this phenomenon is rather naïve: a return to narrative innocence, or a retreat to parables. TeSelle retreats to parables because they do not call 'for the same degree of faith in cosmic or even social ordering' as is required in novels.[6] If one argues for the importance of literature – be it on a purely technical level or on the level of content as well – one cannot exclude a major part of that literature or prominent tendencies in such a way.[7] Estess, referring to American writers like TeSelle, warns against uncritical enthusiasm for the story form. The disruption of the story form by authors like Samuel Beckett creates an important challenge to narrative theologians (or religionists, as Estess calls them). Beckett does not present a 'successive among interrelated elements', a 'linear development with hierarchically arranged parts', but 'a puzzling interrelation of disrelated particles', a 'contraction of attention to particulars of experience', a juxtaposition of elements in a 'desultory fashion'.[8] Theologians should not succumb to the temptation to exclude 'renovative chaos', to 'disorder life by violent imposition of the order of story' for such an imposition can undermine 'the attitude of wonder towards the relatively chaotic flow of life-experience'.[9] Theologians often imply that life is a well integrated plot: 'one sometimes receives the impression that instead of literature imitating life, the religionists interested in story want life to imitate literature'.[10] The complexity of life should not be obscured by a simple plot. Similar points are made by Mieth when he says that a more positive attitude towards the so-called destructive tendencies in modern literature is required.[11] Weinrich's return to narrative innocence is not desirable for the same reasons, and it is doubtful whether this return would solve anything: would story-telling become more innocent if less reflection took place? This leads to the problem of criteria.

1.3.2 *Criteria?*

Do narrative theologians indicate criteria that determine, when changes occur in the process of retelling a story, which of these changes are permitted and which are not? Do they mention norms for the selection of some new stories and the exclusion of others? Do they allow for safety measures to prevent possible abuse? The necessity of this kind of question is clear in the light of the criticism of religion as being an ideology, and in the light of the need to preserve the specific character of the Christian tradition, for if every story can be part of that chain, it seems difficult to claim a distinctly Christian nature for it.

There are elements in the writings of the narrative theologians that can be understood as criteria: they are all concerned with the effect of the story. Stories should move people, should create insight, should start a process of coming to belief, should result in action and imitation. But the same story or metaphor can have opposite effects and can result in quite different actions. The story of a world-wide Jewish plot as told in the *Protocol of the Elders of Zion* can result – and has resulted – in both anti-semitism and the rejection of anti-semitism. 'Life is a tale told by an idiot' can evoke feelings of despair and feelings of protest (dangerous memory), can result in resignation and in feverish action to change one's life. So, some further specifications are necessary, and these can in fact be found in the writings. In her discussion of the (re-)sources of parabolic theology, TeSelle argues that apart from the stories and the images of Scripture, poetry, novels, and autobiographies can serve as sources. The selection criterion here is 'the distortion of the familiar, for the purpose of providing a new and extraordinary context for ordinary experience'.[1] As TeSelle acknowledges, this criterion applies to all good literature, or can be used as such, and states a characteristic feature of poetry. But, as it stands, this criterion is not sufficient, and the introduction of 'anonymous Christian' in this context reinforces the suspicion that 'good' literature and 'Christian' literature are to be identified.

The criteria used in the evaluation of the examples of the sources are not of much help either. Some poets, TeSelle says, are better than others, because they see where others see nothing; some novels are not satisfactory because they do not tell the story of people on the move towards belief; some biographies are Christian because they are vocationally oriented, while others are self-oriented. But these criteria are still too general: to see what? to believe what? to be called to what? On one occasion something like an external check is mentioned. 'The New Testament images and stories serve as a rough guide to keep us from calling everything that is merely hopeful or positive "Christian", and to make clear that such phenomena as racism and Manichaeism are definitely out'.[2] The problem with this remark is not just the vagueness of 'rough', but the presupposition that those images are clear, that their meaning is obvious and not in need of explanation. The cases of racism and Manichaeism quoted defy this presupposition: how could they have played such an important role in the Christian tradition, how could they have occurred at all, if it is so obvious that they are excluded? The problem of criteria is not a real problem to TeSelle.[3]

Weinrich's introduction of the notion 'narrative tolerance' can be seen as a specification of criteria. Stories are told and retold with changes, but these changes are permitted within a story-cycle, like the stories in Boccaccio's *Decameron*. 'The point of the story cannot be extracted by an examination in terms of "true" and "false", but becomes part of the wisdom of the ages as a succession of stories gradually builds up our experience of life and salvation'.[4] Weinrich's example of such retelling is the chain: the murder of the children of Bethlehem – the persecution of the Jews by the Nazis – Vietnam. But this example provokes several questions which cannot be answered satisfactorily by reference to this notion of 'narrative tolerance' – questions like: are these stories limited to children (Jewish and Vietnamese), or are they about everybody who is helpless in the face of violence? Can one include abortion stories in this chain? Or, to change the example: it is a common feature in the Christian tradition that people understand their suffering in relation to the suffering of Jesus, as for example Paul (Phil 1:12f; Col 1:24). But can a bishop whose authoritarian actions provoke a strong reaction and criticism identify his 'suffering' with that of Jesus? Can the wife of an alleged war-criminal link the arrest of her husband to that of Jesus? One cannot deny that in the history of Christianity the passion story has been connected 'in some way' with pogroms, in the sense that the passion story functioned as the argument for the persecution. Is this a sign of the 'wisdom of the ages'? What is the status of that 'wisdom of the ages'? Is it an institution beyond questioning, a supra-critical authority? These questions are even more pressing since Weinrich rejects questions about the truth of stories and considers them irrelevant. Would the discovery that the *Protocol of the Elders of Zion* was a forgery, written by an anti-semitic member of the Tsarist secret police, make no difference to the way we react and respond to that story?

In Metz's view not all stories are acceptable: only those that have emancipatory power and express a social criticism are admissible. In other words, 'dangerous memory' serves as the criterion. But stories about oppression, failure, and suffering have been used for what turned out to be just a change of personnel or the consolidation of an oppressive society. So there is still some ambivalence left, and still a need for a discussion about the interpretation.[5]

One could object that these criticisms are unjust, since it is impossible to formulate less general and more specific criteria. One cannot decide before the stories are told whether they are admissible or not. Insistence on more specific criteria is therefore unrealistic and should not be used against narrative or metaphorical theology. At first sight this seems a reasonable objection – certainly if it is understood as relating to content criteria – for if one tries to formulate more specific criteria one quickly discovers the problems. An example of further specification would be: all stories advocating the killing of people, all stories reducing the godhead of Christ, all stories denying the almight of God, are excluded *a priori*. But then someone might tell a story about the murder or the attempted murder of a tyrant – say, Bonhoeffer's involvement in the attempt to murder Hitler; or acclaim Jesus Christ as Superstar, and point out that 'he is just a man but scares me so', is a 'Christology with parabolic indirection', as TeSelle does;[6] or tell stories about evil and disaster; and people might even refer, in these contexts, to stories in Scripture – to the story of David killing Goliath, to the story of Jesus in Gethsemane, or to the silence of God in the period between Joseph and Moses. And even if one tries to reformulate these criteria in a somewhat more general way without losing all content – e.g., stories that stress the commandment of loving one's neighbour, that recognize the importance of Jesus, that accept God's activity – the problems are not solved. For it is not so difficult to find groups of people in past and present who told and tell stories covered by these criteria and who considered and consider themselves Christians, but who were not and are not considered to be Christians by others who told and tell stories falling under the same criteria. So, it seems that the insistence on criteria is misguided: it is difficult to give criteria for stories that have been told, and it is impossible to give criteria for stories that will be told in still unknown situations.

The answer to this important objection does not consist in insisting upon the necessity of content criteria, but in showing that a formal scheme can be produced that fulfils the requirements and that has built-in precautions against abuse.[7] The first step towards such a formal scheme is the recognition that a story can belong to one of three different 'streams'; to Scripture, to tradition, or to the present time. A new story can be said to be a genuine Christian story if it can be linked with stories in Scripture and tradition. But this is clearly not enough, and two further steps have to be introduced. First, the nature of the linkage has to be defined; and secondly, the one-way check from Scripture and tradition on the new story has to be changed into a two-way check. The first of these two steps is connected with the problems that appeared in the attempts to formulate more specific criteria. The problem there was that it is possible to quote example from Scripture (or tradition) to support a story that seemingly ought to be excluded from the Christian story chain. The second of these steps is the result of the realization that faith is a living faith and that the expression of faith is always determined by historical and cultural circumstances, whether this expression is recognized by the Christian community as canonical, or belongs to tradition, or is contemporary. These last two steps imply, though, interpretation, analysis, and argumentation in all three 'streams'. Relevant questions for this interpretation and analysis include: Is the concept of neighbour the same in all three streams?; Is God's omnipotence correctly understood and invoked here?, etc. Since these two further steps are necessary, and since they necessarily imply the use of arguments, analyses, and interpretation, which is only possible by means of abstraction – i.e., by leaving the level of narrative and metaphor – it is clear that narrative or metaphorical theology necessarily has to be supplemented by argument. This conclusion becomes unavoidable from the moment one becomes aware of the problem of criteria: this problem can only be solved if one leaves the level of narrative and metaphor. The danger of the exclusive and radical version of narrative (and metaphorical) theology as defended by TeSelle and Weinrich is not so much that the available elements that could serve as criteria are insufficient, but that there is little or no concern about this important question regarding the criteria. On this radical view everything is possible and everything permissible, which leads to a Christianity void of content and rightly denounced as ideology.

Metz escapes this danger by giving argument a place. But if the necessity of another type of language is recognized, the question arises how this conceptual or argumentative level is related to the metaphorical or narrative one. Metz allows argument to play a minor role within the framework of the narrative. One of the reasons he gives for denying argument a more important place can be found in his already-quoted thesis that an argumentative and conceptual mediation between the history of salvation and the history of suffering is 'out of the question', since such a solution implies either a 'gnostic perpetuation of God's suffering' or 'the reduction of suffering to its concept'. The dilemma cannot be escaped by 'more subtle reasoning'.[8] One may presume that Metz does not intend to say that, since the available conceptual solutions are not satisfactory, no conceptual solution will ever be satisfactory. In order to make sense he has to present other arguments for that conclusion. An argument that Metz seems to indicate is the following: conceptual solutions and speculative reasoning do not solve the problems of suffering and salvation, because those problems are only solved when something is done, when the suffering is removed and the salvation realized. In this sense conceptual solutions are always inadequate: practical problems are not solved by speculative arguments. This is a point that might be necessary to make in those cases where conceptual power is overstated or the expectations with regard to discursive reasoning are too high.

Once the point is seen, though, it loses much of its initial force,[9] and one can ask whether in the case of narrative the same or a similar point cannot and should not be made. Why should narrative be better in mediating between the history of suffering and the history of salvation? Metz suggests a connection between narrative and praxis when he uses formulations like 'the theological language of Christians has a narrative-practical feature'[10] and mentions the lack of pretence and small scale of narrative: insofar as this presupposes that narrative language exerts great influence on people and on their acting, the problem of the criteria returns. Another possibility is that history and stories are so related that this link constitutes the basis for Metz's claim, viz., that stories are themselves explanatory, as is maintained by some philosophers of history. Is the philosophy of history, to which some authors appeal, helpful on this or other points?[11]

1.3.3 'History tells stories'

The narrative historians hold two related claims: first, that narrative is not a stylistic ornament, but a feature which belongs essentially to historical work; and secondly, that the understanding which is typical of history is reached through narrative.[1] If this position is taken to maintain that every historical work must show an overall narrative pattern, the position is, according to some critics, untenable. Works that undeniably belong to history – like Huizinga's *The Waning of the Middle Ages* – would have to be excluded. If the position is understood as maintaining that all the important works are narratives and that the non-narrative ones are ancillary,[2] that would still conflict with the practice of historians. Although these counter-arguments have some force, they are only decisive if one accepts the general opinion about what history is and historians do. But if one sees it as the task of the philosophy of history not only to describe what in fact takes place, but also to criticize, if necessary, what historians do, one can still argue that those works are wrongly considered to be historical or central. This means that the second point – the nature of historical understanding and the contribution of stories to that understanding – is the central point of the discussion.

Gallie says that a narrative is self-explanatory and Louch calls narrative 'a distinct kind of explanation': 'it focuses attention on the fact that describing a chain of events from a certain perspective in itself reveals the connection among events'.[3] Danto states that 'to ask for the significance of an event, in the *historical* sense of the term, is to ask a question which can be answered only in the context of a *story*'.[4] This answer can be given because a narrative is 'a form of explanation', it 'describes and explains at one and the same time'.[5] There is a class of sentences, characteristic for historical writings, which exhibit this feature of narrative. These sentences 'refer to at least two time-separated events, though they only *describe* (are only about) the earliest event to which they refer. Commonly they take the past tense and indeed it would be odd . . . for them to take another tense'.[6] Words like 'anticipated', 'cause', 'began' are typical for such narrative sentences. An example of such a sentence is: 'The Battle of the Marne was one of the decisive battles of the world, not because it determined that Germany would ultimately lose or the Allies ultimately win the war, but because it determined that the war would go on'.[7]

According to Danto, the role of narrative in history is to explain a change which may be a process that covers a long period of time. These processes have a beginning and an end which are both part of the explanandum, while the middle is constituted by the explanation. For example, 'Louis XIV died unpopular' (end) presupposes that he once was popular (beginning) and the changed attitude towards the king is then explained with reference to his foreign policy, etc. (middle). The selection of the beginning is determined by the end, and the explanation looked for is a causal one, pointing to one or several causes. This implies that to tell stories is to make a choice: 'stories, to be stories, must leave things out'.[8] A complete description of events in the sense of a complete order-preserving transcription of absolutely everything that happened, as, when, and how it happened, is not the aim of history and the historian, since narrative sentences and causal connections could not be included in such an 'ideal chronicle'. A complete description that is interesting from a historical point of view – i.e., that locates an event 'in all the right stories' – is impossible to obtain, since the future is open and the meaning of an event might be revealed only much later. What the historian does is to give a narrative organization. And this implies an 'impugnable subjective factor', and 'element of sheer arbitrariness'.[9] We organize events relative to some events we find significant in a sense not touched upon here. It is a sense of significance common, however, to all narrative, and is determined by the topical interests of this human being or that'.[10]

The explanatory power of a strictly narrative sequence is questioned by Mandelbaum (among others), who argues that even in the cases where narrative seems most adequate, like reports of an election campaign or a biography, the historian has to appeal to non-narrative elements. A biographer must appeal to intelligence, temperament, personality, the society the subject lives in, etc. – to elements, in other words, that are not events which form part of a sequence; a historian writing about an election-campaign has to refer to voting habits, the cultural and social background of the constituents, etc., in order to explain why what happened did happen. Historians must appeal to background factors that cannot be formulated in terms of narrative.[11] Or, to put it differently: 'narrate' can be used in connection with events, but not in connection with situations.[12]

But there is another argument against the narrativist's claims about the role of stories, and it is concerned with the underlying linear model of history. It regards 'the events which form a unitary strand of history as a linear sequential series: a leads to b, b to c, c to d, and so on'.[13] This model assumes that 'what occurs in history is to be construed as if its occurrence were primarily or even exclusively due to human actions'.[14] Reference to antecedent human action then suffices as an explanation of what happened, and this can only be done in narrative, because narratives concentrate upon human agents and therefore prevent a distorted view. Mandelbaum and Ely argue that this model cannot be maintained, since it leaves no place for conditions, and conditions are necessary, since they have causal significance. Historians in fact appeal to conditions in their work, and those that make history use conditions – as, for example, a politician who takes advantage of a certain crisis. Moreover, if in laboratory experiments the conditions have to be controlled, it is clear that conditions have a causal influence.[15]

This short survey of the discussion about narrative in history shows that the suggestion that narrative theologians can appeal for support to the philosophy of history is not a useful one. First, there is a considerable difference in the understanding of narrative. In the discussion 'narrative' is used to characterize an explanation and a description of a process that is past: the future is excluded from this understanding of narrative. Danto is very clear about this point. His analytical philosophy is developed in opposition to what he calls a substantive philosophy of history, i.e., 'a systematic interpretation of universal history in accordance with a principle by which historical events and succession are unified and directed towards an ultimate meaning'.[16] To interpret history this way is 'a misconceived activity, because it supposes that the history of events can be written before the events have happened'.[17] In this view the meaning of an event is seen in the context of the whole of history – past, present, and future. But, according to Danto, this is unacceptable 'because we are temporal-provincial with regards to the future'.[18] The meaning of an event may become clear later and it is the task of the historian to bring this to light, but this 'later' is always a part of the past with regard to the historian. Only after 1940 can historians talk about 'the first world war', although prior to 1940 they could have said that 'the great war' lasted four years. This is the reason why narrative sentences do not have a future tense. It is significant that Danto, agreeing with Löwith, calls the substantive view 'essentially theological'. For, 'from a theological point of view history becomes history, when it has hope, when it has future', as Mieth puts it.[19]

Secondly, even if this difference in understanding can be removed without damaging consequences for the historical view and theory, the criticism of the self-explanatory character of narrative seems unsurmountable. A possible way of meeting this criticism – namely, by arguing that these objections are typical to history – is not open to theologians, and certainly not to theologians like Metz, for it would imply that faith has no connections with or consequences for life and society, that faith is concerned with events, persons, human agents, but not with society, with the conditions these persons live in, etc. These criticisms of the self-explanatory character of narrative also casts doubt on biography and autobiography as 'pure' sources for an exclusive narrative theology.

Thirdly, one of the unquestioned claims in the discussion is that historians present a subjective organization or construction of what happened.[20] The emphasis on subjective selection, and thus on the difference between the data and the narrative construction, resembles Estess' remarks about the difference between life and literature. The dangers of reducing the one to the other are in both cases aggravated by too simple an understanding of literature and history, namely, a well-integrated plot and a linear model of history. But this means that narrative history faces the same problem as narrative theology – the problem how to decide whether a narrative construction is correct or not. One can escape cynicism about history, the work of historians, only when one allows for arguments to settle the differences.

This all means that the appeal to the philosophy of history for help is not very useful, except that it underlines the importance of the question of criteria. But this line of inquiry does answer another question, namely, the question about the relation between the two types of language which was raised by Metz's position. It answers this question in a somewhat surprising way, though, since it points to a more important place for argument than Metz is prepared to acknowledge. Mandelbaum's criticism of the thesis that stories are self-explanatory shows that stories cannot be understood without some general knowledge derived from analysis. Or, as Jones puts it, using a comparison with a game of cricket; 'Understanding depends not only on following the progress of play (or of the story) but also on recognizing that this or that event breaks the pattern of generalized expectations we wrongly or rightly hold in regard to the game (or story) . . . Following the story of Israel or the Church depends upon a framework not of stories but of certain non-narrative descriptions, analyses and generalizations which we or others have worked out (well or badly) in a process of discussion and argumentation. Stories would then be parasitical upon this argued or at least arguable framework'.[21] This realization has of course some consequences for the claims about the unique and exclusive relation between narrative and the experience of newness, etc. These experiences and narratives can only be recognized within such a framework and by using this framework.

With regard to metaphors, a similar feature was mentioned when it was said that metaphors depend upon their literal meaning and presuppose the accepted order of reality, for otherwise they would not be discovered or recognized as metaphors. The complexity of the relations between language and reality is again relevant. Strangely enough, Metz does recognize this complex relationship, when he says that the reality we encounter is in fact a 'secondary world', i.e., a world determined and formed by theories and systems. Only within these world systems are we able to experience and change reality.[22] The examples he gives of the two world systems dominating European-American culture are the evolutionist interpretation, which can be found in Western bourgeois cultures, and the materialist-historical interpretation which can be found in East European societies. As is clear from the examples, these world systems are not narratives. Metz was earlier quoted as saying that the linguistic content of Christianity is an exclusive story containing argumentative elements and structures with the explicit denial of a reverse relation, and that contradicts this point. Even if one recognizes that Metz at this particular point conducts a polemic against the view that narratives are just means of illustration, this contradiction is not resolved, for the view of theology is too limited and not in accordance with Metz's own practice. While in the one case the argument arises out of the narrative and the narrative remains primary, in the other the argument is outside the frame of the narrative; in the one case, theology consists in following the narrative and protecting it, in the other theology analyzes the narrative in the context of the secondary world and looks critically at the relations between them. Ambivalence about the view of the task of theology can also be found in his indiscriminate use of 'theological language'. In his arguments about the fundamentally narrative structure of theological and Christological knowledge and language, Metz uses 'theology' and 'Christology' in a broad and non-technical sense, but the technical sense of these terms appears in his argument about deficient soteriology. Only if this ambivalence in the understanding of theology and theological language is removed can a solution be found for the contradiction.

1.3.4 *Conclusion*
The discussion of these three groups of remarks shows that the reconstruction of a metaphorical theology on the basis of arguments used in support of two types of narrative theology is unsatisfactory. An exclusive narrative or metaphorical theology is not able to counter the charge that it is a form of ideology, or that it empties Christianity of any specific content. Only by allowing for arguments and interpretation, by allowing for another type of language, can the questions about criteria be answered. The recognition of another type of language as an integral part of language is also the result of the criticism of the presuppositions about narrative innocence and the purity of the narrative sources. It is the all-pervading presence of 'argumentative', 'analytical', and 'abstract' language in language generally that reveals the unsatisfactory character of the solution presented in the moderate version. The complexity of the relationship between language and reality is not sufficiently recognized in this view.

2. *Models*
There is, apart from the type of argument presented in narrative theology, another type of argument in favour of the importance and necessity of metaphors in theology and theological language: the argument that theology, like science, uses models. This type of argument rests upon three distinct claims: metaphors and models are similar in important respects, models play a crucial role in the formation of theories in science, and similar functions in theology are fulfilled by models.

For a proper discussion of the first claim, it is necessary to recall both the distinction between the structure and the function of the metaphor and the importance of an adequate explanation of the structure. It is not enough to defend a similarity in function: a similarity in structure is required as well. With regard to the second claim, an extensive examination of the different positions in the philosophy of science goes beyond the scope of the present discussion. It is enough to explore one position that gives models an indispensable role in scientific research and theory formation, for if on this account no sufficient case can be made for metaphor models in theology, it certainly will not be possible to do so with the help of other positions that give models less prominence.

The term 'model' is used for a bewilderingly wide variety of phenomena: in order to structure the field somewhat and to limit the discussion to types relevant to theology, a classification of the use of 'model' in science is necessary. In the literature several classifications, or principles for classification, are proposed. Apostel classifies models on the principle of their relation to their prototype. 'Models and prototypes can belong to the same class of entities or to different classes of entities'.[1] Harré makes a similar remark when he distinguishes between models whose source and subject are identical (homoeomorph) and whose subject and source are different (paramorph).[2] Black's classification is used by some philosophers of religion and he distinguishes four types: scale models, analogue models, mathematical models, and theoretical models.[3] Scale models cover 'all likeness of material objects, systems and processes, whether real or imaginary, that preserve relative proportions'.[4] Analogue models are 'some material object, system or process designed to reproduce as faithfully as possible in some new medium the *structure* or web of relationships in an original'; in these models a 'change of medium' occurs.[5] The theoretical model comes close to the analogue model, for here, too, an identity of structure is basic. The difference between the two is that the theoretical model does not need to be constructed; it is enough to describe it: 'the heart of the method consists in *talking* in a certain way'.[6]

A more elaborate classification is given by Bertels and Nauta.[7] They base their classification on three main principles: the type of entity out of which the model consists, the mechanism of the model, and the function of the model. The various sciences study three types of entities and each of these can be used for a model: concrete, conceptual, and formal entities. Each of the three types can be a model for one of the three entities (an empirical or concrete model of a conceptual system, a conceptual model of a conceptual system, etc.). They further distinguish six different principles according to which a model works (*mechanism*): change of scale (*scale models*, like miniature cars or samples), change of medium with isomorphism as result of analogy (*analogy models* – these include Black's analogue and theoretical model – like measurement of the temperature of stars by means of light, or the representation of the electrical field in terms of an imaginary fluid as Maxwell proposed), idealized circumscription (*ideal model*, like 'ideal gas'), presentation of qualitative structure (*structural model*, like blueprints of an organization) and *mathematical* and *abstract* models. All types of models have a number of functions in common: they visualize, reduce, and represent, and they are didactically and heuristically helpful. The different types have, moreover, specific functions: so, for example, an analogy model can explain phenomena.

Most writers on models in theology are interested in what in this classification falls under 'conceptual models'. This does not mean that empirical or abstract models do not occur in theology: iconography and logic can play a role in theology, but the point is that they do not play a central role. The limitation to conceptual models excludes scale models and abstract models, since the first type belongs to the empirical models and the second type is only used in the formal sciences; mathematical and empirical analogy models can be excluded as well, which leaves analogy models (Black's theoretical models), ideal models, and structural models as the types of model that can occur in theology. This narrows down the field sufficiently for the following discussion. In the course of the discussion a further refinement will be made.

2.1 *Models and metaphors*
One of the philosophers who compares models to metaphors is Black, and he refers explicitly to a theory of metaphor to support his claim.[1] He invokes the similarity between models and metaphors in his discussion of two problems connected with theoretical models. The first of these problems is

concerned with claims about reality which are implied in the use of models. According to one view, the use of models is a heuristic device: it presents something 'as if'. This view 'uses a detached comparison reminiscent of simile and argument from analogy'.[2] In this view models do not have explanatory power, since they do not claim that reality is such and such. The other view maintains that in using models the scientist makes an existential claim: something is said to be such and such. This view requires 'an identification typical of metaphor'.[3] Models understood in this way are able to explain, but there is a danger of self-deception. The second, closely related problem is one about the status of models. Some philosophers argue that models are not necessary and that, even if used, they can be replaced adequately by a clear and logical language: models are 'props for feeble minds', 'surrogates', but not 'a rational method having its own canons and principles'.[4] This argument resembles the discussion about the possibility of an adequate translation of paraphrase of metaphors. Referring to his interaction theory of metaphor, Black points to the extended meaning of the metaphor that 'can neither be adequately predicted nor subsequently paraphrased in prose . . . Metaphorical thought is a distinctive mode of achieving insight, not to be construed as an ornamental substitute for plain thought'.[5] Similar remarks can, according to Black, be made about models. And an objection about the use of models in science as irrational is answered by Black as follows: a model must be isomorphic with the domain it is applied to, and 'in stretching the language by which the model is described in such a way as to fit the new domain, we pin our hopes upon the existence of a common structure in both fields. If the hope is fulfilled, there will have been an objective ground for analogical transfer'.[6] So, the irrational charge is countered with a defence that appeals to the existential commitment.

Hesse, like Black, mentions a theory of metaphor in connection with her views on models, and the theory she mentions is basically Black's interaction theory. But there is an interesting point of difference. Black says that metaphors can create a similarity, but Hesse thinks that, although this may be the case in poetry, it is not the case in science. 'The question that *any* scientific model can be imposed *a priori* on *any* explanandum and function fruitfully in its explanation must be resisted. Such a view would imply that theoretical models are irrefutable ... no model ever gets off the ground unless some antecedent similarity or analogy is discerned between it and the explanandum'.[7] The danger of the comparison view, with its implication of an adequate translation, can be avoided on the interaction view, and also by realizing that 'as long as the model is under active construction as an ingredient in an explanation, we do not know how far the comparison extends'.[8]

Both Black and Hesse acknowledge differences between (poetic) metaphor and model. A metaphor, Black says, is a short statement, while models are like sustained and systematically developed metaphors. In a metaphor common-place associations are at work, while in a model a known scientific theory is used, and a typical and essential requirement for a model is 'the systematic complexity of the source of the model and the capacity for analogical development'.[9] Hesse sees the main difference in the reference and the application of 'true', and the other points of difference follow from this basic difference. Poetic metaphors are striking, unexpected, even shocking, and are not meant to be analyzed, and several formally contradictory metaphors can be used for the same subject. Models on the other hand may be unexpected, but they are meant to be analyzed, and contradictions or inconsistencies are a challenge to reconcile the models or to refute one of them. 'We can perhaps signalize the difference by speaking in the case of scientific models of the (perhaps unobtainable) aim to find a "perfect metaphor" whose referent is the domain of the explanandum, whereas literary metaphors, however adequate and successful in their own terms, are from the point of view of potential logical consistency and extendability often (not always) intentionally imperfect'.[10]

But these differences are apparently not so great that they sever the link between metaphor and model. The question is whether the metaphor theory used can support this near-identification: that is to say, are the reasons for appealing to metaphor for the solution to the problems concerned with the structural features of the metaphor? In the previous chapter the argument was put forward that the interaction theory cannot sufficiently explain the mechanism of the metaphor, because it wrongly supposes that what has to be explained is the change of meaning of a term, i.e., metaphorical meaning. The two points concerning the structure of the metaphor that Black uses to defend the necessity of theoretical models are 'extended meaning' and 'the inadequacy of translation', and the basis of the second point is the first. So, if extended meaning is the characteristic feature of models, one cannot use that to link models to metaphors, for no extension of meaning occurs in a metaphor. The point on which Hesse disagrees with Black – the necessity of some antecedent similarity – does not strengthen the case for a link between model and metaphor: on the contrary, it makes the gap between the two even greater.

One can also ask whether the differences mentioned by Black and Hesse are not such that the connection is less obvious than they suggest. Is a sustained, systematically developed and analyzed metaphor still a metaphor? Is there only a small difference between common-place associations and a known scientific theory? Is the 'perfect metaphor' in the sense Hesse uses this phrase still a metaphor? Both Black and Hesse emphasize the claims about reality made in the use of models, but does that not show that a scientist when using models is not just proposing a possible redescription of reality, but is redescribing reality? This seems to be the motive behind Hesse's critique of Black.[11] These questions require a further discussion of the place of models in science. Harré's transcendental realism is a theory that gives models a prominent place and that shares some basic interests expressed by Black and Hesse (the existential commitment). Moreover, Harré employs a somewhat different theory of metaphor, which broadens the discussion.

2.2 *Transcendental realism*

A scientist has two distinct tasks: first, to single out patterns in nature and experience, and secondly, to explain those patterns. The explanation should not only include the conditions under which the pattern occurs, but also the description of the mechanism that causes this pattern. This second task of explaining receives most attention in the analyses of the philosophy of science, and is of special interest to the present discussion.[1]

A look at the practice of scientists shows that when they provide a causal explanation a regress or an ongoing stratification takes place. The description of a phenomenon that can be observed and that has to be explained constitutes one level, while the explanation of the phenomenon, that is, the description of the mechanism that causes it, constitutes another. This mechanism can in turn become the subject of an explanation, and so on. For example, 'the liquid corroded the metal' can be explained by 'the liquid in this case contained acid' and this can lead to research into the nature of acid.[2] This development in scientific explanation implies, according to Harré, the presupposition of three 'zones' of reality: a zone of actual experienced reality, a zone of reality that can be experienced in principle, and a zone of reality that is for ever beyond experience.[3] The first two zones can be combined in 'realm 1' while the third zone constitutes 'realm 2'. It is impossible to settle in advance what can and what cannot be experienced, and the dividing line between actual and possible experience is therefore flexible and revisable: the factual division is determined by the state of science at a given time. The development of more powerful microscopes, slow-motion films, etc, have enabled scientists to prove the existence of causal mechanisms like viruses, whose existence could only be presupposed before these developments.

This ongoing stratification means that perception and imagination both play a role in science. Perception alone is not enough for the required causal explanation: structures and mechanisms have to be imagined and postulated as well. Using Coleridge's analysis of imagination, Harré distinguishes two phases which correspond to the second and third zones: a reproductive and a creative phase. The first is concerned with the anticipation of possible perception and experience. It conceives of things that are too slow or too quick, too small or too big to be perceived by us due to the limitations of our senses, and it conceives of these things parallel to what we experience and perceive. The second phase is concerned with what can never be experienced, with what transcends all possible perception. The imagination conceives of these things in a way different from the reproductive phase: it 'dissolves, diffuses, dissipates in order to recreate; or where this process is rendered impossible, yet still at all events it struggles to idealize and to unify'.[4]

The imagination is subject to two constraints in science. First of all, the mechanism is imagined in order to give a causal explanation of a certain pattern of behaviour. So it must be structure that could produce such behaviour: the behaviour of the imagined world must match the behaviour of the real world. Secondly, since the model must be satisfactory as the source of the content of the theory, the structure must be possibly existent. So our experience of reality, existing scientific knowledge and theories, and our concepts of what reality looks like determine also what can and cannot be accepted as a causal structure.[5]

The notion of models enters into science because models are the product of imagination. But since the term 'model' is used by philosophers indiscriminately for the non-verbal and verbal products of imagination, which sometimes leads to confusion, Harré introduces a more precise terminology: icon-model for the non-verbal product and sentential model for the verbal product, for the description of the icon. This refinement in terminology has a consequence for the discussion of models and metaphors: the more precise question now is whether metaphors occur in the sentential model, in the sets describing the icon.

A scheme can present the outline of the theory of transcendental realism and can serve for our discussion about the role of metaphors.[6]

	perception		imagination	
subject matter	observed pattern	causal mechanism	icon-model	source
sentential sets	I	II	III	IV

Sentential set I contains the description of the pattern of behaviour that has to be explained; sentential set IV contains the description of the source of the icon-model. Sentential set II is empty but can be filled in two ways, either via set III if the icon-model becomes more and more plausible, or directly if existential hypotheses are generated and confirmed. This explanatory framework is used in the case of the realm of possible experience as well as in that of the realm of reality beyond experience. In both cases an 'analogy of behaviour' between the icon and the mechanism is present, but only in the case of the realm of possible experience is there also 'an analogy of being'. That is to say, the claim for an icon-model in realm 1 includes a similarity between the characteristic items of source, icon and reality: the icon is like the source and is like reality. The item constituting the source forms the genus of which the item is in reality a species. Such a claim cannot be made when the icon-model represents reality beyond experience, since the relation between the unknown mechanism and the source is not one of species to genus. This difference is reflected in the language used. In the case of realm 1 the predicates used for the unknown mechanism are similes, for an investigation of the negative, positive, and neutral analogies is possible. In the case of the predicates for realm 2, they are metaphors, since the positive, negative, and neutral analogies cannot be investigated. The predicates used in the similes keep the same literal meaning in the context of the icon as they have in the context of the source and when at some stage, through research or the further development of instruments, the icon becomes the true representative of the causal mechanism, the terms preserve their meaning. But the discourse about reality beyond experience is the result of the creation of new semantic fields, of new meanings. For it is difficult to find a language that describes adequately and intelligibly the reality beyond experience: only metaphors can do that. This conclusion Harré reaches via an analysis of metaphors that is influenced by linguistics.[7] The Saussurian notion of the 'meaning-field of a lexical item' that includes all the syntagmatic and paradigmatic dimensions of that item, can be rendered in terms of rules: syntactical rules summarizing the syntactical dimension (verb, noun, etc.), and selectional subcategorial rules summarizing the paradigmatic dimension. A metaphor is generated by violation of the subcategorial rules, while the syntactical rules are preserved. Subcategorial rules reflect our experience and are therefore not violated when we talk about our experience (realm 1), but are necessarily violated when we talk about what is beyond our experience, given the differences between the two realms. Metaphors are thus required to talk about realm 2. In this view metaphors are characteristic of a particular sentential model, namely, that dealing with reality beyond experience, while the language of models dealing with the realm of possible experience is characterized by similes.

At first sight this conclusion is rather different from what Black and Hesse say, and does not seem to be very helpful in solving the problems about metaphors and models. But they share ideas that seem to point to a general agreement: like Black and Hesse, Harré maintains that models are not just heuristic fictions, but indispensable parts of scientific theory; and, like Black and Hesse, Harré maintains that existential claims are made by scientists when they use models, for it is the aim of science to push the dividing line between actual and possible experience further. And it is on the basis of this agreement that doubt arises about this disagreement about the use of metaphor. What are the features of language that motivate this opposite conclusion?

Black rejects the 'as-if' thinking as an adequate rendering of what takes place when a scientist uses models, and he stresses the 'as-being' thinking: the first he associates with simile, the second with metaphor. But that first connection is somewhat strange: a simile or comparison is normally not used to express an 'as-if', but to present a similarity, a likeness between two entities with regard to one or more particular features. Metaphor is correctly associated with 'as-being', but it is not quite correct to characterize model-thinking as 'as-being-thinking' *tout court*, since there is an element of caution in the identification between model and metaphor. Black himself uses terms like 'putative' and 'hope'.[8] And what is hoped for is a similar structure. One of Hesse's arguments for not using a simile, or, more precisely, for not using a comparison view of metaphor, is that models allow for the exploration of neutral analogy, i.e., the comparison is not limited to one particular feature or to a set of particular features, but is open. The argument employed by Harré for using 'simile' is in fact the same as Hesse's argument against its use: the likeness can be established because the positive, negative, and neutral analogies can be explored. But the use of simile or metaphor in this context is also a little strange, for interest in neutral (and negative) analogy is not typically connected with the normal use of simile and metaphor. Terms like 'open comparison', 'perfect metaphor', and 'extended metaphor' are witnesses of a terminological uncertainty: 'metaphor' and 'simile' do not fit the phenomenon described and it would be better if a new term could be found. So, Black, Hesse, and Harré agree basically about the language used, but this agreement is clouded by the 'uncertain' terminology. This conclusion directs our attention to the models used for the second realm and to the language describing them. Is Harré correct to characterize this language as metaphorical? Is the theory explaining metaphors an adequate one?

In the discussion of the linguistic approach to metaphor at the beginning of Chapter II, it was argued that certain presuppositions and concepts make it impossible for a number of linguists to give an adequate explanation of metaphor. Like the linguistic theorists, Harré uses as one of the central concepts in his theory of metaphor 'violation of subcategorial rules'. As was shown, this concept is not able to distinguish between metaphors, mistakes, lies and grammatically correct nonsense. Since it is one of the presuppositions of the structuralist approach that meaningful behaviour, including speech, is governed by rules, the violation of a rule must result in non-meaningful behaviour or in non-sense. The awkwardness of this appeal to the violation of rules is here, too, disguised by the other notion Harré uses: the change of the meaning-field of a lexical item. This notion directs the attention to two features, the lexical item and the change of meaning, and neither of these is of much help in a theory of metaphor, since a metaphor is a sentence in which words keep their ordinary and original meaning. A change of meaning implies a change of rules, but this is not consistent with a violation of rules, if they are understood to take place at the same time. The solution is to see the violation of the rules as a comment about the history of the meaning-change, and that implies, as was argued before, a diachronic approach to metaphor.

It is clear that one of two things has to take place: either the term 'metaphor' has to be dropped, or a better theory has to be invoked to replace the one that is used currently. One way of deciding which of the alternatives should be chosen is to look at the language that is labelled 'metaphorical', i.e., the language describing the realm beyond experience. One of the problems Harré sees with regard to the realm beyond experience is how to talk about that realm in an intelligible and adequate way. He argues then as follows: since realm 2 is probably different from realm 1, the language must show this difference. And since metaphors create new fields of meaning, metaphors must be used to express this difference. The premiss about the difference between the two realms requires some elucidation. What does the difference consist in? The realm beyond experience is beyond experience, not because of the limitations of our senses, but because it is a realm which cannot be experienced and which is not meant to be experienced: it is the realm of concepts, the realm where representations fall short and only abstract thinking is adequate. It is the realm of metaphysics. Harré indicates this not only by using the term 'metaphysics', but also by selecting 'power' and 'structure' or 'nature' as his key-terms for the realm beyond experience.[9] These terms are chosen because we can conceive of mechanisms and structures of powers, but we cannot visualize them or represent them (cf Aristotle's *hyle* and *morphe* or Aquinas' *materia prima*). But these terms show also that metaphors are not necessary. What is necessary – and this is valid for realm 1 and realm 2 alike – is a precise, technical, and theoretical language. The aim of the imagination in both realms is to reach a scientific explanation, a theory of causal mechanism. The description of the source of the icon-model, of the icon-model itself, and of the causal mechanism contain theories and the terms used are determined by this context. Whether they are arrived at by way of a change of meaning, whether their meaning could in certain cases be called 'metaphorical', is only of historical interest: at present they are understood and learned by reference to the theory they belong to. Their meaning is a technical and theoretical one. These arguments suggest that the first alternative – viz, to drop the term 'metaphor' as a qualification of the type of language describing the models of realm 2 – should be followed.

So these two sections show that the appeal to metaphor in the explanation of what scientists do when they use models is not very helpful. Metaphors and models are not the same, and the invocation of 'metaphor' appears to rest upon inadequate theories of metaphor and upon the idea that extension of meaning or change of meaning form an essential part of metaphor.

2.3 *Models in theology*
Two of the three claims that constitute the argument in favour of using metaphors in theology by appealing to the use of models in science have now been examined. For the decisive phase of the discussion attention is again going to be directed to the first claim that relates models to metaphors, and to the third claim which states that theologians, like scientists, use models. After the arguments of the previous sections it is sufficient to see whether Ramsey, Ferré, and Barbour, who present this type of argument, introduce new concepts that improve theories of metaphor in such a way that the connection between models and metaphors becomes acceptable.[1]

2.3.1 *Metaphor and model*
Ramsey links models and metaphors very closely: he uses the terms indiscriminately.[1] In his *Models and Mystery*, which contains a more elaborate discussion of models than his earlier books, Ramsey mentions the similarity between his treatment and that of Black, but notes some differences as well. A first difference is partly a terminological one. Ramsey renames Black's scale model and analogue model as picture model and disclosure model.[2] The disclosure model, as Ramsey understands it, is not only central to natural and social sciences, but also to theology, and this disclosure model resembles the metaphor closely. Ramsey prefers the label 'disclosure model', since the structural similarity, or the similarity with differences, which is typical for this type of model 'generates insight . . . leads to disclosures'.[3] The condition that has to be fulfilled, in science and in theology, in order to achieve a reliable understanding is that 'structurally the model must somehow or other chime in with and echo the phenomena. In this way the universe itself authenticates a model. The model arises in a moment of insight when the universe discloses itself in the points where the phenomena and the model meet. In this sense there must be at the heart of every model a "disclosure". Such a disclosure arises around and embraces both the phenomena and their associated model'.[4] Disclosure

is also at the heart of metaphors: 'metaphors like models are rooted in disclosures and born in insight'.[5] This is the reason that they are distinctive. Richards and Black locate 'the secret and the mystery' of metaphor in the connection between two contexts; but, Ramsey asks, how does this mystery arise? His answer is that it arises out of the connection 'when and because the point of connection expressed in the metaphor itself generates a disclosure . . . Hence, the "is" of a metaphor has to be understood as a claim that (i) A and B in contact have generated a disclosure, revealing some object and (ii) what it is that has been disclosed demands discourse which infiltrates B into A'.[6] The introduction of 'disclosure' into the theory of metaphor is another difference with Black.[7] Ramsey wants to stress the cognitive significance of insight and imagination, their objective reference. The reason why he prefers to talk about models rather than metaphors is that 'model' 'prejudices less the discussion and points more likely to logical, epistomological and ontological issues'.[8]

Are the points of difference between Ramsey and Black such that Ramsey presents a better case for connecting metaphors and models than Black does, and consequently a better case for metaphors in theology? The central notion of his treatment is 'disclosure', so the question becomes whether 'disclosure' improves the interaction view, and, if so, whether it facilitates the transition from metaphor to model. 'Disclosure' is introduced to explain the interaction of the contexts: the point of connection is rooted in and generated by a disclosure. Although this might be the case for metaphors, it does not constitute a sufficient explanation for the following three reasons. First, the term covers too broad a field of experience. The stories of the judge who recognizes in the accused an old schoolfriend and of David and Nathan are not metaphors – not even if they are reduced to one sentence – although they are examples of disclosures.[9] Disclosures happen without the use of metaphors. But, secondly, even if disclosures were experiences that only happened in connection with a metaphor, that were only caused by a metaphor, there would still be the problem that a metaphor becomes a subjective phenomenon. Ramsey repeatedly says that a disclosure cannot be forced or guaranteed. This leads to the conclusion, undesirable in a theory of metaphor, that the same sentence might be a metaphor to one and not a metaphor to another. Finally – and this is implied in the last objection – to consider 'disclosure' as an explanation for metaphor is to give an explanation in terms of function and not in terms of structure. So, disclosure does not improve the interaction view as an explanation of metaphors, and a reconsideration of the position reaches *vis-à-vis* the relation between metaphor and model is therefore not required.

Like Ramsey, Ferré identifies models and metaphors.[10] Models share 'the logical essential characteristics of all metaphors, they are not supposed literally true of their referent, and they have a point, they are illuminating in some respect when created'.[11] It is obvious that these two points are not sufficient to characterize metaphor, let alone to explain the structure of metaphor. The first point is concerned with structure, but covers mistakes and falsities, and presupposes that the notion of truth and falsity can be used in a theory of metaphor. The second point is concerned with function. The same conclusion can therefore be drawn as in the case of Ramsey.

Barbour does not equate metaphors and models.[12] He points, following Black and Hesse, to a series of similarities between the two: both have positive, negative, and neutral analogies; in both cases neutral analogies invite further exploration and prevent reduction to a literal paraphrase; and the interaction between metaphorical and literal language finds a parallel in the interaction between theoretical and observational language.[13] Models differ from metaphors in that they do not evoke 'emotional and evaluational responses'; they are systematically developed, the positive and negative analogies are specified, and they lead to theories that can be tested.[14] In his theory of metaphor as well, Barbour follows Black, and marks as the important structural characteristics the analogies, similarities, and dissimilarities between 'the normal context of a word and a new context into which it is introduced',[14] and the fact that a metaphor is not literally true and is open-ended.[15] These remarks do not improve Black's interaction theory and even show a return to the word approach. So, none of the three philosophers has been able to make a convincing case for the identification of metaphor and models or for a connection between metaphors and models. This also means that the purpose of our discussion has been achieved. But there remains the question whether or not it may still be helpful to talk about models in theology.

2.3.2 *Models in theology?*
When these authors use 'models' to describe typical procedures in theology, they presumably see enough similarity between the procedures in science and theology to validate the use of the same term. Do they mean to claim that the procedures in both cases are exactly the same, or do they point to some important points of difference as well? Ramsey, Ferré, and Barbour differ in the answers they give to these questions.

Ramsey does not see fundamental differences between science and theology for 'all disciplines combine understanding and mystery, which means that we shall expect to find in every discipline words and phrases which witness to the insight as well as models which ensure literacy'.[1] He refers here to his notion of 'qualifier', i.e., to words that are witnesses of the mystery, directives which prescribe a special way of developing a model.[2] As examples in theology Ramsey cites terms from negative theology like 'impassable' where 'im-' is the qualifier, and from the attributes of God, like 'first cause', where 'first' functions as the qualifier. In theology the presence of qualifiers is 'an absolute *sine qua non* declaring the inadequacy of all models':[3] the qualifier not only points to the mystery but is also a 'built-in stimulus' for the endless construction of variants.[4] In science, too, qualifiers can be found, because single words can combine in them model and qualifier,[5] the ultimate basis of which is the claim that 'all language has its intimations of divinity as theology has its essays in literacy'.[6]

While Ramsey does not see fundamental differences, Barbour does. He makes a distinction between the cognitive and non-cognitive function of models in comparing science and religion. With regard to the cognitive function, the difference is one of degree and not of absolute contrast.[7] But with regard to the non-cognitive functions the difference is fundamental: one of the primary functions of religious models is to express and evoke attitudes, to recommend a way of life.

Models in science do not have similar functions.[8] And Ferré mentions other points of difference. First, he sees a difference in the type of models used: while in science several types are used, in theology only the conceptual type is employed.[9] The second difference is a difference in scope: while in science models have a limited scope, in theology models have an unlimited scope. In science models belong to 'the order of limited theories', in theology to 'the order of metaphysical theories'.[10] 'The role of theological models with respect to understanding is to help conduct a complete comprehensive conceptual scheme in which every possible event can be interpreted as exemplifying it'.[11] Related to the difference in scope is a difference with regard to adherence to models and theories. In science models are changed or replaced rather easily, while changes on the highest level of theoretical constructions only occur when there is an absolute need for it. In theology the reverse is the case: models are changed less easily than theories. A change in 'prime theories' of science brings about a scientific revolution, a change in the key models of religion a religious revolution.[12] The third point of difference concerns the status of the model: 'The model ... is a necessary condition of theological theory. The dependence [is] not shared by scientific theories'.[13] The basis of this difference is that 'cognitive assent cannot be given to theological theories alone, stripped of their models, as can be done (in principle at least) for scientific theories'.[14] In the case of theology, the need for models is also related to 'the non-cognitive dimensions' of meaning. 'For it is without doubt the imagery of the models in theology which evokes communal adoration, obeisance, awe, ecstasy, courage....'.[15]

All three positions require some comment. Ramsey seems to be too positive. Apart from the different aims of science and theology, there is a serious problem attached to his broad understanding of 'model'. This broad understanding is revealed in remarks like: 'Sometimes a single word, perhaps indeed most single words when they are used significantly, combine in themselves the possibility of models and qualifiers', or, '... we "see" what "energy" means when we pick up from the interaction of bodies at rest and bodies in motion some sort of "invariant"; when despite the changes and chances within a system, something overall is disclosed'.[16] This understanding of model and its combination with qualifiers differs considerably from that of transcendental realism, where a sentential model is not just a word but a theoretical description. Another feature of Ramsey's broad understanding can also be found in Ferré's and Barbour's views: the application of 'models' to both religious and theological language.[17] This is possible because of his broad understanding – and because of his identification between models and metaphors – but at the same time it questions the parallel with the use of models in science. The distinction between religious and theological language is similar to the distinction between ordinary language and the technical language of the sciences, philosophy, etc. Religious language is the everyday language of faith and it is the language of Scripture, prayer, sermons, catechesis, etc., while theological language is a technical language, developed and used by theologians for their scholarly, systematic, and methodical work. As in the case of ordinary language and (any) technical language, this distinction between religious and theological language implies neither a complete separation nor an exclusive one-way relation between the two. A failure, though, to distinguish the two can lead to dangerous confusions, certainly if the same words are used in both types of languages.[18] Only by employing a distinction like this is the right perspective gained for discussion of the question whether models are used in theology in a way similar to that of science. Moreover, the parallel between ordinary language and religious language casts doubt upon the introduction of terms like 'the religious model' or 'the model of religious language', for only in a very imprecise way can one talk about the use of models in ordinary language, and it is far from clear what is explained by such a use.

The need for this distinction is shown by the confusion in Barbour's position. If one tries to find similarities and dissimilarities between theology and science with regard to the use of models, it is beside the point to see the differences in the non-cognitive functions.[19] The same criticism has to be made with regard to Ferré's views, for he, too, introduces non-cognitive dimensions as a support for his claim that theology needs models. Despite terminological appearances, he does not make a distinction between religious and theological language. Terms like 'metaphysical model', 'biblical model', 'biblical model of reality', 'biblical metaphysical model', 'theological model' 'models of theology', and 'models of theological theory'[20] are all concerned with biblical language, with religious language. If we were to divide these terms as referring to either religious or theological language according to the word they use, Ferré's argument would become incomprehensible. Ferré is concerned with 'the vividness and immediacy' of biblical language.[21] Moreover, Ferré's account of the use of models in science does not pay enough attention to the role of theory in the use of models. When he remarks that 'the physicist must not permit himself to become *committed* to the point by point relevance of the theory of wave dynamics, when he is studying the behaviour of light, even though the theory is fully established in its own domain',[22] he suggests that theory is not the most important part. But, of course, it is. It is precisely the possibility of using an already established theory which makes this process of thinking in terms of models more than adding a picture or some imagery to an abstract calculus. But it is this very view which Ferré suggests when he contrasts 'model' with terms like 'abstract' and 'theoretical'.[23] 'Model' thus comes close to 'imagery'. The question whether 'model' is used here in the same sense as, for instance, in the theory of transcendental realism, must be answered negatively, despite Ferré's own analysis of the discussion in the philosophy of science.[24] An interesting feature of his broad understanding of 'model' appears when he talks about the 'metaphysical model'. It refers to the conception people have of what reality looks like. 'The function of this model [the biblical metaphysical model of nature, man, and God], indeed, would seem to be that of laying down guidelines for what may be counted as being real!'[25] It is not clear why such a metaphysical view should be called 'model', or why such a view should constitute a difference between theology and science.[26]

In these accounts, therefore, we discover too broad an understanding of 'model' and a confusion between theological and religious language. The two are related, for the lack of distinction between the two types of language makes it necessary to broaden the meaning of 'model' to accommodate (for example) biblical imagery. The interesting question that remains is whether models understood in the stricter sense can be used to qualify processes and procedures in theology. There seem to be no decisive arguments against a recognition of a structural or formal parallel between the two. In both cases material is organized and explained with the help of imagination; in both cases theories developed with regard to the source of the icon are imported; and in both cases these imported theories may have to be adjusted to explain the new phenomenon. In theology one can point to the development of dogma, as Auer does, to the Christological formulations of Chalcedon, to the dogma of the Trinity or to the dogma of the eucharist, which according to Auer employs 'the substance model'.[27] But as is clear from these examples, the imagery that may or may not be present (cf 'substance model') is not important; it is the available theory which is crucial. And this means that, although it may make sense to talk about models in theology, it does not constitute an argument in favour of metaphors as central terms in theology.

3. Thomas Aquinas

As in the previous sections, two main questions are important with regard to Aquinas' view of the role of metaphor in theology: How does Aquinas explain the mechanism or structure of metaphor?, and What does he say about the function of metaphor in theology? On two occasions Aquinas explicitly discusses the function and role of metaphors in theology, but his view of the mechanism and structure of metaphors has to be distilled from remarks scattered throughout his works.

3.1 *Aquinas' view of the structure of metaphor*

Thomas uses *metaphora*, *metaphorice*, etc. some five hundred times, and frequently a few other terms occur in the immediate context: *similitudo*, and the couple *proprie-improprie*.[1] Aquinas uses *similitudo* to point out that in the case of a metaphor there is only a similarity with regard to one specific point. This makes it possible to use the same metaphor for two different things or persons or to use different metaphors for one thing or person.[2] *Improprie* is used to qualify the metaphor and to distinguish it from proper language. Although Aquinas refers only a few times explicitly to Aristotle's view of metaphor,[3] one can conclude from this first observation that his view resembles that of Artistotle. The broader theoretical context will make clear how one has to understand Aquinas' appeal to similarity and to proper-improper, and how he places his own emphases.[4]

Aquinas remarks that with regard to a term or a word two things have to be distinguished: its signification and its supposition, i.e., the meaning of a word and what it stands for given that meaning.[5] For Aquinas, but not for him alone, a basic presupposition in the discussion about signification is that words do not signify things immediately, but that they signify them via intellectual concepts, also called the *ratio nominis*.[6] Naming and knowing are related for we name things as we know them. This leads to the distinction in the *ratio nominis* between *res significata* and *modus significandi*, between the thing signified and the way it is signified. The way of signifying, expressing the way of knowing, is either abstract or concrete, that is, is either signifying the form or the composite of form and matter. E.g., 'humanity' and 'man' signify the same thing, but 'man' signifies it concretely while 'humanity' signifies it abstractly. This example shows also that this distinction between *res* and *modus* is not to be understood as if the *res* could be encountered or known apart from the *modus*: the distinction draws attention to the fact that we know things in a certain way and that other ways are possible as well.[7] *Suppositio* indicates that a term given its meaning stands for something. It can do this in different ways: it can stand for itself, as in '"man" is a noun' *(suppositio materialis)*; it can stand for the nature it signifies considered as universal and common, as in 'man is a species' *(suppositio simplex)*, and it can stand for something in which the *res significata* is found, as in 'every man is an animal' *(suppositio personalis)*, which is in most cases meant when *suppositio* is mentioned.[8]

With the help of these notions the difference between univocal, equivocal, and analogical language can be explained and metaphors can be located with regard to these language-uses.[9] When things are said to be univocally named the same word and the same *ratio nominis* is used, as e.g. in 'man and horse are animals'.[10] But when things are said to be named equivocally they have only the name in common, and not the *ratio nominis*, as is the case with 'dog' referring to an animal and to a star.[11] When things are said to be analogically named, the same word is used, and they also have the *res significata* in common, but they differ in the way of signifying it. 'There is diversity because the name signifies different proportions or relations or references; there is unity because these proportions or relations or references are to one and the same thing'.[12] This unity and diversity results in a certain order: in one of the analogous words the *ratio propria*, that is, the *res* signified in the primary and regulative way, is retained, while the others signify it in so far as they refer to what preserves the *ratio propria* perfectly. Aquinas' favourite example is 'healthy'. 'Healthy' is used for urine, medicine, animal, etc. as in 'the urine is healthy', 'the medicine is healthy', and 'the animal is healthy'. In all these cases the same *res* (health) is referred to, but each sentence does it in a different way, for urine shows health, medicine restores it, and an animal has it. Among these, the way 'healthy' is used in 'the animal is healthy' expresses the *ratio propria*.[13] Since equivocal, univocal, and analogical use of language belong to the level of *significatio* and not to the level of *suppositio*, a word like 'man' can be used for different individual human beings without becoming an equivocal term.[14]

In the context of his discussion of analogy, Aquinas also uses the term *ratio communis*, and he refers then to the extension of meaning which makes the analogical use of words possible.[15] In the case of the 'healthy' examples, the *ratio communis* is 'with regard to health'. Aquinas uses this notion to distinguish analogy from metaphor, as a discussion about the question whether 'light' is properly used of spiritual things shows.[16] Aquinas starts with two opposite opinions: Ambrose and Dionysius hold that 'light', if used of spiritual things, is used metaphorically, while Augustine maintains that 'light' is used properly of spiritual things and even more properly of these than of corporeal things. Aquinas analyses the difference as a difference in understanding 'light'. If light is understood as that which makes things visible *(ratio propria)* it can only be used metaphorically of spiritual things, for nothing which is *per se* sensible belongs to the spiritual except in a metaphorical way. Ambrose and Dionysius understand 'light' in this way. But if light is understood as 'the principle of manifestation' *(ratio communis)* the reference to corporeal things is removed and 'light' is used properly of spiritual things. Augustine understands 'light' in this way. In a parallel text Aquinas uses the contrast between the first application and the usage of a term: if 'light' is understood in its ordinary usage, it is understood as having received an extended meaning in the course of time and as covering all cases of manifestation. And if this is taken into account, as Augustine does, 'light' applied to spiritual things is not a metaphor, but an example of analogical use.

So, *ratio communis* plays an important role in distinguishing metaphor from analogy. In analogy the *ratio propria* is preserved only in one term, but the *ratio communis* is present in all. Because the difference between the *ratio propria* and the *ratio communis* lies in the way something is signified, and not in what is signified, and because there is a *similitudo analogiae,* analogical names are properly applied to something, and the thing to which these names are applied belongs to the proper supposition. In the case of metaphor, though, there is no question of a *ratio communis*: there is only a univocal term with a *ratio propria*, but the term is used improperly, that is, it is used for something which does not fall under its *significatio*. The basis of the metaphor is a similarity of effect or property which Aquinas qualifies as a *similitudo proportionalis*. But this effect or property is not mentioned: what is mentioned is the thing that has this effect or property.[17] When a man is called 'lion' or God is called 'fire', this is done on the basis of the similarity in strength between man and lion, or the similarity in power to purify between God and fire. But since this effect or property is not named, but rather what has this effect or property, no new way of signifying the *res* is involved. Metaphor is a case of improper supposition. If all suppositions of lion and fire were collected, man and God would not be among them. On this account of metaphor it is impossible therefore to talk about analogy as a kind of metaphor and metaphor as a kind of analogy.[18]

The development of analogy and its contrast with metaphor, the use of the distinction between *significatio* and *suppositio* form differences with Aristotle's view, but these differences do not remove the grounds for the criticism voiced in Chapter II. On the contrary, they bring out – in an interestingly sharp way – the problems attached to this rhetorical view. First, there is a problem in connection with the starting-point, namely, that the metaphor is a word applied or transferred to something which is not part of its signification. If a metaphor is a question of improper supposition, it is implied that a metaphor is a predication and that it belongs to the level of a sentence. For, as McInerny remarks, 'a term has a supposition, it would seem, only as used in a proposition'.[19] But this means that there exists a discrepancy, which, if noticed, calls into question either the starting-point (the metaphor is a word) or the explanation (a metaphor is a case of improper supposition). Secondly, the contrast with analogy makes clear that no change of meaning or extension of meaning occurs in a metaphor. The consequences attached to this correct observation seem less correct, though, and puzzling, for what is left of the meaning of the word if it does not constitute the basis of the transfer? Why is this particular word chosen if not for its meaning? Moreover, Aquinas' remark that 'brave' does not mean the same if applied to God and lion, seems to undermine the explanation even further.[20]

On the basis of this theory of metaphor no arguments about the role of metaphor in theology can be accepted. But, as in the case with narrative theologians, the question has to be asked whether Aquinas' argument about the role of metaphor in theology can be based upon the theory we proposed in Chapter II. An answer requires the outline of Aquinas' view on theology as far as it relates to the role of metaphor.

3.2 Aquinas' view of the role of metaphor
At first sight, on the two occasions on which Aquinas explicitly discusses the role of metaphor in theology – at the beginning of his commentary on Lombard's *Sentences* and in the first *quaestio* of the *Summa Theologiae* – he uses similar arguments, which suggests one consistent view can be constructed out of the two texts. But a closer look reveals important and crucial differences. According to Corbin, we approach these differences correctly and are able to explain the dissimilarities

if we consider these two texts as the beginning and the end of a life-long process of thinking and experimenting with ideas and solutions to the question what theology is – a question which had become especially pressing for Aquinas' generation because of Artistotle's so-called 'third entrance'. The two texts will therefore be analyzed separately.[1]

3.2.1 *The* Scriptum

Aquinas' task as a *baccalaureus sententiarum* (1254–1256) was to lecture on Peter Lombard's *Sentences*. The way these *Sentences* were used from 1152 when they were written, up to the middle of the 13th century, showed some important changes: while at the beginning of this period the commentators provided glosses and kept close to the text, later on they inserted *quaestiones* which had a fairly loose relation to Lombard's text and whose contents were mainly determined by more recent theological discussions. This is the case with Aquinas' *Commentum in libros Sententiarum Magistri Petri Lombardi*, which was the result of his lectures. It contains his first personal reflections and views on content and method in theology.[1] The first *quaestio*, discussing problems about the nature and the method of the *sacra doctrina*, is a good example of this personal approach. These problems do not occur in Lombard's prologue, and Aquinas' discussion is determined by the contemporary situation, by Artistotle's third entrance.

In this first *quaestio*, Aquinas' view of the function of metaphors appears under the heading *utrum modum procedendi sit artificialis* and forms part of a further specification of the way in which theology proceeds. Aquinas' starting-point is the thesis that the way a *scientia* proceeds is determined by its principles, by its material. He develops this in three sections.[2] First, the principles from which theology proceeds are accepted by revelation, and since the acceptance of revelation can be divided into the way it is received and its content, Aquinas is able to connect to this a classification of the literary genres of Scripture: *modus revelativus* and *modus orativus* on the one hand, and *modus narrativus* and *modus metaphoricus, symbolicus* or *parabolicus* on the other. The *modus revelativus* considers the reception of revelation from the point of view of the giver (prophetic visions) and the *modus orativus* considers it from the point of view of the recipient (psalms). The two other *modi* concerned with the content are embedded in epistemological arguments: since we grasp the principles via sensibilia, the narration of miracles is necessary, and since the principles are not proportioned to our earthly minds which always proceed from sensibilia, we have to be led to these principles via sensible likeness, i.e., via metaphors and symbolic language. Secondly, in theology we proceed from the principles with three aims: the refutation of error, the instruction of morals, and the contemplation of truth. For the refutation of error and the contemplation of truth one needs arguments. When ethics are mentioned, Aquinas refers to three biblical genres: the law (prescription), the prophets (promises), and the histories (examples). Thirdly, because of this, Scripture has four senses: historical, moral, allegorical, and anagogical. The historical sense is related to the truth of faith, the moral one to the instruction of ethics, the allegorical and anagogical ones to the contemplation of truth of things in this life and in the future life. The historical sense is the only adequate one for arguments and the refutation of error.

In this article Aquinas makes two types of remarks about metaphors; one could be called 'epistemological', the other 'logical'. The first type of remark is concerned with the disproportionality between revelation and the human mind or reason. Revelation has necessarily to be couched in metaphorical language, i.e., in similes taken from sensibilia. Without metaphorical language we would not be able to understand revelation, for our minds take their point of departure in sensibilia. It is due to this fact of disproportionality that theology and poetics, although very different, have the *modus symbolicus* in common.[3] The second type of remark is concerned with argumentation: metaphors cannot be used in arguments, and therefore cannot be used for the refutation of error. Since arguments have to be used for the contemplation of truth,[4] we may conclude that metaphors cannot be used for the contemplation of truth either. Aquinas quotes a saying of Dionysius, 'symbolic theology is not argumentative', which he uses later in the *Scriptum* and also in other works.[5] The reason why symbolic theology is not argumentative is that symbolic or metaphorical language is not simply true, but true only with regard to some point.[6] But these remarks state two opposite claims, one about the necessity of the occurrence of metaphors, and one about the necessity of the non-occurrence of metaphors.[7] It is not easy to reconcile these two claims, for this tension is part of a broader tension.

The three sections on the *modi*, the aims of theology, and the four senses of Scripture that make up the *solutio* seem to be interlinked and to form a coherent whole, for the *modi* are recalled in the section on aims and the historical and literal sense is related to the aim of refuting error. But this appearance is deceptive: the transitions between the three sections are rather abrupt and it is not clear why the starting-point should lead precisely to these three sections. Corbin points to the fact that the title, the *sed contra*, and two of the four responses (2 and 4) indicate that the central point of concern of this article is the argumentative way in which theology proceeds, but that this argumentative way does not receive much attention in the *solutio*. Despite the fact that theology as *scientia*, as argumentative discourse, provokes the discussion, argumentation is only one way – and not even a well developed way – among other equally possible ways.[8] The tension of the *solutio* is one between traditional elements (sections 1 and 3) and new elements (section 2); the traditional elements are the grammatical, rhetorical, and dialectical tools and devices developed for reading and explaining Scripture, and they belong to the conception of theology as 'exegesis', while the new elements are related to the changing attitude towards reason and to the conception of theology as *scientia*. Because of the occurrence of these elements and because of their tensive relation, this article belongs to that development in theology that Chenu characterizes as the transition from dialectics to *scientia* and to the process of specialization into biblical studies and systematic studies.[9] This whole process is realized in the practice of teaching before it is clarified theoretically; the variety of terms and the imprecision of their meaning *(sacra pagina, sacra doctrina, theologia)* is a symptom of this.[10] Aquinas' article reveals the features of that development and process. Reason is not just limited to apologetics, but is given an important place in the pursuit of truth; the term *quaestio* used in the fourth response is also an indication of the new ideas.[11] But the ideas are not well integrated in the rest of the *solutio*. This raises the question about Aquinas' conception of theology as presented in the preceding articles of this first *quaestio*: does it show similar tensions between traditional and new elements? According to Corbin it does.[12] There are four other articles in the prologue: one on the need of the *sacra doctrina*, one on its unity or plurality, one on its speculative or practical character, and one on its subject.

The central question of the first article of the prologue shows the far-reaching consequences of Aristotle's third entrance: the whole system of physics, ethics, and metaphysics presents itself as a rival system to Christian doctrine and sets an ideal of knowledge *(scientia)* that seems unattainable for theology. In this situation it is not enough to point to the possibility of theology: it is required to argue for the necessity of theology.[13] The objections express all the sufficiency of the philosophical *scientiae* with regard to action and to knowledge, with the consequence that faith and theology are reduced to arbitrary opinions without foundations. In his argumentation for the need of theology, Aquinas proceeds in two ways: in the *sed contra* he adduces an argument from Scripture about the necessity of faith, and in the *solutio* an argument from 'common sense' *(omnes qui recte senserunt)* about the contemplation of God as the aim of life. In both cases philosophical knowledge is said not to be sufficient. The argument from common sense is developed further by Aquinas saying that the contemplation of God is realized in two modes, namely, mediately via creatures and immediately via God's essence. The first mode of contemplation occurs *in via*, the second *in patria*. The doctrine that leads to contemplation is characterized by a similar double mode: philosophy and theology. But since the way via creatures or effects (philosophy) is imperfect, the other (theology) is necessary for achieving the aim of life. The relation between the two ways is then defined by Aquinas in feudal terms: principal and vassal.

This first article shows two remarkable and related features. First, philosophy is taken seriously and not dismissed out of hand. The hierarchical structure of the relation between theology and philosophy implies in fact the proper and independent value of philosophy, for according to the subsidiary principle of the feudal system, the vassal has freedom, responsibility, and autonomy in his own region or on his own level. And the phrase 'the contemplation of God, though, is twofold'[14] shows that philosophy is a way that leads to the contemplation of God. Unlike some of his contemporaries, who treat the philosophical *scientiae* as introductions and merely instruments, Aquinas gives the philosophical *scientiae* a place within the whole movement towards God. He does not want to treat the whole of philosophy as previous generations had treated grammar and dialectics.[15] The second feature is that because of this, philosophy is placed face to face with theology, which is expressed in a parallel between the two, based upon the parallel between *in via* and *in patria*.

The dissimilarities and similarities implied in the parallel and further developed by Aquinas in the two following articles. Given this parallel, the plurality of the philosophical *scientiae*, caused by the different topics and methods, seems to imply a plurality in theology as well. This suggestion is rejected by Aquinas, because the philosophical *scientiae* use *rationes creaturarum*, while theology uses the *divina ratio*.[16] In other words, Aquinas now explores the difference between knowing *in via* and knowing *in patria*: the always-inadequate, partial, fragmentary knowledge of *in via* is contrasted with the all-embracing knowledge of *in patria*. In the discussion of the question whether theology is a practical or a speculative *scientia*, both the similarities and the dissimilarities between philosophy and theology are mentioned: both aim at the contemplation of God and both use arguments, but philosophy proceeds in a human way, while theology proceeds by divine inspiration. The similarity is further developed in a *quaestiuncula* discussing whether theology can be called a *scientia*. *Scientia* in the Aristotelian sense is described as a movement from first principles to conclusion, and this discursive movement in which arguments are used can, according to Aquinas, be found in philosophy and in theology.

Some commentators think that Aquinas establishes theology as *scientia* on this point, but Corbin argues that this part is only a development of the first article and that the first article contains the argument for theology as *scientia*.[17] For, if the *scientia*-character of theology is established here, the previous articles would not really have been arguments about the necessity and the unity of the theological *scientia*. Moreover, this section clarifies only three objections and does not give a separate argument, and as such it occupies a place only on the secondary level in the argumentation as a whole. The first sentence preceding the clarifying remarks – 'as is said' – refers to that separate argument and can only refer to article 1. Aquinas establishes the *scientia* character of theology by arguing for the need of another doctrine than philosophy, and the parallel between *in via* and *in patria* is the foundation for the claim that theology is a *scientia*.[18]

But if this is the case, it is understandable that this could not be Aquinas' final answer, because there are at least two major problems attached to this view of theology. The first is related to the basic distinction *in via – in patria*. The couples immediate knowledge – mediate knowledge, *in via – in patria*, and philosophy – theology are central to the first *quaestio*, and Aquinas identifies philosophy with mediate knowledge *in via* and theology with immediate knowledge *in patria*. But that identification turns theology into something that is not human and not belonging to this world: theology is identified with divine knowledge. This returns in the discussion about the difference between theology and philosophy, where the difference is located in the origin of the arguments used: the arguments of philosophy are from creation, those of theology are from God. The diversity of philosophy and the unity of theology are based precisely on the multiplicity of creation and the unity and simplicity of God, i.e., on the difference between human and divine knowledge. The problematic aspect of the use of *in via* and *in patria* is reinforced by the positive parallel, namely, by the fact that both philosophy and theology have a discursive movement from principles to conclusions (*scientia* proper). This discursive movement is typically human. Aquinas does not recognize the incompatibility of this aspect with the divine status of theology. The two aspects of the parallel between philosophy and theology are not thematically related but are treated separately in the first *quaestio*. Corbin refers to this as the immediate character of the prologue.[19]

The second problem is related to the development of the distinction *in via – in patria*. Aquinas locates the similarity in the likeness of the discursive movement, but this is only a formal feature pointing to a logical procedure. That it remains a formal feature attached to a conception of theology already found in (e.g.) Anselm's writings becomes clear in the third *quaestiuncula* of article 3. It is an answer to an objection about the certainty of the principles in theology, which is faith. Faith, it is objected, is placed between *scientia* and *opinio* and does not have the degree of certainty required for a *scientia*. Aquinas' answer consists in three steps: the first two steps involve an analysis of two aspects of faith: the certainty, which has a base in God, and the incapacity of the human mind fully to capture what is given. This tension leads to a movement, indicated in Aquinas' third step, away from an initial, incomplete grasp, an initial obscurity, towards a better, although not complete, understanding of what was obscure.[20] This process is the *intellectus fidei*, that is, theology as understood by e.g. Anselm and Richard of St Victor.[21] The reason for saying that the parallel structure is attached to this traditional understanding of theology in a formal way without influencing it or changing it, is the following: Aquinas changes his perspective in the course of his answer to the objection about certainty. The certainty required for a *scientia*, i.e., for reasoning, is an initial certainty, an initial *intellectus*. Aquinas' first step is in fact a sufficient answer to the objection. But he goes on and introduces an *intellectus* that is the result of the discursive movement. So there is a change from an initial prior understanding to a posterior understanding, and these are not the same: in the first case the conclusions do not illuminate the principles accepted by faith, while in the second they do.[22] This argument shows two things. First, it shows that Aquinas limits the concept of *scientia* to the discursive movement, i.e., to the use of arguments, to syllogism, which is a formal feature. While he starts in the first article with the problems caused by the discovery of the whole system of philosophy, and while he indicates that he wants to take the whole system seriously and to provide a redefinition of theology, his answer given in the parallelism of structure makes use of only one part of philosophy, namely logic, which was known before Aristotle's third entrance. So, the redefinition of theology, made necessary by that third entrance, turns out to be a translation of a traditional conception in a scheme which was known before that entrance.[23] The mixture of old and new constitutes the ambivalent character of the first *quaestio*. But the argument of a. 3 q^a. 3 also shows – secondly – Aquinas' uneasiness about his solution, for the introduction of the *intellectus fidei* is not required for answering the objection. The first step, pointing to divine inspiration, suffices to answer the objection about certainty, and in fact the objection is answered earlier (q^a. 2). The second step, pointing to the obscurity of faith, due to the weakness of the human mind, which leads to the *intellectus fidei*, is part of an analysis of faith, that cannot be done justice within the previous treatment of the principles. The complete analysis of faith as a mixture of obscurity and clarity cannot be done justice because of the way Aquinas uses *in via* and *in patria*: the identification of theology and *in patria*, of theology and vision and immediate knowledge, prevents him from incorporating the aspect of the obscurity of faith into reflection on theology. But since this aspect cannot be forgotten, it is introduced via the *intellectus fidei*.[24]

So, Aquinas' first conception of theology is a somewhat uneasy old answer to a new question. Against this background the introduction of old material in the discussion on how theology should proceed and the tension between the two elements is understandable. Corbin sees a parallel between the introduction of the *intellectus fidei* in a.3 q^a. 3 and the appeal to the theory of the *modi* and the senses to solve the problem of the method.[25] It is also understandable that Aquinas can make such different and opposing claims with regard to the role of metaphors. The analysis also makes clear why a logical argument can occupy such an important place, for in the end Aquinas uses mainly the insights of logic.

3.2.2 *The* Summa Theologiae

The other place in which Aquinas explicitly discusses the role of metaphors in theology can be found in a.9 of the first *quaestio* of the *Summa Theologiae*, written around 1266. There are several differences between this and the article dedicated to the same problem in the *Scriptum*. Some of the ideas already present in the *Scriptum* are now developed more fully and are given a place of their own. While in the *Scriptum* literary genres, metaphors, arguments, and the theory of the four senses were all discussed under one heading and in one article, the literary genres have disappeared completely, and the other elements are discussed in separate articles, namely 8, 9 and 10.[1]

The ninth article deals with the question 'whether Holy Scripture should use metaphorical or symbolic language'. The argument Aquinas proposes is an argument from convenience, repeated a little later: it is convenient that Scripture treats divine and spiritual things under corporeal likeness, under corporeal metaphors.[2] Two premisses lead to this convenience argument; first, God provides for all things according to their nature; and secondly, the nature of human beings is such that their knowledge starts from sensible things. A quotation from Dionysius – 'the divine ray cannot enlighten us unless wrapped in a variety of sacred veils' – expresses this too. The first argument is followed by a second argument from convenience: revelation is intended for everyone and because Scripture presents spiritual things under corporeal likeness, everybody, including the uneducated who cannot understand these things through reasoning, can understand Scripture. The contrast between metaphor and concept here introduced via the uneducated, does not imply a disqualification of the metaphor: on the contrary, it gives metaphors a crucially important place. In his answer to the objection that symbolic or metaphorical language obscures the truth, Aquinas returns to the distinction between metaphor and concept.[3] Following Dionysius, he says that veiling by image and metaphor does not extinguish the divine light, since metaphors are not end-points but starting-points. People are not meant to remain on the level of metaphor but have to move on to knowledge of the intelligible. This unveiling is only a relative one *(expressius)*, however, and never complete, for, as Aquinas stresses in the next response (ad 3m), in this life we are not able to have a complete knowledge of God. So the place and the function of metaphors is determined by this tension between necessary veiling (in revelation) and partial unveiling (in theology).

As is clear, this argument is not about the role of metaphors in theology – or, at least, not only about the role of metaphors in theology. The use of *S. Scriptura* in the heading of this article, while in the previous articles Aquinas has used *sacra doctrina* over and over again, is an indication that he is here talking mainly about the language of Scripture, about the language of revelation.[4] A look at Aquinas' conception of theology as outlined in the other articles will make clear whether this observation is correct, and what the implications and consequences are. Of these articles, articles 1, 2, 3 and 8 are of special interest.

The first article deals with the question whether, in addition to the seemingly sufficient philosophical *scientiae*, another *doctrina* is needed. The *responsio* offers the thesis – that a divinely inspired *doctrina* is necessary for human salvation – supported by two arguments from convenience. The first argument states that God is the end, the aim of man, but that this end exceeds human comprehension and that man, in order to direct himself to God, needs thus some pre-knowledge, i.e., revelation. The second argument is a kind of *nota bene*: even when human reason is able to think about God, revelation is still necessary.

In the second article Aquinas discusses the question whether the *sacra doctrina* is a *scientia*. The argument for an affirmative answer involves an analysis of the Aristotelian concept of *scientia* and an analysis of the structure of the *sacra doctrina*. The examination of the Aristotelian concept appeals to a distinction made between two kinds of *scientiae*: some *scientiae* proceed from self-evident principles, e.g., geometry, others from principles received from higher *scientiae*, e.g., optics, which uses the principles of geometry. The difference between the two is that the first has evidence for its principles, while the second takes its principles on trust. These principles are not beyond the human mind, but they cannot be grasped within that particular *scientia*. The analysis of the *sacra doctrina* shows that it proceeds from principles, known in a higher *scientia*, namely, the *scientia* of God and the blessed. So, the *sacra doctrina* is a *scientia* of the second type.

In the third article on the unity of the *scientia*, Aquinas uses a procedure similar to that of a.2: an analysis of a philosophical doctrine and an analysis of the *sacra doctrina*. This article is a continuation of the previous one. The Aristotelian theory Aquinas uses this time is part of the philosophy of mind. It is not the material, but the form, involved that determines the unity of the faculty of the soul: e.g., sight considers many things (man, animals, stones, etc.) but sees them with regard to a form – say, colour. The unity is therefore the result of human organization. The analysis of the *sacra doctrina* is rather short: 'Since Holy Scripture considers certain things as far as they are divinely revealed, . . ., all things whatsoever, that can be divinely revealed, share the one formal reason of the object of this *scientia*'.[5] The key to the understanding of this analysis is *revelabilia* – the things which can be revealed – a term that also occurs in the ad 2m. In the above quotation one can discern three couples: Scripture – *scientia*, particular things – all things whatsoever *(aliqua – omnia quaecumque)*, and revealed – that can be revealed *(revelata – revelabilia)*. The first terms of these couples refer to Scripture and state in combination that Scripture presents in some statements what is revealed; the second terms refer to the *sacra doctrina* as *scientia*, and in combination state that the *sacra doctrina* as *scientia* relates everything whatsoever to the particular statements that are revealed, that is to say, treats everything whatsoever as *revelabilia*, as clarifiable by revelation. So, the unity of the *sacra doctrina* consists, despite the diversity of topics and despite the variety of the philosophical disciplines, in the fact that all these topics are seen in the light of revelation and can be clarified by revelation.

The questions discussed in these three articles resemble those of the *Scriptum*, but the treatment of the questions and the answers is rather different. The first article establishes the need of the *sacra doctrina* by showing the convenience of the revelation to man of his aim: without revelation he would not know it, since it surpasses his natural capacities. There is no distinction between *in via* and *in patria*, between a human and a divine mode of knowing God. The first article simply states the need of foreknowledge of the aim of man's life and therefore the need of revelation. It establishes the need of a *sacra doctrina*, but not of theology.[6] Aquinas does not use the word *theologia* in this part of the *Summa*, while he employs it frequently in the *Scriptum*: in the *Summa* he uses *sacra doctrina*, which does not refer to Scripture, or tradition, or theology, but to the whole complex.[7] While the *Scriptum* (a.1) treats the need of revelation as the need of theology, the *Summa* separates the two: a.1 is about the need of revelation, a.2 is about theology, about the *sacra doctrina* as *scientia*. The second article does not use the theory of subalternation as a formal solution invoked on the second plan, but places it in the centre of the argument.[8] This means that the previous attention to the parallel structure of the discursive movement is now replaced by a focus on the principles. This is more in accordance with Aristotle, for in his theory a *scientia* is a true, a real *scientia* not only because of its use of logic, but also because of its principles in which reality is encountered. This means that the *scientia*-character of the *sacra doctrina* no longer depends upon fulfilling formal requirements of the Aristotelian theory (the parallel structure) but that the revealed principles, revelation, form the basis of the *sacra doctrina* as *scientia*. The *sacra doctrina* is a *scientia* not because of an Aristotelian theory, but because of revelation, and the Aristotelian theory helps Aquinas to express this.[9] And in the third article (cf. a.5) the philosphical arguments are not placed alongside the theological arguments: they are now completely integrated. In a.5 ad 2m Aquinas relates the use of philosophical disciplines to the weakness of our minds, to our way of knowing, and in this context he uses the term *manuductio*. The knowledge obtained via natural reason is a 'guide' towards what is above reason. This upwards movement forms, together with the downwards movement expressed in the couple *revelata-revelabilia*, one circular movement: natural knowledge, the philosophical *scientiae*, are guides if seen as leading towards revelation, and are *revelabilia* if seen in the light of revelation.[10]

Article 8, on the question 'whether this (sacred) doctrine is argumentative' discusses the relation between faith and reason, faith and proofs (see objections), and is related to article 2 on the *sacra doctrina* as *scientia*. The *responsio* starts with a short analysis of the role of arguments in *scientia* and the same role is recognized in the *sacra doctrina: scientiae* do not prove their premisses, but argue from their premisses, principles, in order to show something else. The second part of the *responsio* is concerned with the question how to deal with people who deny the principles. In metaphysics, the highest of the philosophical *scientiae*, Aquinas observes that one can start a discussion if an opponent accepts something in common, but that, if he denies all the principles, no discussion is possible, except an exposition of the weakness of his arguments. The same is the case for the *sacra doctrina*.

The first part of the *responsio* is often interpreted as the outline of a conclusion-theology: 'to argue from the principles in order to show something else' is then equated with setting up syllogisms. Corbin mentions two arguments against this interpretation. First, one would expect Aquinas to use this type of deductive argument frequently in his *Summa*, but that is not the case.[11] Secondly, there is a crucial distinction between logic and the real *scientiae*, for logic is a formal instrument and an abstraction from the real *scientiae* that are constituted by their principles, their object. This distinction is forgotten if Aquinas is interpreted as advocating a conclusion-theology. Moreover, this interpretation denies the insight expressed in article 2, where Aquinas locates the *scientia*- character of the *sacra doctrina* in the principles and not just in the use of reasoning (cf. the similarity in formulation between articles 2 and 8). In other words, this interpretation denies the difference and the development between the *Scriptum* and the *Summa*.[12]

How this 'proceeding from principles to show something else' has to be understood instead is indicated by the example Aquinas uses. Paul, he says, argues from the resurrection of Christ to the resurrection of all men. The resurrection of all men, though, is not a theological conclusion, but an article of faith, and that means that Aquinas sees the typical task of theology as to exhibit the internal coherence of the articles of faith.[13] There is an important relation and similarity between the view Aquinas expresses here and his view on the articles of faith. When, later in the *Summa*, he discusses faith explicitly, he presents a picture of a whole complex of related and interlinked articles. 'Article', Aquinas explains means 'any sort of fitting together of distinct parts'.[14] So, if one talks about 'articles of faith' one sees the content of the Christian faith as an organic complex of distinct but interrelated and mutually linked parts.[15] This unity-in-diversity is related on the one hand to the fact that all these articles are ultimately reducible to one, namely, that God exists and cares for man, and on the other to the fact that the number of articles has grown because in the course of time things that were implicit have been made explicit.[16] This view of the content of the Christian faith as an organic complex is also presupposed in the second part of the *responsio* of article 8, when Aquinas mentions the possibilities of discussion with opponents. If an opponent accepts a principle, the discussion takes the form of contrasting that accepted principle with the contrasted one; if the opponent denies all principles, there is no way of using this type of argumentation. This procedure only makes sense if there exists a whole complex of connected and interrelated articles, for only then can it be shown that the acceptance of one article or principle implies the acceptance of another.

In the *Scriptum* discursive movement, reasoning, and argumentation were disjoined from the principles which led to the formal parallel between theology and philosophy, but here reasoning arises out of the principles. After article 2, in which Aquinas discusses the principles as the source of the *scientia*-character of the *sacra doctrina (procedere ex principiis)*, in article 8 he focuses his attention upon the development of these principles *(procedere ex eis ad aliquid aliud ostendum)*. This close relation between principles and argumentation or reasoning accords with Aquinas' understanding of Aristotle as expressed in his theory of knowledge, which is part of the *Summa*'s treatise on man, and in his commentary on the *Posterior Analytics*.[17] Understanding, i.e., grasping the principles, and reasoning are not two separate powers, but two aspects of the same power. Aquinas compares it to movement which starts with a rest and ends with a rest: the beginning and end are formed by the principles.[18] If there is complete understanding to start with, development or discourse is not necessary, and if there is no initial understanding whatsoever, discourse cannot begin. Arguments develop initial understanding towards a fuller understanding. It is not strange to find a strong similarity between these insights concerning the circularity between understanding and reasoning and the circularity between revelation and philosophical *scientiae* as *revelabilia* and guides (a.3 and a.5 ad 1m and ad 2m), for these circular movements reflect the workings of the human mind. In the *Scriptum* the distinction *in via – in patria* prevents Aquinas from acknowledging fully the human aspect of practising theology, but in the *Summa* there is no such barrier: he presents theology as a thoroughly human activity in which revelation and everything studied and discussed in the philosophical *scientiae* are related to each other, so that everything is clarified by revelation and revelation is clarified by everything. It is an activity which has its source in revelation and receives its impetus from faith, for it develops and explores and interprets initial understanding and the internal coherence of faith. Theology is *intellectus fidei*. Corbin concludes that, with this conception of theology, Aquinas adequately responds to Aristotle's third entrance and that theology has again become *intellectus fidei*, precisely in comparison to the philosophical *scientiae*. The agreement with Aristotle is at the same time an agreement with Anselm.[19]

If principles play such an important role – that is, if the *sacra doctrina* is a *scientia* because of its principles – and if reasoning arises out of the principles, it is understandable that, after completing the exposition of the *sacra doctrina* as *scientia*, Aquinas turns his attention to where these principles can be found: Scripture.[20] Article 9 on the metaphors of Scripture sets out to show that development and interpretation and exploration are possible and necessary, and article 10 on the theory of the senses to show how this development and interpretation is related to the spiritual interpretation of Scripture.[21]

The earlier observation that Aquinas talks mostly about metaphors in the language of Scripture can now be developed further. Corbin points to the parallelism between articles 9 and 1 that exists not just on the level of the type of argument (convenience), but also on the level of content.[22] Both articles refer to the need of revelation, to the need of some foreknowledge: that this foreknowledge must be intelligible is presupposed in article 1 and thematized in article 9. Aquinas does this by invoking the human way of acquiring knowledge, namely, starting from sensible things. Metaphors that present spiritual things as corporeal and sensible things enable man in this way to understand revelation. But because metaphors present divine and spiritual things as sensible things, or because they present them improperly, the same aspect of obscurity and clarity that is characteristic of faith is characteristic of the language of faith.[23] It is these two aspects which make theology possible and necessary: because there is some understanding, further development and clarification is possible, and because this understanding is initial and not complete, a development and clarification is required. The two opposite claims of the *Scriptum* concerning the occurrence and the non-occurrence of metaphors have now been reconciled by Aquinas acknowledging the difference between original language and interpretative language, between religious language and theological language. Moreover, the logical formulation has disappeared together with the external parallel in structure between philosophy and theology and the emphasis on logical technique.

3.3 *Reconstruction*

As in the case with narrative theology, the evaluation of Aquinas' arguments requires a reconstruction, for the theory of metaphor he uses is insufficient. Can Aquinas' argument against the use of metaphors in theology and his view on the role of metaphors in religious language be restated on the basis of the theory of metaphor proposed in the second chapter?

A preliminary problem is raised by Corbin in his analysis of article 9 of the *Summa's* first *quaestio*. On the basis of the parallel between articles 1 and 9 Corbin concludes that the article on metaphor is not just discussing a problem concerning a part of the language of Scripture but is dealing with the whole of the language of Scripture. According to Corbin, this is not a minor issue, for, if Aquinas were here discussing only a part of that language, it would follow that there would be a type of language which is completely clear and unveiled, that metaphors would become inessential to revelation, and that the presuppositions of Aquinas' theory of knowledge would be undermined.[1] For the reconstruction this conclusion implies the question whether a completely metaphorical language is possible.

Corbin's conclusion, however fascinating, is not correct, for it does not acknowledge Aquinas' important distinction between metaphor and analogy. Corbin alludes to that distinction by contrasting the metaphorical names of God with names like 'wise', 'good', etc.,[2] but he interprets the distinction as one between 'veiling' and 'complete unveiling', between an indirect and a direct access to the spiritual realities.[3] By so doing, he construes the problem in a confusing way, for Aquinas does not imply in his argument (or in the way he uses these names) that the names give a direct access or that they are completely unveiling. On the contrary, he is at pains to point out that our knowledge of God is imperfect, because it is a knowledge of the cause via what is caused, namely, creation.[4] The same confusing construction leads Corbin to interpret Aquinas' remark in the ad 2m of article 9 that 'truths expressed metaphorically in one passage of Scripture are explained more expressly in other places',[5] as referring, not to other scriptural passages where a complete unveiling takes place, but to that 'game of biblical images that interpret each other mutually'.[6] 'More expressly' *(expressius)* does not mean 'complete unveiling', and Aquinas' remark therefore does not constitute an argument in favour of 'complete intelligibility'. And given the preceding remarks about metaphors as starting-points, the appeal to the mutual interpretations of metaphors or biblical images is not one that can and has to be made, as the formula used by Corbin already indicates: images do not interpret each other mutually, people interpret them. *Expressius* points to interpretation and theology as well. There is consequently no danger of undermining the theory of knowledge which emphasizes the sensible as the starting-point of knowledge. Aquinas does not argue that all knowledge is limited to the sensible, and he does not argue that every time knowledge occurs the whole procedure is to be repeated.[7] Corbin's move to obliterate the difference between analogy and metaphor is not surprising or completely unintelligible, however, for Aquinas does here emphasize an aspect of metaphor which also can be found in analogy: similarity.[8] But as the analysis of Aquinas' theory of metaphor shows, the kind of similarity is not the same in both cases. As McInerny remarks: 'It would be confusion confounded to equate the analogical name with analogy in the sense of proportional similarity, since the latter itself is not an analogous name'.[9] In the evaluation of the theory of metaphor this notion appeared problematic: would the withdrawal of this notion and the introduction of the theory of metaphor we have proposed support Corbin's strong thesis? It is unlikely, for a complete metaphorical (religious) language is difficult to conceive of, not just on Aquinas' own theory, but also on the one proposed in the previous chapter.[10]

The answer to the question whether Aquinas' argument can be restated on the basis of the proposed theory can be given now, and it is a positive one. In fact, Aquinas' arguments are strengthened by a reconstruction. On his own theory – namely, the emphasis on proportionate similarity – the implication of the ornamental view and the possibility of an adequate replacement endanger the importance of metaphors on the level of religious language, the need of interpretation, and initial intelligibility, the understanding already present. The central elements of the proposed theory – that words are used in their ordinary sense but that the concepts are presented in an extraordinary combination – fits these last points well.

But there is another remark by Corbin which seems to contradict this, namely, the argument that the theological interpretation of Scripture is necessary because of the lapse of time. Corbin makes this remark when he elaborates his conclusion that Aquinas, in his final conception of theology, presents theology as a way of reading Scripture. Referring to Aquinas' saying that the truth of faith is contained in Scripture 'but diffusely, in diverse ways and sometimes darkly',[11] Corbin remarks that the greater the cultural distance between biblical times and the time of theology, the harder the work. The language of Scripture had become distant by the 13th century, and its already-present intelligibility had become obscure and for Aquinas an object of research.[12] It is certainly correct to point to the cultural circumstances of the 13th century and to argue that Aquinas was able to clarify the relation between Scripture and its interpretation and to establish the status of theology as *scientia* by means of Aristotelian theories, as Corbin does.[13] But that is not the same as locating the need of the interpretation or the problems of interpretation in the distance of time. In Aquinas' own view Scripture always need to be interpreted, for the language of revelation is always and to everybody a mixture of the plain and the obscure. The difference in time and culture is not irrelevant, but the difference and distance cannot be seen purely in negative terms. Aquinas acknowledges that in the course of time – and this is not just limited to the time up until the New Testament – an increase in understanding can occur.[14] So, Aquinas locates the need and the possibility of an interpretation and explanation in the metaphors of religious language and in nothing else, and this argument is strengthened by the theory we have proposed.

The main point of criticism of the two reconstructions of narrative theology concerns the role and place of arguments. The criticism of radical metaphorical theology is obviously not applicable to Aquinas' view: he not only allows for arguments, he calls for them. But the criticism of moderate metaphorical theology is not applicable either: without saying that Aquinas presents a picture of an argumentative frame in which metaphors can be understood, his view of the interaction and the mutual influence of revelation and Scripture on the one hand and of human knowledge and the philosophical *scientiae* on the other evades in principle the criticism of a one-sided view of this complex relation – the criticism necessary in Metz's case. Moreover, the analysis shows that Aquinas, in the way he uses Aristotle, reveals the relativity of Aristotle's conception of *scientia*. This creates the situation in which it is not necessary to reject Aquinas' argument if Aristotle's conception, or elements in his theory, are no longer adequate. Finally, the way Aquinas discusses metaphors does not result in a replacement view or in the conclusion that they are superfluous. On the contrary, they are allocated an important place and an irreducible role. The correct criticism on the part of narrative theology of the devaluation and disqualification of metaphor and religious language is not applicable to Aquinas, and the dangerous confusion of the different tasks of metaphors and concepts, which is the consequence of this criticism in (e.g.) TeSelle's case, is avoided by him.

4. Conclusion

One of the main conclusions of the exploration of these three different answers to the question whether metaphors should play a central role in theology is that a level of language other than that in which metaphors are central or a type of language different from the metaphorical is required. The criticism of the presuppositions of narrative innocence and pure narrative shows how pervasive and fundamental the 'analytical' and 'argumentative' language is in the whole of language. A completely metaphorical language, and thus a completely metaphorical theological language, is not a coherent conception. The radical version of narrative or metaphorical theology appears to be dangerous as well, for by its rejection of the level of reflection and argumentation and the corresponding language, it also rejects the possibility of answering questions about orthodoxy and orthopraxy, and disqualifies itself as ideological by so doing. Related to this distinction between the two levels is the distinction between religious and theological language. The lack of that distinction results in some confusing claims with regard to the emotional quality of theological language, as becomes clear in the discussion about models. These confusing claims again underlie the criticism of systematic theology which is a part of narrative theology.

Another conclusion is that two suggestions about the relation between these two levels of language do not prove correct or sufficient. The moderate version of narrative or metaphorical theology presents an overall narrative or metaphorical structure with some argumentative elements inside that structure. This view appears to present a picture which does not sufficiently interpret the mixed character of language and the fundamental complexity of the relation between language and reality. Moreover, it does not give an adequate picture of what a theology that claims to be a justification of hope in fact does. Aquinas' final conception of theology, in which everything is related to Revelation and Revelation to everything, is able to give a better explanation. The attempt to link the two levels via an identification of metaphors and models is not successful either, since the identification rests upon incorrect suppositions and explanations of metaphors, or upon too broad an understanding of 'model' which does not pay enough attention to the role of theories in this way of thinking.

How, then, should the relation between the two levels be seen? How is it possible to avoid the danger of *de facto* reduction of religious metaphors to emotional ornaments, a denial of the important insights of modern theories of metaphor? How is it possible to determine the specific task of theology with regard to these religious metaphors? Can the suggestion implied in Aquinas' view of theology be further developed?

Chapter IV

Methodological Considerations

In this final chapter the results and insights of the two previous chapters have to be related to the analyses of the first chapter. First, the conclusions of the arguments and criticisms of the previous chapter are developed and the relation between metaphorical language and theological language is specified. In the writings of the theologians analyzed in the first chapter we can find two types of arguments that prevent a hasty application of this view of the relation to the problems discovered in the first chapter. The first type of argument appears in relation with 'the linguistic status' of 'people of God' and 'body of Christ' and can be centred around the question whether a definition of the church is possible. Apart from the fact that an appeal to metaphors plays a role in the question of the definition, an important point of consideration too is that, if a definition were impossible, the development of a systematic theological treatment would be severely hampered. A second type of argument is the way theologians proceed and actually make use of metaphors in their theology. After a discussion of these counter-arguments (2 and 3) the way is open for us to propose a central term or a basic statement that can take full advantage of the perspective opened up by *Lumen Gentium* and Vatican II.

1. *Two levels of language*

1.1 *The fear of reduction*
The analyses of Chapter III point to the need for a level of language in which metaphors are not central. A clarification and determination of the relation between the metaphorical and non-metaphorical level, and especially of the specific task

of theology with regard to religious metaphors, must take into account an element of the theory of metaphor that returns in the fears expressed by narrative (and non-narrative) theologians. That element is the discovery of the cognitive value of metaphor, which is the other side of the criticism of the traditional, rhetorical, ornamental view of metaphor – the fear that acceptance of a non-metaphorical, theological level leads to an impoverishment and a reduction. The original richness of religious language, its evocative and emotional and cognitive power would disappear. And there is also a fear that the need for such a level would further suggest that what is really meant by metaphor is revealed on that non-metaphorical level, reducing the original language to a transitory stage, or even calling into question the need for such a language at all.

These fears resemble remarks that are made in the discussion about the possibility of an adequate paraphrase of the metaphor. In that discussion two main arguments can be found, one in the context of the word-approach and one in the context of the sentence-approach. The first one presupposes that a metaphor is a word used to replace another word, and since this word can be put back, the metaphor word is an ornament. If a metaphor is seen this way, a replacement is easily considered to be an improvement: it means properly what the metaphor word meant improperly, and it presents clearly what the metaphor hinted at in disguise. If applied to theology and religious metaphors, the acceptance of another level of language implies the exposure of the original religious language as serving some kind of (ideological) function. But since it was shown that upon this presupposition no explanation can be given of metaphors as metaphors (metaphorical use), the basis for this argument collapses.

In the other argument the two parties agree that a loss of evocative power occurs when a metaphor is paraphrased, and the disagreement is about the eventual cognitive loss. Those who defend the thesis that a paraphrase necessarily results in an evocative and cognitive loss can argue that in the case of religious metaphor a paraphrase leads to a reduction of cognitive content, and those who argue against the strong thesis can defend a position similar to that of the rhetorical approach: a paraphrase states exactly the same as the religious metaphor

Methodological Considerations 195

and different answers are then possible to the question why metaphors are used at all. The analysis of the discussion about the 'indispensability thesis' shows, however, two things: first, that when the incorrect presuppositions and inconsistencies are removed, the two parties agree on the semantic indeterminacy of metaphors; and secondly, that the characteristic features of the metaphor-paraphrase are not sufficiently recognized. These two elements are connected. The semantic indeterminacy is the result of the extra-ordinary combination that is made in a metaphor, and because of the kind of combination that is made not all the connections and the implications are immediately clear. The semantic sketch given in the metaphor cries out, so to say, for development and interpretation.[1] A paraphrase of a metaphor tries to explore the implications and tries to present a coherent interpretation.

The resemblance between arguments in the paraphrase discussion and the fears of some theologians suggests that theology, when dealing with metaphors in religious language, can best be seen as a form of metaphor paraphrase. The fear that a theological treatment necessarily implies a reduction, or that it necessarily makes the original language redundant, is then clearly without foundation. On the contrary, seen in this light the dependence in a certain sense of theology on religious language is quite clear. The loss of evocative power, though, is not solved by talking about theology as a form of paraphrase. This loss is accepted by both parties in the paraphrase dispute, and there is no reason to suppose that such a loss would not occur in the case of the paraphrase of religious metaphors. But since the paraphrase is not meant to replace the original, but to create a better understanding of it, the rejection of a paraphrase solely on grounds of this loss of evocative power is an unnecessarily negative attitude confusing the different tasks of the different types of language. This suggestion that the relation between the two levels can be seen in terms of a paraphrase has to be developed further. How helpful is it? And how is the form of paraphrase to be understood in the light of the analyses of the previous chapter?

1.2 Theology: a form of paraphrase
There are three elements that shape the paraphrase: inter-

pretation, understanding, or explanation of a metaphor. First, it is a paraphrase of a *metaphor*; secondly, it is an *answer* to some question about the meaning of the metaphor; and thirdly, it is given *in a certain way*.

As mentioned in the discussion on the possibility of an adequate paraphase of metaphors, a metaphor-paraphrase is not like a paraphrase of another kind of sentence, for it does not consist in one sentence capturing exactly the cognitive content of the metaphor. A metaphor-paraphrase attempts to reveal the implications of the extraordinary combination, to explain the connections, to interpret the associations, to explore the consequences, and to reach a coherent understanding of the metaphor overall.

Paraphrases, interpretations, and explanations are normally asked for or given when something is not clear or self-evident. Up till now, 'paraphrase', 'interpretation', 'understanding' and 'explanation' have been used rather indiscriminately, but in discussion about the methods of natural sciences and the humanities some of these terms have received a technical sense, referring to specific procedures and methods. This discussion can clarify further how theology as paraphrase should be seen.[1] Some of the participants in this discussion defend the ideal of a unified science and try to show the universal validity of one particular method. This method consists in explaining an event or state of affairs (the explanandum) by pointing to other events or states of affairs and to one or more general laws (together forming the explanans).[2] This is called the covering-law theory or the subsumption-theory, for an individual case is subsumed under a general law. Others resist this methodological monism and claim an independent, different, and equally 'scientific' method for the humanities. The first method, the causal one, is characterized by the term 'explanation' *(Erklären)* while the second, or teleological, method, by the term 'understanding' *(Verstehen)*.

An interesting feature in the discussion is that the defenders of methodological monism take 'to explain' and 'explanations' as answers to 'why-questions', or to causal why-questions.[3] G. von Wright does question the limitation of the causal explanations to 'why-necessary-questions', for he thinks that 'quasi-teleological explanations', answering 'how-possible-questions' have a 'distinct causal character'.[4] He argues, moreover, that in sciences that try to explain human actions, like history and social sciences, causal explanations play only a minor and subordinate role: the major role is played by a type of explanation that employs the practical syllogism.[5] In a practical syllogism the major premiss includes what is aimed at, or intended, the minor expresses some action to reach that aim, and the conclusion consists in the decision to perform that action in order to achieve the aim or intention. In a teleological explanation the order of this type of argument is reversed: one starts with the action and the premisses serve as the explanation. This is a genuine alternative to the causal explanation since 'intentions', which are crucial to actions, cannot be called 'causes' in the same sense as the term is used in 'causal explanation'. In causal explanations, cause and effect are logically independent, while in the case of action and intention the relation between action and intention is a logical one. 'Nothing can be an act of volition that is not logically connected with what is willed – the act of willing is intelligible only as the act of willing whatever it is that is willed'.[6] In discussing the question whether for the same 'explanandum' a causal and a teleological explanation can be given, von Wright turns his attention towards the description of the explanandum and remarks that behaviour must be 'intentionally understood', otherwise it does not become 'teleologically explicable'.[7]

In the case of a causal explanation, intentionalistic language may be used, but it is irrelevant to the answer.[8] 'The explanandum of a teleological explanation is an action, that of a causal explanation an intentionalistically noninterpreted item of behaviour, i.e., some bodily movement or state'.[9] And he remarks also that 'the mere understanding of behaviour as action, e.g. button pressing, without attributing to it a remoter purpose, e.g. making a bell ring, for the attainment of which the action is a means, is itself a way of explaining behaviour. Perhaps it could be called a rudimentary form of a teleological explanation'.[10] But he adds that it might be better to distinguish this from the explanation proper. In this line, he makes another distinction, namely, a distinction between interpretation and understanding on the one hand and explanation on the other.

Interpretation and understanding belong to the level of description, or, are answers to the question what something is, while explanation is then the answer to why- and how-questions. Intepretation in this sense is an explicative activity. But since interpretation and explanation are interconnected in the sense that an explanation can lead to another interpretation, one can discern layers of interpretation and understanding. For example, somebody dies and subsequent investigations show that he is killed intentionally by a certain group, and that the group calls it an execution, while others call it murder and qualify it as an act of terrorism. This line of thought has some consequences for the opposition between understanding and explanation. If understanding is the same as grasping what something is, understanding is a prerequisite for every explanation, but as von Wright observes, this is trivial. Understanding has to be further specified as 'understanding what something is like', which is the beginning of a causal explanation, and 'understanding what something means or signifies', which is the start for a teleological explanation. 'It is therefore misleading to say that understanding *versus* explanation marks the difference between two types of scientific intelligibility. But one could say that the intentional or non-intentional character of their object marks the difference between two types of understanding and of explanation'.[11]

Von Wright talks here about understanding in a somewhat ambivalent fashion: on the one hand he seems to limit understanding to a heuristic phase – albeit not in the trivial sense – prior to an explanation, and on the other he lifts this restriction by recognizing the interrelation between understanding and explanation. By accepting that an explanation 'at one level often paves the way for reinterpretation of the facts at a higher level'[12] explanation becomes a process between two forms of understanding.[13] But because he does not thematize this, the ambivalence towards 'understanding' goes unnoticed and the validity of the distinction between 'explication' and 'explanation' is not questioned. The point is not so much that there is no difference between what he calls 'explication' and the two ways in which an explanation can be given, but that, if there is a reason to call both the causal and the teleological procedure 'explanation', the same label can be applied to 'explicative' procedures. In all three cases there is a process leading from some form of understanding to a fuller understanding.

In Pannenberg's view of the relation between 'explanation' and 'understanding' this ambivalence towards understanding is not present. He rejects the division between two types of science on the basis of explanation versus understanding, but he does not defend the supremacy of the covering-law theory. On the contrary, he argues that this type of explanation requires a broader 'systematic theoretical concept' of explanation to make sense. Every attempt to explain arises out of the experience that something does not fit the understanding of reality and every explanation consequently consists in providing a new context or frame in which this particular event, behaviour, action, etc. makes sense. The procedure of subsuming a case under a general law becomes only an explanation in the situation that an explanation is required.[14] Given that the general structure of explanation consists in providing a context or placing something within a whole, the various procedures can be seen as special cases of this general pattern.[15] Explanation thus appears as the link between, on the one hand, an original understanding which is related to an undetermined, unshaped horizon, and, on the other, an understanding that is related to an especially provided frame of sense.[16]

Pannenberg and von Wright agree in points that are helpful for the present discussion about theology as paraphrase, although these points have to be developed.[17] They both reject the presupposition that only why-questions are relevant to scientific explanation and agree that explanation can take place in a number of ways. They both recognize, too, the importance of the description or the understanding that is presupposed for any explanation, and realize the complex relation between understanding and explanation. These points of agreement open up the possibility of taking into consideration another kind of question and answer. Apart from the question about the meaning of words used in a description which can be asked for any sentence whatsoever, and apart too from questions about causes and purposes, there is another type of question:

questions about presuppositions and conceptions of those things, processes, states of affairs, etc. which are referred to in the starting-descriptions of the explanations. In contrast to the why- and how-questions these can be called 'what-questions'. And since these questions do not consider things, processes, states of affairs in their historical or empirical dimensions, but consider their ultimate grounds and foundations, these what-questions can be further specified as 'transcendental', while the why- and how-questions can be called 'categorical'.[18] And since these what-questions are not so much concerned with causal or teleological mechanisms, but with concepts and conceptual systems, their answers can also be specified as 'conceptual explanations'. As is the case with causal and teleological explanations, the starting-point is some understanding, but the direction, so to speak, is a different one: it aims at discovering the conception of something, the presuppositions that are implied in understanding what something is like and in understanding what something signifies. Given Pannenberg's and von Wright's views, there does not seem to be a reason for not calling this kind of answer an 'explanation'. Pannenberg does not explicitly discuss this kind of question, but since it shows the general pattern of explanation as outlined by him, a positive answer may be supposed. And von Wright's argument for distingushing between explication and explanation, which might be invoked here as a counter-argument, does not appear strong enough.

In the case of metaphors, the need for and the importance of such what-questions and conceptual explanations is especially conspicuous because metaphors challenge by their extraordinary combination, or by being proposals to redescribe reality, the conception of how things are and the presuppositions of what reality looks like. In paraphrasing and explaining metaphors conceptual explanation is likely – at least at first sight – to feature more prominently than the other types. Moreover, the need for a conceptual explanation becomes apparent in the discussion about the possibilities of a metaphorical theology, for without conceptual explanation no criterion can be found as to what is and what is not a correct conclusion or consequence, and no reason can be given to support the decision to accept or to reject a (new) metaphor.

But the need and the importance of conceptual explanation can also be seen in other cases. The theory of transcendental realism shows that a realm beyond experience is presupposed in the practice of the scientists and that reflections about that realm are required for a complete and coherent theoretical account. Harré does this by means of an analysis of the concepts 'power' and 'structure'.[19] Gilkey reaches a similar conclusion with regard to history. On the basis of a phenomenological analysis of the current awareness of history and of an examination of tendencies in the philosophy of history he concludes that ontological categories like freedom, destiny, and ultimacy are presupposed, and that a coherent acccount requires a reflection on these categories.[20] These examples show, too, that Pannenberg is not completely correct when he argues that the need for an explanation is only felt when a contradiction occurs in the available theory or theories: the need for a conceptual explanation can also arise out of the realization or discovery that for the construction of a coherent theory reflection upon and development of the presuppositions are required.

If this kind of conceptual answer is a kind of explanation, the question arises whether this can be further specified. This leads to the third element shaping the paraphrase: the way it is done. Although it is possible to consider Picasso's *Guernica* as an interpretation of 'homo homini lupus' and Ravel's *La Valse* as an exposition of 'I live in the autumn of the world', the previous reflections point to a 'scientific' way in which the semantic sketch of the metaphor is further developed by conceptual analysis and explanation, and in which its intensions are brought to light via a system of termini.[21]

'Concept' refers to a fundamental feature of language. To speak a language and to understand it requires the ability to use words that are learned in a certain situation again in different but appropriate situations, including those in which no example of the concept is at hand. 'Concept' is not limited to substantives, but covers all kinds of words that can be used to complete 'that is . . .' like 'dog', 'hilarious', 'to weep'. To use a language requires the ability to employ concepts according to the rules specifying their place and role in the language as a whole. In Chapter II 'concept' is used in this sense when language is described as a system or web or interrelated concepts and sets of concepts, and metaphor is described in terms of the extraordinary combination of sets of concepts. The analysis of how a concept is employed can result in two different types of descriptions. One kind of description consists in the registration of the actual use, and the second in the legislation of how a certain word should be used or is going to be used. The registration of how concepts are used in the ordinary, everyday language shows the elasticity and the richness of that language. This richness is related to the context-dependence or context-openness of words and to their polysemy. The context – i.e., the sentence functioning in a whole communication situation – determines the selection from the available word-meanings. The other side of this aspect of language is that it is rather vulnerable to misunderstanding, for the context does not always determine sufficiently, or does not reduce the polysemy fully. Such an analysis shows also that ordinary language is mixed with fragmentary comments and residues of reflection and theory. An example of this is the way 'metaphor' is used by the theologians mentioned in Chapter I, which shows also that, however revealing a registration is, it is not adequate for the creation of a type of language that is both precise and critical. Since such a language is necessary (cf. again the use of 'metaphor') apart from registration, there has to be legislation. This can happen *ad hoc* and for one specific concept, but it can also happen more systematically by moving from ordinary language to 'scientific' language, i.e., by developing concepts into termini. When the use of a concept is agreed upon by explicit argument or by stipulation and the rules are so specified and tightened that the context-dependence is minimal, the concept becomes a terminus. Although the explicitly specified rules make the terminus already independent of the actual communication context, this independence is further strengthened by a 'terminology', by other termini that form together a coherent system or theory in which the termini influence and support each other and which also can be used in the formulation of rules.[22] Such a terminology can be specially developed, or it can be an already existing system that is used with or without modifications. In a terminology one can distinguish between formal and substantial terms: understanding and explanation are concentrated in the substantial terms, while the formal terms structure the original and the secondary language. Formal terms can be general terms like 'concept', 'terminus', 'metaphor', or specific to a certain field of research like 'ecclesiology'.[23]

The discussion of metaphor and metaphor theory in Chapter II is an example of describing the precise use of a concept and of relating the terminus 'metaphor' to other termini and locating it within a terminology. Since 'metaphor' is a formal, metalinguistic concept, the starting-point is formed by a series of examples of what are commonly called metaphors. The analysis of these sentences reveals some features that are not adequately captured by the rhetorical descriptions in their unsophisticated and sophisticated forms. The explanation in terms of rules and sets of concepts and the discussion of alternative theories aims at relating this terminus to other termini in a coherent system, in an already existing terminology.

The transition from a relatively loose concept to a much stricter terminus can be expressed by the choice of a specially coined word (e.g., eschaton), but need not (e.g., 'hope', which occurs in ordinary language, in religious language, and in theological language). In the latter case the danger of confusing the different levels or shifting unwittingly from one level to the other is greater than in the first case. The transition from the level of loose concepts to the level of termini encounters some special problems where metaphors are concerned. While in other cases the rules of the relevant concept can be tightened and another word may be chosen which forms some kind of continuation with the ordinary one, the application of such a procedure to metaphors would deny the specific character of metaphors. If, for example, 'life is a tale told by an idiot' was the starting-point, then 'tale' would not do as the central terminus, for it would direct attention to the 'metaphorical word' and not to the sentence, to the metaphorical combination, and thus imply a rhetorical view of metaphors. Moreover, in religious language, but not only there, various different metaphors are used for the same person, thing, group, etc. (the church is 'the people of God', 'the body of Christ', 'the bride of Christ', 'the temple of the

Holy Spirit', etc.). The selection of one – e.g. 'body' – plus a specification and tightening of the rules would create severe additional problems about selection and the relation to the various metaphors. So, the transition from metaphor to an explanation by means of terminology, to a precise conceptual explanation, requires another method – namely, the selection of a terminus that in combination with (e.g.) 'church' forms a basic statement that is *open* enough to elicit and reveal the myriad of connections, if present, and *precise* enough to determine which of the possible interpretations and explanations is coherent and thus possibly correct or not. The first requirement is obvious, but the second needs some clarification.

The question about truth or falsity, about correctness or incorrectness, can be asked of a statement that is coherent, i.e., a statement 'which it makes sense to suppose is true; one such that we can conceive of or suppose it and any other statement entailed by it being true; one such that we can understand what it would be like for it and any statement entailed by it to be true', as Swinburne puts it.[24] It does not seem to be erroneous to require the establishment of coherence in the case of metaphor explanations as a preliminary to the attempts to answer the questions about their correctness. Swinburne states as a formal condition of coherence that a statement should neither express nor entail a contradiction, for a statement is incoherent if it expresses or entails a contradiction. If the status of a certain statement is doubtful, its incoherence can easily be shown by revealing that it entails a contradiction, but its coherence cannot so easily be shown by means of the same procedure. 'Generally, we cannot prove a statement p to be coherent by proving what it *entails*. The fact that it entails many coherent statements would not show it to be coherent; for all statements, coherent or not, entail many coherent statements. "Some squares have five sides" is incoherent, but it entails "some squares have sides" which is coherent. Our only hope of proving a statement p to be coherent is by showing that it *is entailed* by some other statement r; and that would prove it to be coherent if and only if r was coherent'.[25] The reason for this is that, since r is coherent, no contradiction follows from it, and 'since p deductively follows from r and so is involved in the claim that r,p must also be coherent'.[26] Swinburne remarks that the success of this procedure depends on the assumptions about the coherence of the other statement (or combination of statements) and about entailment, and this may require some discussion.[27] And he adds that, apart from deductive arguments, inductive arguments may show the coherence or the incoherence of a statement.[28]

Swinburne's remarks suggest a way of dealing with metaphor paraphrases, a way of judging which ones qualify for further investigation. Suppose p, q and r are metaphor-paraphrases and all concern the same object A, and suppose their coherence is not obvious or doubted. Then a statement s, also about A and obviously coherent, must be found, and if p,q and r can be shown to be entailed by s or if s counts in favour of p,q and r, p,q and r are coherent and the discussion about their correctness can start. It is clear that s should not be a metaphor, for that would push the problems away, not solve them. This aspect, together with the first aspect, can be captured in the formula that for the transition from the metaphorical level to the terminological level a basic statement is required that can function as an interpretation-key and a coherence-criterion. Such a statement makes the extraordinariness fruitful and available for further reflection.

These three elements together and understood in this way determine theology as paraphrase of the metaphors that can be found in religious language. And although at first sight the suggestion of theology as paraphrase may seem to lead to a view like Metz's, in which argumentation occupies a minor role within an overall story-frame or metaphor-frame, the specific character of the metaphor and the kind of explanation it provokes originate a paraphrase that does not remain 'inside' the metaphor, but that, due to the presence of the basic statement, has a foundation 'outside' the metaphor.

2. *The definition of 'Church'*

Before these ideas can be applied to ecclesiology two preliminary problems have to be resolved. The theologians discussed in Chapter I present both in their practice and in their arguments an alternative to what is proposed in the previous section, and the strength of it has to be tested. Their arguments can be grouped around the question whether a definition of the church is possible. Some think it is possible and argue in this context against the use of metaphors, while others deny such a possibility and accept metaphors, and in most cases a number of metaphors, as necessary in any fundamental description of the church. Apart from the various presuppositions about metaphor which influence these arguments, both parties share some presuppositions about definition, and these presuppositions require further examination. In the light of this examination the arguments against the possibility of definition have to be restated and can then be judged.

2.1 *The arguments*
The thesis that the church cannot be defined in principle is often implied, sometimes mentioned, and occasionally discussed explicitly.[1] The distinction between nominal and real definition, mentioned by Congar in an article dedicated to this question, is a first indication of what is declared to be impossible.[2] A nominal definition is concerned with words and its purpose is to settle or to state the meaning of words.[3] A real definition is concerned with things, with reality. The discussion among the theologians is about real definition, about the possibility of stating and establishing the essence of the church by citing those features that constitute the church as church. Congar questions the possibility of a real definition according to the rules of formal logic and he supports this with two arguments: 'the reality we now call church is too rich to be captured by one concept and to be called by one name'; and, the church is not just a human, social reality with some Christian addition, the species 'supranatural' of the genus 'society', but a substantially supranatural reality.[4]

These arguments return repeatedly in the discussion and are in fact two aspects of the one central argument: the church is a mystery and can therefore not be defined. In a book by Commer on the essence of the church, to which Congar refers for his second argument, and which is quoted by other theologians as well, the relation between the two aspects can be seen clearly.[5] According to Commer, no logical definition of the church can be given for logical definitions are about natural things and the church is not a natural thing: the church consists of spiritual and corporeal elements. And even a 'quasi-definition' of the church is impossible, for the church does not have a higher genus in common with other things: because of its uniqueness and infinite and divine character it cannot be listed among the finite and non-unique natural things. The impossibility of the definition is not due to a deficiency of being, but to an excess that defies all categorization by finite concepts and distinctions. God and Christ cannot be defined, and neither can the church, for Christ and the church are in a certain sense identical. The only way one can talk about the church is in images derived from Scripture.[6] And in a later article he writes that if one were able to know the mysterious essence of the church completely, one would have to show this by capturing all its properties exactly in a formal concept. But all attempts so far do not fulfil the logical requirements and are not without metaphors.[7] Commer's views are an important source for other theologians, e.g., Holböck and Schmaus. According to Holböck 'the church in its proper essence participates in the incomprehensibility of God and Christ'.[9] The church is a mystery and that implies that its essence can only be captured in faith and that no proper definition can be given, but only a description. Referring to Commer, he qualifies this further by saying that not even a description, but only a 'circumscription' by means of images, is possible.[10] And following Semmelroth he stresses the dangerous illusion of mastery given by concepts.[11] Schmaus, too, quotes Commer with approval on the question about the possibility of a definition of 'church' in the strict sense. And in a later work he adds that for such a definition of the church a complete knowledge of the church, including its future to the end of time, is required; since that knowledge is not available such a definition cannot be given.[12] But Schmaus allows for a definition in the broad sense, an 'essence-description' employing analogical language.

Although Dulles uses a somewhat different terminology, he, too, mentions that the church is a mystery and in that connection makes remarks about definitions and images. When 'mystery' is used for the church, it signifies that the church is 'not fully intelligible to the finite mind of man', that the church 'pertains to the mystery of Christ', and that the church cannot be fully objectified because of our involvement in it.[13] This has methodological consequences: 'the proceeding from clear and univocal concepts, or from definitions in the usual sense of the word' is ruled out. One can nevertheless talk about the church indirectly, that is, via images.[14]

Of these arguments Schmaus' remark about the lack of knowledge of the future and Dulles' remark about the lack of full objectivity, if taken seriously, do not only apply to the church or to theology in general, but also to such different phenomena as nature, man, marriage, history, time, space, and state. Valid or not, these points do not have a special force in ecclesiology and can be left out in the following discussion. That means that the following elements are relevant: the type of definition that is declared impossible is the real definition; such a definition has to fulfil certain requirements and obey certain rules – it has to indicate, e.g., the genus and to specify the differentiating features, and it should not contain metaphors, but because of the mystery-character of the church these requirements cannot be fulfilled.[15] Moreover, a number of metaphors and images are better equipped to express the mystery, than just one metaphor or image alone.

A special problem in this discussion consists in the declaration of the encyclical *Mystici Corporis* that 'to define and to describe' the church 'no more noble, no more excellent and no more divine' expression can be found than 'the mystical body of Christ'.[16] Holböck tries to solve the discrepancy between this declaration and his own position by distinguishing between a 'descriptive definition' and a 'defining description', between a descriptive determination of a concept and a conceptual determination of a description. According to Holböck, Pius XII proposes a defining description: it is defining insofar as 'mystical body' is given prevalence above other descriptions that are possible, and it is description, because it does not become a definition, but remains a description.[17] Semmelroth maintains that the declaration of the pope does not mean that one has to analyze the components of 'the church is the mystical body of Christ' with the help of natural logic and so find the essence of the church. The exposition the encyclical gives is not intended as a word analysis, although the encyclical proceeds in this way, for it is a magisterial proclamation of the faith of the church and it is the only valid interpretation, inspired by the Holy Spirit.[18] And Congar quotes Pius' declaration and accepts it without relating it to his previous doubts about the possibility of definition.[19] These reactions are not adequate. Holböck's distinction is not clear and the interpretation of 'defining' as 'giving prevalence above' does not have much foundation in either ordinary or technical language. Semmelroth's argument opposes magisterial teaching to analysis, but such an opposition is not necessary and leads in the end to a position of the teaching of the church outside the frame of common human language, understanding, and analysis. And Congar does not even try to solve the discrepancy.[20]

Koster criticizes the formal counter-arguments within his own defense of the possibility of a definition in 'Ekklesiologie im Werden'.[21] He defends the thesis that the (German) ecclesiology of that period still belongs to the pre-theological level and he points to those arguments against the possibility of a definition on principle and to the connected arguments about metaphors and images as symptoms of the pre-theological state. He rejects the various arguments that are given in support: the historical argument that since up to now no adequate definition is given, no definition is possible at all, and the argument that the mystery of the church cannot be known and defined. The first argument concludes incorrectly from the fact that a definition never has been given to that it never can be given, and the second does not acknowledge the analogical character of theological definitions, statements, and conclusions. This second argument Koster develops further by analyzing the presuppositions about the analogy of faith and the theological analogy that determines the radical negative position. It is said that the church is without any analogy or comparison, but, Koster remarks, this contradicts Scripture and the teachings of the church in which the church is presented by means of several comparisons. Moreover, without analogy no conception of the church would be possible and in consequence no faith could be asked for. Another point he criticizes is the deification and idolisation of the church and the identification with Christ: this rests upon neglecting the analogy between the order of the supranatural and certain things in the order of the natural.[22] And he points also to the strange phenomenon that the defenders of the impossibility-thesis suddenly leave their 'theological agnosticism' by accepting metaphors about the church in theological language. They consider these as second best, degrading by this evaluation the language of Scripture to the second rate.[23] In his criticism of attempts to see 'mystical body' as the real definition of the church, Koster reveals his own views on what a definition should be and what kind of tasks it must be used for.[24] A definition should not be a mere 'fixing of the use of the word' *(Festsetzung)* but an 'essence-determination' *(Wesensbestimmung)*, and it should present the 'conceptual determination' and the 'linguistic expression' of the essence named by means of such a fixing of the use of a word. The test-case for deciding whether a proposed definition is merely fixing the use or determining the essence, is the truth-question, for there is only one essence-determination possible. 'The definition of the church is thus the true conceptual expression of the essence, understood in a human way, of what God has let Paul name "Body of Christ"'.[25] The functions such a definition has to fulfil are fourfold: it has to explain the essence of the church and to distinguish it from other things; it has to explain the essential properties that can be deduced from the essence; it has to indicate and reject theological errors; and it has to evaluate other theories.[26] Metaphors and images also play a role in Koster's understanding of definition. Another element in his analysis of contemporary ecclesiology is the 'theological ethos' and the way of thinking related to it. He refers here to the positive evaluation by certain people of the pre-theological level for pastoral or other reasons. On that pre-theological level metaphors and images dominate, and these are more helpful for preaching, etc. But for the theological level metaphors are not sufficient.[27]

This means, though, that despite criticism and differences in the evalution Koster does share important presuppositions with (e.g.) Commer whom he criticizes: both parties agree about the nature of the definition and about the implications of this nature, namely, that a definition should not contain metaphors or images. This disagreement is about the possibility of an essence-definition in a particular case – the church – but not about the possibility or the feasibility of a real definition as such. Yet philosophers have called the correctness and the coherence of such an enterprise into question: some have declared it a totally misguided undertaking, while others have distinguished various activities, of which some are important and valuable and others are incorrect, all confusingly combined under the same label. A look at these analyses is necessary before a decision can be taken as to whether a definition of the church is possible or impossible.

2.2 *Real definitions*

Definitions, both nominal and real, are normally given and asked for when a speaker or hearer is not certain or clear about a word that is being used or about something that is being mentioned. Real definitions can be understood as answers to 'what is . . .' questions. To see what kind of answers a real definition cannot give, the remarks about the relation between language and reality made earlier in the context of metaphor-theory have to be recalled. Language has a conventional character, i.e., cannot be conceived of as merely reporting or mirroring a pre-existing structure of reality. The conceptual structure of a language is not necessitated by reality. Consequently, it is not possible to point to reality as supporting evidence for certain concepts – nor is it possible to use sentences like 'but there are really four primary colours' or 'but all triangles are really rectilinear' as backing for certain statements. Such appeals are, in Wittgenstein's words, 'justifying a sentence by pointing to what verifies it'.[1] Moreover, they do not take into account that the conceptual structure of a language is the result of human activity.[2] The relevance of these general remarks for a discussion of real definitions is that if real definitions are understood as stating what makes something what it is, the definitions neither state, nor report, nor establish something completely independent of human structuring, but state how language is used to structure reality. In other words, real definitions give an answer to a what-is question by stating the defining characteristics.

But if this remark is taken as the only remark that can or should be made in connection with what is traditionally called 'real definition', the complexity of the 'what-is . . .' question is overlooked and the possibility of discovering a number of valuable activities is blocked. It would also mean that what theologians in fact do when they discuss the church does not receive enough attention: it is too easy to dismiss their disagreement as purely disputes about words.³ Apart from stating the defining characteristics, there are several other answers that can be given to 'what-is . . .' questions, since questions like 'what is music?', 'what is art?', 'what is time?', 'what is man?', etc, are vague and general. The type of answer expected is not specified in the question itself – although it may be clear from the context. This means, though, that several correct answers can be given to the one question, and that one should expect this variety to be reflected in what is normally offered as a real definition.⁴

A real definition can state a key-element which structures the whole and from which other elements follow, e.g., 'music is melody'. It can present a rejection or recommendation of a certain ideal, as (e.g.) in 'music is the art of making pleasing combinations of sounds in rhythm and harmony'.⁵ That is to say, a real definition can be a 'persuasive definition'; if it is, it is often formulated with the help of terms like 'true', 'real' or 'really' as in 'true music is . . .' or 'the real function of music is . . .' A real definition can point to the cause or the conditions of something as (e.g.) in 'music is the noise produced by man by means of his vocal chords or by means of an instrument'. And finally, a definition can give some kind of analysis, and 'analysis' covers here a number of activities. First, it is used to refer to processes of abstraction and naming, e.g., to the process of becoming aware of a certain pattern within noises and naming it 'music'. Secondly, it can refer to the activity of realizing the complexity of a general element by acknowledging its parts, as (e.g.) in the case of music distinguishing between melody, scales, major-minor, rhythm, etc. Thirdly, analysis can also refer to the activity of placing something in a greater whole, defining something in terms of something else (music as one of the expressions of man's emotions) or by classifying it (music as man-made noise opposed to noises caused by brooks and birds). Fourthly, analysis can also mean the improvement of an idea or concept.⁶ Of these four kinds of analyses, the first type – abstraction and naming – should not be called a definition.⁷ This activity is presupposed in all of the others, for without abstraction and naming the question would not arise and an answer would not be possible.

So, what is traditionally called *definitio realis* can be one of these activities, but quite often such a definition is a mixture of more than one of them: the persuasive definition quoted presents a key-element as well. Further, it may not always be possible to tell whether a definition presents a key-element or an improvement of the idea. Another complication is that a real definition can entail some kind of nominal redefinition. In the case of definition as analysis, the realization of the complexity can lead to the improvement of the concept and this often entails a stipulation about how the word should be used in the future, resulting in a refining of the defining and accompanying characteristics. If the complexity of music is analyzed, it may lead to an improvement by making it more general and to the stipulation that 'music' should not be restricted to certain man-made noises, but that it should include bird noises as well. Or it may turn out that the search for a key-element requires a more precise delineation. Of these different types of answers, the persuasive definition is commonly judged to be an undesirable one. The correct argument for its rejection cannot be that it expresses a value judgement instead of facts, for this would imply an over-simplistic view of factual language. The correct argument should be that such an answer does not clearly or openly show that it recommends or rejects an ideal. The recognition or exposure of this deceptive feature of a particular definition may be sufficient and a complete rejection of the answer not necessary.[8]

Traditionally, too, a number of rules or requirements are cited that an adequate definition has to fulfil: some of these rules have been mentioned by the theologians in their arguments. For present purposes, three such rules are relevant. First, a definition should establish the essence of what is defined and not state accidental properties; secondly, a definition must state the genus and the differentiating species; and thirdly, a definition should not use metaphors or figurative language.[9] Of these rules the first one becomes rather obvious when the misunderstanding based upon an incorrect view of the relation between language and reality is removed. If the definition is a nominal one, the rule merely says that a definition should state the defining characteristics, i.e., should define, and if the definition is one of the types of answers distinguished the rule has to be translated to bring it into accordance with the type of question asked. This implies that it is rather difficult to formulate rules about definitions since context, purpose, etc. cannot always be specified. This is even clearer in the case of the two other rules. If the second rule is applied to nominal definitions, 'genus' has to be interpreted rather loosely, e.g., in terms of grammar indicating the possible combinations with other words (Ryle, Wittgenstein).[10] And even then, the rule cannot be used to exclude other ways of defining a word, for the rule would mean that a word can only be defined analytically when it may be perfectly adequate to define it by ostension, by denotation, or by giving a synonym. If applied to real definition, 'genus' has again to be understood broadly, for such a real definition is not limited to questions about natural species or objects, nor is it limited to one particular type of analysis as is implied in the rule. The rule forbidding figurative language or metaphors cannot be maintained in its generality. 'Life is a tale told by an idiot', or 'man is a thinking reed', or 'architecture is music turned into stone' can be perfectly adequate answers to a 'what is . . .' question, depending on the context and the purpose. Moreover, such a metaphorical definition can be the starting-point of an analysis, for it may suggest a line of thought which results in a refinement or improvement of the idea and in a stipulation of how a word should be used in the future.

2.3 *The arguments reconsidered*

In the light of these reflections about the nature of real definitions, the arguments of the theologians have to be considered. Both parties maintain a view on real definitions that supposes a possibility of circumventing language and that denies the human participation in structuring reality. Insofar as theologians understand essence-descriptions or real-descriptions as attempts to reach the essence without language or as ways to determine the essence separated from naming, their arguments are signs of a misguided concern. The way (e.g.) Koster employs the distinction between 'fixing the use of a word' and 'essence-determination' and the remarks made by him and other theologians that the name does not matter so much, is an illustration of this attitude. If this misunderstanding is removed, the negative argument can be restated either as an answer about defining characteristics or as an answer to a 'what is . . .' question. Are there arguments in favour of declaring either answer impossible in the case of the church?

A denial of the possibility of giving an answer to a question about the defining characteristics amounts to saying that no rules whatsoever can be specified for the use of the word 'church'. But only if a word is meaningless can no rules, no defining characteristics be given.[1] The negative argument interpreted this way results in saying that 'church' is a word without meaning, without a place in language as a whole, and this conclusion is clearly not intended by the theologians. With regard to the real definition as an answer to a 'what is . . .' question there is, apart from a possible negative judgement about persuasive definitions, no argument on general grounds for denying the possibility of such an answer. But are there arguments in the case of the church which makes such an answer impossible? The central argument is 'the church is a mystery and can therefore not be defined' and this argument could be used here. But how is 'mystery' to be understood? The theologians mentioned do not always clearly indicate how they understand 'mystery' and their views contain elements that are incompatible, as Koster observed.[2] For the sake of argumentation and clarity the different interpretations and elements are presented schematically in what follows.[3]

There is first of all 'mystery' as it is used in ordinary language, and there are two notable features to this understanding: we can express intelligibly why something is puzzling or mysterious, and the mystery can in principle be solved.[4] When the church is called a mystery, this type of understanding is not commonly used. Two other interpretations are discernible in the case of the church: one in terms of the supra-natural, and one in terms of God's plan for mankind.

The first theological interpretation defines mystery as a revealed truth that cannot be found out by human reason and that, even if believed, remains obscure and beyond human reason and human concepts. There is some ambiguity in this formulation for it can imply either no grasp whatsoever, or a partial grasp.[5] If understood in the strong sense, 'the church is a mystery' does not allow a definition, but neither does it allow any predication and forbids sentences like 'the church is the most real relation of people with the God-man',[6] or 'the church is the mystical body of Christ'.[7] It blocks the development of any ecclesiological thought, and it means that 'church' becomes a meaningless and vacuous term. If understood in the weaker sense, however, 'the church is a mystery' allows some grasp via analogous concepts. The combination between mystery and analogy is a somewhat awkward one: a strong emphasis on the difference undercuts the whole procedure, since a certain similarity is required. The example given by Scheeben of an explorer reporting about a flower whose colour, blossom, and smell hardly resemble those of the flowers we know shows this problem in an interesting way. Why should the explorer call it a 'flower' except for some similarity?[8] This classification may turn out to be incorrect, for subsequent research may reveal that it is in fact an animal or something that belongs to another category of vegetation (cf the case of the whale) or that it is something that requires a category of its own. But in all those cases it is related to things we know and fits into our system. Moreover, there has to be some understanding of the subject of the analogous predication itself, or it would not be possible to say that these predicates are analogical or to what degree they are analogical, nor would it be possible to say which predicates are allowed and which not. That this knowledge is presupposed is clear from the fact that disagreements occur and are discussed. That is to say, as soon as analogical predicates and concepts are allowed the appeal to 'mystery' loses much of its initial force. The appeal to the mystery of the church then becomes a comment upon the limitations of all human knowledge and it is not surprising to find Scheeben claiming that one cannot know the essence of things.[9] Such a comment may be correct in the case of theology, or even in the case of all human knowledge, but it requires some specification or indication that the other approach to something or to everything is presumptuous and an overstatement of human capacities. The introduction of the appeal to the mystery of the church in the ecclesiology of the 19th century forms a good example of this further specification: it was the reaction to a treatment of the church which only paid attention to the external structure and which was thought to be a reductionist treatment. It was an appeal to realize the complexity of the church (visible-invisible, the relation to Christ, the importance of grace) and was made in order to reach a better understanding of the church. 'The church is a mystery' does then not exclude any of the procedures and analyses that form an answer to the 'what is . . .' question. On the contrary, the appeal uses and points to precisely those procedures.

The second theological interpretation of 'mystery' is given in terms of the history of salvation. God's plan for mankind is called 'mystery' by Paul, but is not something secret or inexpressible for it is revealed and preached.[10] In the course of the early centuries of our era the original meaning of God's plan was further developed by canonical and other writers and by the end of the second century it covered either God's plan revealed in Jesus, or Jesus himself, or the prophecies and prefigurations in the Old Testament of the mystery of Jesus.[11] The change within the Pauline letters from 'mystery' as the revealed plan of God towards Jesus as the summary and the revelation and the realization of God's plan implies a change in emphasis: the change is concerned with the way God's plan is realized and has become accessible.[12] Nor does this understanding of mystery contain arguments for denying the possibility of a definition, for mystery is closely related to revelation and preaching. Or, as Pope Paul VI expressed it in his opening address of the second session of the Council: 'The Church is a mystery. It is a reality imbued with the hidden presence of God. It lies, therefore, within the very nature of the Church to be always open to new and ever greater exploration'.[13] Precisely because it is 'open to new and ever greater exploration', this understanding cannot be used to defend the thesis that the church cannot in principle be defined.

Related to the appeal to mystery is the argument that only images, and even only a number of images, can be used to talk about the church, and this argument is brought forward against the possibility of defining the church (cf. the synthesis view). Can these positions be maintained? The rule forbidding metaphors to occur in definitions appears to be less obvious and that does call into question the positiveness of this thesis. But since an answer in metaphorical language to a 'what is . . .' question can be an adequate answer, these theologians could appeal to this line of argument and still claim that the church can only be discussed by means of metaphors or even by a number of metaphors. If such a conclusion could be reached the development of an ecclesiological terminology would be prevented, for a systematic treatment requires more than a definition that may indicate a line of research or that is only a semantic sketch. The transition from metaphorical language to the terminological level requires a definition or basic description that can be used for discovering the possible paraphrases. (See the previous section.)

There are several aspects to this argument that for talking about the church metaphors are better suited than concepts. Dulles and Mühlen apply the distinction 'directly-indirectly' to conceptual as opposed to metaphorical or analogical language, albeit with contradictory evaluations added: about mysteries one cannot talk directly, but only indirectly via images (Dulles), and metaphors express only one aspect of the mystery, while conceptual formulations express the mystery itself immediately (Mühlen).[14] Apart from the problem in Dulles' case – that to know predicates are used indirectly implies some direct knowledge – the formulation of the difference between metaphorical and conceptual language in terms of 'indirectly' and 'directly' points to the conception of the relation between language and reality that was criticized earlier, and to the rhetorical conception of metaphor that proved to be inadequate. There is no reason to disqualify metaphorical language as less related to reality and therefore less suited for definitions. Besides, Koster has already correctly observed that it is rather awkward to hold that metaphors are second best in view of their use in Scripture, and the qualification 'indirectly' suggests precisely this.[15]

Another aspect is the suggestion that concepts, unlike metaphors, give the illusion of mastery and that metaphors are thus better protectives for the mystery. Is it clear though that in its generality this cannot be maintained. For example, Ramsey points out that often the metaphor, or the model, is seen as a picture and that this creates severe problems and misunderstandings, because people have not been sufficiently aware of the metaphorical character.[16] Mühlen, putting forward a view similar to Aquinas', warns about the danger of metaphors,[17] and the criticism of the radical version of metaphorical theology also reveals the problematic side of the use of metaphors. Even the proviso that a number of metaphors should be used is not enough, for the danger lies not so much in the metaphor or in the concept, but in the people who use the language and in the conception they have of language. In the case of both metaphor and concept the illusion of mastery is possible or not possible, but is not necessarily linked to either. And the argument about the number of metaphors as better expressing the mystery is not valid either in the case of metaphors only, for the same can be said of concepts. Moreover, the complementarity is not necessarily the final stage, for there seems to be no *a priori* argument that a more encompassing metaphor or concept cannot be found.[18] It is because the thesis that only images can be used occurs in the context of the appeal to a mystery that surpasses all knowledge that another aspect of these arguments is the contrast between cognitive (concepts) and non-cognitive (metaphors). But in metaphors as in most other sentences, one can discern a cognitive element. This content aspect is precisely the aspect which is responsible for the peculiar feature of the metaphor, and it is precisely this aspect which makes a conceptual development possible, if required. So, instead of a sharp contrast between metaphor and concept on this point, there is more of a link, continuation, or transposition. So this line of argument employing various differences between metaphorical and conceptual language in support of the claim that only metaphors can be used in talking about the church proves to be unsound because these differences rest upon confusions.

The only argument left is the one that appeals to the rule that a definition should state the *genus proximum* and the *differentia specifica*. This rule has become less important since this analysis has been shown to be relative to other types of analysis. But the arguments against the application of this kind of analysis that could be drawn from (e.g.) Commer's view are not correct either. It is only by making the church part of the Trinity (cf. Koster's criticism), or by calling the church a mystery in the incoherent way, that an argument can be made against this type of analysis. The points raised by the appeal to 'uniqueness' are not decisive either, for the statement that something is unique presupposes some kind of classification: complete uniqueness, like complete newness, can neither be noticed nor conceived.[19]

So, the overall conclusion is that the arguments from the mystery of the church are not convincing and are not sufficient for a denial of the possibility of a real definition of the church, if 'real definition' is understood in the sense outlined earlier.

3. *The practice of the theologians*

Several theologians who argue against the possibility of a definition of the church present, nevertheless, some kind of formula or description that forms the basis or direction for their further reflections on the church. What are they doing? Does their practice constitute a counter-argument? Does it present an alternative to the conclusions of the previous section? Do these theologians propose a type of basic statement argued for in the first section of this chapter? And what are the theologians who accept the possibility of a definition actually doing about it? The various solutions to the problem created by *Lumen Gentium* that were analyzed in Chapter I, including those by theologians who do not explicitly discuss the issue of definition, can be evaluated here from a methodological point of view by means of answers to these questions.

Some of the theologians who argue against the possibility of a definition of the church defend the synthesis-view (Schmaus, Congar). As the analysis of Chapter I shows, they and other synthesis-proponents proceed along the same lines: they analyze the advantages and disadvantages of certain images used for the church and cancel the disadvantages via a synthesis. Schmaus proposes basic formulas like 'the church is the people of God living and acting as the body of Christ', 'the church is the New-Testament people of God . . . existing as Christ's mystical body', or 'the church is the people of God because and insofar as it is the body of Christ'.[1] With regard to the last formula he remarks that 'people of God' is the encompassing and 'mystical body of Christ' the determining concept.[2] Congar formulates it as follows: 'Under the new dispensation . . . people of God receives a status that can only be expressed in categories and theology of the body of Christ'.[3] Dulles proceeds like Schmaus and Congar, although he starts with some remarks about models which seem to lead to a pure pluralism. In order to talk about the mystery of the church, he says, we have to use models, and unlike aspects, models cannot be integrated 'into a single synthetic vision on the level of articulate categorical thought . . . we must work simultaneously with different models. By a kind of mental juggling act, we have to keep several models in the air at once'.[4] But in his evaluation of the models he discusses, he advocates some kind of harmonization. The pluralism of the models provokes questions about compatibility, adequacy, and correctness; since each of these models has certain values and, when taken in isolation, disadvantages, the solution of a super-model suggests itself. But Dulles, referring to the mystery-character of the church, is sceptical about the possibility of finding such a super-model and concludes: 'we are therefore condemned to work with models that are inadequate to the reality to which they point'.[5] He proposes instead a method of harmonization in which the different models become 'complementary rather than mutually repugnant'.[6] This means that one model can be taken as the starting-point and that the values of the others can be integrated into it. Of the five models he discusses and analyzes – the church as institution, as community, as sacrament, as herald, and as servant – he excludes the church as institution as a model that can function in such a primary way for 'of their nature . . . institutions are subordinate to persons'.[7] Of the five, Dulles himself prefers 'the church is a sacrament', not only because it can integrate the values of other models – as he shows, 'the church as servant' can do that too – but also because it is the 'theologian's model', so to say. It proves fruitful for theological systematics enabling an integration of different themes into a 'single overarching unity'.[8]

These formulas are as such adequate answers to the question 'what is the church?'. Points mentioned in the enumeration of the various types of answers to 'what is . . .' questions can be recognized in this procedure: the starting-point is formed by two or more descriptions of the church, each indicating a key-element from which other elements follow; the concept of the church is then improved by making one key-element, people of God, more specific and precise via the other, body of Christ, or in Dulles' case, by taking one model and by integrating into it the values of other models. But there are also theologians who follow a somewhat different procedure: while the proponents of the synthesis-view use the terms of the starting descriptions in their final formula, Semmelroth, Holböck and Mühlen propose a new term.

Semmelroth's starting-point is that important biblical images for the church – people of God, body of Christ, and bride of Christ – seem to contradict and not to supplement each other.[9] How can the church, he asks, appearing as a state with juridical structure (people) at the same time be called 'bride', i.e., a person drawing its life from love and not from structures? And how can the church be called 'bride', indicating a separate identity from Christ, and at the same time 'body', not indicating a separate identity? As the way Semmelroth poses the problem already shows, he sees 'people of God' as the scriptural basis for the organizational and juridical view of the church, and he remarks that when Scripture and the early Christian tradition apply this term to the church, they envisage primarily, and correctly, the external juridical and societal reality of the church. The genitive 'of God' is too vague, though, to determine the underlying divine reality.[10] 'Mystical body' is interpreted as pointing to that inner side, or seen as the invisible soul of the visible body. But Pius XII rejects this solution in *Mystici Corporis*, which raises the question about the relation between the two concepts 'people of God' and 'mystical body'. The two sound so different that we cannot readily suppose they mean the same: nevertheless, they are said to be referring to the same reality. The problem is even aggravated by 'bride', for it implies the opposite of 'body'.[11] Semmelroth's solution is to propose 'primordial sacrament' *(Ursakrament)*, not as a church-concept alongside others, but as a 'reflection upon the supranatural ontology expressed in the revealed statements about the church . . . To see the church as sacrament means to explain the nexus between the different partial aspects of the church, especially between its meta-empirical divine reality and its societal human outer reality'.[12] 'Sacrament' indicates a complex connection of inner and outer, of divine and human, related as sign and signified, cause and result. (Cf. Trent's formulation of sacrament as the 'visible form of an invisible grace'.)[13]

Holböck qualifies his basic formulation as a quasi-definition: it is neither a definition nor a figurative circumscription. Like Semmelroth he starts with people of God, body of Christ, and bride of Christ. He extracts these biblical images from the schema on the church that was not fully discussed at the first Vatican Council and examines their respective advantages for the quasi-definition. Although 'bride of Christ' contains in a sense the whole of ecclesiology, it is not very helpful for reaching a precise quasi-definition, while 'people of God' and 'body of Christ' are very useful in this respect.[14] In the notion 'body of Christ' Holböck discerns two aspects: the external aspect (visible organization founded by Christ and managed by Christ through his vicar) and the internal aspect (vivified by the invisible principle).[15] In 'people of God' understood in its special meaning distinct from the ordinary and the Old-Testament meaning, the important point is the relation to and the difference from the Old Testament people of God. He introduces another element which he thinks important for a quasi-definition and which cannot be found in those images, namely, the cultic task of the church. The result is the following quasi-definition: 'the church is that Christ-shaped hierarchically ordered universal society, which through, with, and in Christ, in unity with the Holy Spirit brings all honour to God the Father and truth and salvation to the world'.[16] The central concept here is that of 'society' *(Gemeinschaft)*,[17] which according to Holböck is implied in both 'mystical body of Christ' and 'people of God', the former indicating the solidarity of all members, the latter the individuality of the members. The images themselves do not appear in the quasi-definition, for they should not appear in a scientific definition.[18]

Mühlen proposes a dogmatic basis-formula, which is neither a definition nor an essence-description, but a 'formal' summary containing all elements of revelation concerned with the church. A definition – i.e., a definition *per genus proximum et differentiam specificam* – is not possible and an essence-description has two disadvantages: it enumerates only the essential properties by which the church is distinguished from other human communities and it contains metaphors. Enumeration of the essential properties alone though does not express the essence of the church completely, and metaphors illuminate only one side precisely because they are graphic representations. Bellarmine's and Möhler's essence-descriptions are the ones mostly quoted and both are dominated by an image: Bellarmine's by that of 'people of God' and Möhler's by that of 'body of Christ'. As basis-formula Mühlen proposes: 'one person (the one Spirit) in many persons (Christ and us)'.[19] This is a further specification of *una persona mystica*, a term found in tradition from Augustine up to modern times *(Mystici Corporis)* and based upon the Old-Testament concept of corporate personality. It is this concept which is the common basis of understanding for 'people of God' and 'body of Christ': both metaphors express different aspects of the reality of the corporate personality which is the church.[20]

Although Semmelroth, Holböck, and Mühlen each propose a different central term, the way they proceed is the same and it reveals elements mentioned in the discussion of the *definitio realis*: they improve the concept of the church by indicating a notion that is more basic or fundamental than those used in the starting descriptions.[21] Aymans, who does not discuss the definition issue, indicates the same procedure when he writes that it is justified to look for the common background of the image concepts 'people of God' and 'body of Christ' and that it is a typical theological task to do so.[22]

Those who propose yet another solution – i.e., either 'people of God' or 'body of Christ' as their central term – follow a somewhat different procedure: namely, an analysis which shows that the various elements thought to be important can be developed from or placed within this central notion, resulting in a redefinition of the term used. The encyclical *Mystici Corporis* exhibits this structure, for it analyzes 'body', 'Christ', and 'mystical' and determines and redefines the meanings of these terms.[23] And Hamer, although he gives a different interpretation to 'mystical body of Christ', proceeds in the same way.[24] In his article on the leading image of the church, Koster employs the following method: he starts from descriptions found in Scripture and liturgy in which the terms 'ecclesia', 'people of God', and 'body of Christ' occur and argues that they have the same 'meaning and content', namely, the people of God and Christ.[25] In developing this central notion he appeals to two more biblical images: bride of Christ, and family of God. The problem with Koster's arguments mentioned earlier reappear here in the choice of two different types of procedures that both fit his strategy: the improvement of the concept by showing first that some of the descriptions can be reduced to one of the descriptions (people of God), or secondly, that a more basic description can be found (people of God and of Christ). The problems noted with regard to Luneau's exposition can also be found in the different types of procedures. On the one hand, he analyzes the notion 'people of God' and shows its complexity and that it contains all important elements; on the other, he follows the type of analysis used by the synthesis-theologians.[26]

The various procedures the theologians follow are like the procedures that lead to the different answers covered by the broad label *definitio realis*, and their proposals are thus adequate answers to the question 'what is the church?' That this is not recognized by them, especially when they criticize other types of solutions and answers, is due to their confusing presuppositions. The fact that the various proposals are adequate answers, though, is not a sufficient condition for their being basic statements central to the systematic development of an ecclesiology. Such a basic statement should not contain metaphors, for if it contains metaphors it cannot serve as the interpretation-key and coherence-criterion that is required for the ecclesiological, terminological development of metaphors in religious language. The presence of metaphors would start a regressive search for interpretation-keys and coherence-criteria.

An over-hasty and too-easy verdict that the first type of basic statements used by the synthesis theologians, and the third type, containing either people of God or body of Christ, do not fulfil this condition, but that the second type does, is obstructed by the variety of terminological qualifications that are used by these theologians. As we remarked in the analysis of Chapter I, most theologians use 'metaphor', 'concept', and 'image-concept' indiscriminately when they refer to 'people of God' and 'mystical body of Christ'.[27] Only at the price of a fundamental confusion can it be maintained that a word is at the same time a metaphor, a concept, and an image-concept. The combination 'image-concept' aggravates the confusion by its suggestive ambivalence. It is not clear why such a hybrid is introduced. It seems to indicate that the term is basically a concept, while the prefix 'image' points to the origin of the concept, or to the possible occurrence of some mental image or picture; both possibilities, however, are irrelevant to the present meaning of the concept. It seems better, therefore, to dismiss 'image-concept' from further reflections. An additional complication is the incorrect presupposition that a metaphor is a word. This means that an evaluation has to examine the various possible interpretations with regard to the status of the proposed formulas.

If the synthesis formula is taken as a metaphor, or as containing metaphors (as the phrasing is when metaphors are seen as words), the synthesis formula cannot supply the basic statement which would be able to function as an interpretation-key and coherence-criterion, since it would require another non-metaphorical statement. The awkwardness of the situation becomes clear when we realize that, on this interpretation, the metaphor can become its own interpretation-key. If 'people of God' and 'body of Christ' are taken as precise concepts, there are two possibilities: first, that the synthesis is still a metaphor, and secondly, that it is a thoroughly conceptual statement. On the presupposition that a metaphor is a word the preciseness of a term may suggest it is not a metaphor, but the discussion of metaphor on the sentence-level shows that the preciseness of the concepts used is not decisive for the metaphorical use of language. In most cases the concepts used in a metaphorical combination are loose ones, but 'life is a tale' remains a metaphor when 'tale' is made more precise by adding 'fairy' or 'horror'. If the synthesis-formula is taken as such a 'precise metaphor' the same problem arises as when it is taken as a 'loose metaphor'. But the stipulation of the meaning of the concepts or one of the concepts can be such that the formula becomes a thoroughly conceptual statement. Such a move normally requires a rather drastic departure from the ordinary meaning. In this case there is first of all a difference with the original, which makes an appeal to (e.g.) Scripture less obvious and possibly even incorrect, and, secondly, the problem that such a stipulation does not yet turn the metaphor into an interpretation-key and coherence-criterion. As argued in the first section of this chapter, the transition from metaphor level to conceptual level cannot take place by just tightening the rules of one element in the metaphor. This may constitute an important phase in the whole process but does not solve the problems about coherence and correctness. These critical remarks about the synthesis-view are also applicable to the proposals in which either 'people of God' of 'body of Christ' is taken as the central term. Whether the basic formula is thought to be or to contain a metaphor, or whether it is thought to be a conceptual statement, either position runs into the problems just mentioned.

Against this background the problems about the way 'mystical body of Christ' is used in the first schema of *Lumen Gentium*, and 'people of God' is used by some theologians, can be clarified. Inspired by the encyclical *Mystici Corporis* the first schema uses 'mystical body of Christ' as its central term. But the thesis that the mystical body of Christ does not consist at all of equal members contradicts the biblical data and the view that the illness of the members does not affect the health of the body renders the image unintelligible.[28] The encyclical itself introduces elements into its analysis of Christ's role that do not follow organically from the image (e.g., founder of the body).[29] These elements are related to or part of current ecclesiastical practice or theory, and a similar feature can be discovered in Koster's arguments. He presents, both in his book and in his article, a juridical and hierarchical conception of 'people of God', as is shown by his discussion of membership and by his statements that anyone who goes against the juridical order of the church goes against the church as people of God, that the people of God is an ordered people, and that the fundamental and unchangeable distinction between apostles (and thus bishops) and other faithful is given with the appearance of the church at Pentecost.[30] Apart from the already-mentioned mistakes with regard to biblical data, this understanding misrepresents the biblical concept of God by leaving out completely the constitutive element of the history of salvation.[31] It is here that we find the basis for Koster's claim that 'the church is the people of God' is not a metaphor. Luneau's argument in favour of 'people of God' is ambivalent and rests in the end (cf. Koster) upon the practical argument that it has some appeal at the present time, and this implies that he uses a contemporary understanding of the phrase. The problematic point in these attempts is not that contemporary theories play a role in the explanation and understanding of 'people of God' and 'body of Christ', or that the selection criterion and the interpretation-key are found outside the metaphors. The analyses and evaluations of the previous chapter and of this chapter have argued for the acceptance of these elements. The problematic points are the fact that a choice is made with regard to such a principle and yet is not explicitly discussed, that the choice is not defended on proper grounds, and that the theories play such a decisive and dominating role that we cannot speak of an influence from both sides, i.e. from metaphor and theory. The process of explanation and understanding is not concerned with eliciting the richness of the metaphor but with employing the metaphor as a formula capturing what is already known; it is not questioned, or is considered as beyond questioning.[32] Because of this strong decisive influence of the theory, the illogical and incomprehensible account of metaphor and the contradictions with the data of faith are neither noticed nor used as a criticism of that theory.

In the case of 'body of Christ' the intrusion of alien concepts is usually easier to notice, but Koster's distinction in the degree of membership is an example of such an imposition in the case of 'people of God'. The problem is not only to be found among these theologians, however: the arguments from content that other theologians put forward in the defence of a synthesis of 'people of God' and 'body of Christ' prove to be insufficient on similar grounds. Especially on institutional issues, the strong influence of the theory and of the current ecclesiastical practice and situation reveals itself and results in this type of imposition and intrusion.[33]

The conclusion is that these two types of proposals are inadequate for the systematic purpose that the central statement has to serve and that consequently the other type of solution – namely, the selection of another term – escapes this criticism.[34] The next question is whether these formally adequate proposals in fact can be used as the central statement in ecclesiology.

4. *The basic statement in ecclesiology: a proposal*

The requirements which a central ecclesiological terminus has to fulfil have been stated and used in the course of the preceding arguments. The necessary transition from a metaphorical to a terminological use of language about the church can only take place if a terminus is found that in combination with 'church' forms a basic statement that can function as an interpretation-key and coherence criterion. (See section 1.) The previous section shows that a metaphor cannot function as such. A reflection upon the systematic place of such a formula can give a further determination in a more positive, albeit formal, way. The ultimate aim is ecclesiology, a systematic theological treatment of the church.

Any scientific systematic treatment of a topic relates the topic it deals with to other topics also discussed within that science and focuses on the approach quintessential to this particular topic. It is not enough to be concerned with the location alone, for it is not an uncommon feature that within a science the same topic is discussed within different contexts: it is therefore necessary – if possible – to indicate the individual typical context of the topic as well, or to specify the quintessential approach as well. That is to say, when and how a topic is discussed depends not only upon the overall structure and the relations of the topic to others, but also on the proper nature of the topic, upon the characteristic features of the topic. This implies that decisions have to be taken as to whether a certain topic is an irreducible element which merits an individual approach or whether it is part of something else. A lack of awareness of this point can easily lead to serious misunderstandings, for characteristic features, if any, are obliterated when the topic is reduced to something else on incorrect grounds.

The narrow apologetic purposes for which the first separate expositions and treatises on the church were written and the subsequent development, heavily influenced by similar apologetic motives, have for a long time determined the way the church is treated in theology.[1] The analysis of the genesis of *Lumen Gentium* shows a growing general awareness and recognition of the deficiency of this narrow approach.[2] From the moment the insufficiency of this type of apologetic treatment – with its often exclusive emphasis on juridical and institutional issues – becomes clear, the problem is not so much the fact that the church is thematized but the way in which the church is thematized. Against this background and against the background of the points raised with regard to a systematic treatment, it is not enough to locate the church in the whole range of theological topics in order to establish an ecclesiology: the question whether the church has its own context, whether an approach quintessential to the church is possible and necessary, has to be discussed explicitly.

An indication of tasks and functions only, or a statement that amounts to giving just a further specification, cannot be accepted as a final answer to this question about the approach quintessential to the church, for who or what fulfils these tasks and functions, or who or what is further specified, has to be named. An indication of tasks or of the further specification is not decisive for acknowledging the quintessential approach; only what fulfils the task, or what is further specified, can establish the need for such an approach. This means that 'sacrament' cannot be the terminus looked for. Semmelroth, who proposes this term, admits that 'sacrament' is not a basic or final term when he remarks – referring to the Council – that 'the church is a sacrament' is a functional qualification, although it has the form of an essence-description. While 'people of God' and 'body of Christ' state what the church is, 'sacrament' indicates the way the church works. But, Semmelroth continues, the two aspects are interrelated: the way the church works implies a statement about its essence, and what the church is points to the way it functions.[3] Semmelroth's appeal to 'modern man' who is more interested in the way an organization reaches its aim than in the organization itself, is not convincing in this context.[4] Apart from the problems of vagueness attached to every appeal to 'modern man', the evasion of any discussion of the presuppositions cannot be accepted in view of the demands of a systematic explanation and understanding (see section 1). And if various types of explanations are called for in a systematic treatment, it seems appropriate to look for a terminus that is so basic that it can function as a pivot and can be used in these various types. 'Sacrament' cannot be such a pivot-terminus since it specifies the task and the function of the church.[5] This point remains valid even if the appeal to modern man is replaced by a more profound argument, as is the case in Boff's study of the church as sacrament. That argument is related to his point of departure and aim.[6] His starting-point is the fact that the obvious character of Christianity and of the church has disappeared, and he sets out to provide an adequate form of legitimation for the church. Under the influence of the historical awareness of the Enlightenment the question about the meaning, function, and essence of the church became the centre of theological reflection.[7] In the present situation the historical awareness is even more all-pervading, and the relativity of the church is further emphasized by the emergence of a secular, pluralistic society. The changes in society which provoke a constant reflection upon the function of institutions, and the disenchantment with ideologies, urge people not so much to ask questions about the nature and the essence of the church, but to turn their attention to the function of the church.[8] This analysis and interest also determine his discussion of the conditions a central statement has to fulfil. Among these there is only one concerned with the systematic and methodological points discussed here: namely, the condition that the basic statement should express the internal link between the various images used for the church.[9] But, as argued in section 1, the argument in favour of a functionalist approach over and against one in which 'the nature and the essence' of the church is discussed, cannot be of a principal character. And however correct Boff's argument that in the present situation the church can only be legitimated functionally may be, from a systematic point of view a pivot-terminus is required and presupposed for such an attempt. And Mühlen's proposal, *una mystica persona*, or 'one person in many persons', cannot be that pivot-terminus either, for the concept of corporate personality that is fundamental in his analysis – the church is a corporate personality – is a further qualification of a group.[10]

A way of finding such a pivot-terminus is indicated earlier in section 1 of this chapter; namely, to register the use of 'church' and, if necessary, to legislate a more strict use. Looking at the way 'church' is used both in ordinary and religious language we may observe that 'church' is not used in a strict sense but that it is not used in a completely undetermined sense either. 'Church' is used to refer to a group of Christians, ranging from a few to a very large number, to the place or building where this group congregates and worships, to the time they gather, and to the leaders or representatives of this group. It is not used for just one Christian, for creation, for sin or grace, for the Trinity or for one person of the Trinity. This does not mean that the church is not related or not normally related to these, but that the church is not said to be identical with any of these. These points reveal that there is a common element in this usage, namely, that the church is a group of believers, not just a number of individuals, but a number of believers forming some kind of unity. In the more technical language of theology we can find a confirmation of this last observation.

But this registration does not need to be the final word. Moreover, there are indications that some theologians tend towards a form of an identification between Christ and church, or to an assimilation of ecclesiology to christology. Is Commer correct when he states that in a certain sense Christ and the church are identical? Can the Christian be called 'Christ'?[11] Are there adequate reasons for reducing the church to any other topic studies in theology? The claim of identity would contitute a necessary and sufficient condition for such a reduction. But it is unlikely that any theologian would be prepared to accept the consequences of such an identity, such as the interchangeability of 'church' and 'Christ' of 'Holy Spirit' in the New Testament or the Symbolum. This *reductio ad absurdum* suggests that the communal aspect of the church, i.e., the fact that it is a fellowship of believers, is irreducible to something else. This indicates what the quintessential approach is: the thematization of the church as the community of Christian believers.

Which terminus should be chosen *in concreto* to express this approach depends on several considerations and conditions. The terminus must be precise, i.e., must indicate this communal aspect, and must be open. This means that two extremes have to be avoided: a completely empty term and an already highly determined term. A terminus can avoid these extremes by being able to be developed into a formal system of relations, a network, which structures and determines the discourse to a certain degree, but which needs to be filled in as well. A completely empty terminus will not be able to lead to such a formal system, while a strictly determined terminus will not leave enough room for subsequent filling in by (e.g.) metaphors. Another point is the clarity of the terminological status of the terminus. If possible, any occasion for misunderstanding and confusion should be avoided, and this means that the formulation itself should reveal that it is a technical term. A final point is that such a terminus cannot be chosen with disregard to terms used in ecclesiological writings of the past and present. These last two points are considerations of a practical kind and do not have the weight of the first condition, but they can play a role if different terms are found to fulfil that first condition.

A number of terms are available to express the communal aspect: 'community', 'fellowship', 'society', 'union', 'congregation' (or their equivalents in Dutch, Spanish, French, German, etc.), *coetus, societas, communitas, koinonia,* and *communio.* Given the second point, terms like 'community', 'fellowship' or their equivalents should not be chosen, for they do not express sufficiently the terminological status of the central term. Nor should *societas* or *coetus,* since they are closely linked with the narrow apologetic approach. A preference for *societas* would not do justice to the developments in ecclesiology and would imply a criticism of those developments without proper argumentation. *Communio* is the translation of *koinonia* and both are interchangeable. Our ultimate option for *communio* is based upon an initial understanding due to the links with terms like 'community', 'communion', 'communication'; *koinonia* lacks this. Moreover, Vatican II uses *communio* quite often, and the term enjoys some popularity in modern ecclesiological writings. By selecting *communio* a critical development and evaluation is facilitated. To express clearly the quintessential approach the complete basic statement should then be: *the church is the communio of the faithful.*

The systematic possibilities of 'communio of the faithful' are formed by what this terminus necessarily suggests and presumes, by the formal network which follows from it. The terminus itself indicates the relationship of the faithful as a whole to God, Father, Son and Spirit. This is a constitutive element, for without this relation it would not make sense to use a terminus like 'communio of the faithful'. Because in ecclesiology this relationship is studied in the context of the communal human aspect, those elements that are characteristic of relationships in which people are involved are part of the formal network. Communal relations have a temporal dimension, for relationships communal or individual imply some duration and normally cover a more or less substantial period of time. Communal relationships also have a spatial dimension, in the sense that they are expressed in some visible, localized form. It might be possible to talk about individual relationships lacking this dimension, although this seems to imply a relationship in which at least one pole is not conscious of the relationship. The question whether this possible element of individual relationships, with its problematic implications, is also applicable to communal relationships has to be answered negatively. It does not make sense to talk about a relationship in which a group or community as group of community is involved without expressing it, and certainly not if the communal relationship to God is a constitutive element. This means that the way the faithful as a community express the relationship becomes relevant to ecclesiology. Because it is not an individual or a number of separated individuals, but the faithful as a whole, that is in the focus of attention, the structure of that whole becomes a significant issue as well, for some form of internal organization is the characteristic feature of communal human behaviour, certainly if it extends over some period of time. In human relationships one can discern a purpose: the purpose of a communal relationship can lie inside the relationship, that is to say, the relationship can be its own purpose, or it can lie outside the relationship, or a relationship can have both types of purposes. Linked to this, but also to the previous point, is the element of the relationship between church and 'non-church', which also becomes a necessary part of ecclesiological discourse.

As a formal terminus 'communio of the faithful' cannot be expected to indicate more than a network which determines the coherence of a possible ecclesiological discourse. The correctness of the discourse which is made possible by this framework, and which consists of filling in the bare structure with biblical and other insights derived (among other sources) from metaphors, is not decided by it. This means that the formal statement 'the church is the communio of the faithful' has a limited but crucial function: it determines which issues can and have to be discussed and which not, which questions are proper and germane and which not, whether it makes sense or whether it is coherent to raise a certain problem. It makes clear where arguments are used and have to be used, and over which points disagreement can therefore arise. So, because the communio of the faithful is related to God, Father, Son, and Spirit, it makes sense to ask questions about Christocentric or pneumatocentric ecclesiologies, that is, ecclesiologies in which either the relationship to Christ or to the Spirit plays the most important role. But it does not make sense within this framework to consider ecclesiology as either a part of Christology or a part of pneumatology. Consequently, the employment of termini belonging to these other fields and specially coined – e.g., 'incarnation' – within ecclesiology becomes highly questionable. On the one hand, an ecclesiology which did not discuss the constitutive relation to God would be incoherent. On the other hand, because of its temporal dimension, it makes sense to apply categories like change, development, and – in combination with the purpose – categories like decline and progress, success and failure. But, because of this dimension, it would also be incoherent to present an ecclesiology in which the church appears as an a-temporal, a-historical, unchangeable entity. Any hypostatization of the church becomes impossible.[12]

A salvation-historical approach to the church is thus not only possible, but also necessary, for it is the result of this temporal dimension combined with the constitutive relation to God. But this does not imply that the history of salvation has to be seen as an automatic process leading to the eschatological fulfilment.[13] Again, because of its form, it makes sense to talk about sacramental and other types of realization of this form and about organizational structure, but it does not make sense to present an invisible, unstructured church. But it is too quick a move to conclude on the basis of 'communio of the faithful' alone to any specific expression or structure. The correctness of either the decentralized and democratic understanding of 'communio' or the hierarchical understanding of it is not established by merely referring to 'communio'.[14]

A final aspect of this formal structure is its consistency, both internally and externally. That is to say, the way one particular element is filled in influences and is influenced by the concretization of others: the way the purpose is determined influences the way the relation to 'non-church' is seen (e.g., in terms of 'state' or in terms of 'world'), the degree of importance attached to the organizational structure and the way that structure is envisaged. Similarly, there are relations and links with other fields and approaches in theology. The way God is seen colours the way the relation between church and God is seen and can be seen, and determines (e.g.) whether the use of categories like 'initiative-response' are proper for the further description of this relation.

This formal structure thus makes a coherent and consistent ecclesiology possible. But the central terminus or central statement should also enable the development of the various types of explanation discussed earlier, or should occupy a pivotal position in the whole of ecclesiology. It is because of the network arising out of 'communio of the faithful' that this terminus can occupy that pivotal position, for there are starting-points in the structure itself for these various types of explanation. The temporal and spatial dimensions not only allow other sciences a place within ecclesiology, but make it necessary to use them. These investigations lead to 'what is . . .' questions, but the communal relationship to God, Father, Son, and Spirit, makes these questions even more obviously unavoidable and a necessary part of ecclesiology.

Thus, 'the church is the communio of the faithful' can stand as the central statement in ecclesiology. With the help of this terminus, this basic statement, the richness of religious metaphors and of biblical and other insights can be made fruitful, and the opportunities created by Vatican II can be used to develop a truly theological vision of the church.

Notes, Bibliography, and Indexes

Notes

The first reference to an authority is shown in the form: Author's (or Editor's) name, *Title* (or 'Title'), page number(s). Second and subsequent references are normally shown in the abbreviated form: Author's name, page number(s). However, where two or more works by the same authority are cited, such subsequent references are shown in the distinguishing form: Author's name, *Short Title*, page number(s).

In all cases the full bibliographical details may be obtained from the appropriate entry in the Bibliography on pp. 279ff below.

Notes to the Introduction

1. Congar, *L'Eglise. De saint Augustin a l'époque moderne*, 269–95, 369–89.

2. Congar, *L'Eglise*, 411–24, 435–37; Nédoncelle (ed.), *L'ecclésiologie au XIXe siècle* (especially the articles by R. Aubert, J. Geiselmann, and H. Davis); Jaki, *Les tendances nouvelles de l'ecclésiologie;* Keller, *'Volk Gottes' als Kirchenbegriff;* Valeske, *Votum Ecclesiae*.

3. Horst, *Das Schema über die Kirche auf dem I. Vatikanischen Konzil*. See also: Mersch, *Le Corps Mystique du Christ* II, 350–57; Koster, 'Ekklesiologie im Werden', 251; Beumer, 'Das für das Erste Vatikanische Konzil entworfene Schema De Ecclesia im Urteil der Konzilsväter'. See further: Valeske, 206; Keller, 65ff.

4. Pius XII, *Mystici Corporis* (ed. Tromp). See also the thesis of the identity repeated in *Humani Generis* (quoted by Tromp, 68). For the situation leading up to the encyclical, see: Congar, *L'Eglise*, 469–72; Valeske, 196f; Jaki; Lialine, 'Une étape en ecclésiologie'; Przywara, 'Corpus Christi Mysticum'.

Notes to Chapter I

I.1

1. *Acta Synodalia Sacrosancti Concilii Oecumenici Vaticani Secundi*. See I.iv 121–61, 172–212, 218–62, 290–315, 327–60, 369–91 for the speeches on the first schema, and 397–639, II.i. 467–604 for other comments. See II.i 282–300 for written comments on chapter 1 of schema 2, version 3; see also 605–801. See 324–9 for the proposal to change the order of the chapters; 343–62, 366–86 for the reaction to the schema as a whole; 391 for the vote on the question whether the schema as a whole was acceptable for further discussion. For the discussion of the introduction and chapter 1, see 391–5 and II.ii 9–63, 68–82; for written comments on these parts, see 129–218 and also III.i 547–796. For the procedure and voting with regard to the relevant parts of *Lumen Gentium*, see III.i 395, 458, 497, and 516.

   For the general history of Vatican II – its preparation, organization and daily routine, and the development of its main ideas and themes – see: Katholiek Archief, *Het Concilie;* Congar, *Vatican II. Le concile au jour le jour;* Fesquet, *Le Journal du Concile;* Laurentin, *L'Enjeu du Concile;* Ratzinger, *Die Erste Sitzungsperiode des Zweiten Vatikanischen Konzils;* Ratzinger, *Das Konzil auf den Weg. Rückblick auf die Zweite Sitzungsperiode;* Ratzinger, *Ergebnisse und Probleme der dritte Konzilsperiode;* Ratzinger, *Die Letzte Sitzungsperiode des Konzils;* Butler, *The Theology of Vatican II;* Rynne, *Vatican Council II;* Schillebeeckx, *Het Tweede Vaticaans Concilie*.

   For the history of *Lumen Gentium*, see: Betti, 'Geschiedenis van de Constitutie'; Congar, 'D'une "Ecclesiologie en gestation" a Lumen Gentium chap. I et II'; Moeller, 'Het rijpen van de ideeën bij de voorbereiding van de Constitutie'; Philips, G., *Dogmatische Constitutie over de Kerk Lumen Gentium*.

   For commentaries on *Lumen Gentium*, see (e.g.): Barauna (ed.), *De Kerk van Vaticanum II; Das Zweite Vatikanische Konzil* I, 137–359; Hampe (ed.), *Die Autorität der Freiheit* I, 291–372.

2. *Acta* I.iv 121.

3. See Betti, 136f. This might well have been the only possible solution, given the differences between the theological schools and the powerful position of the 'Roman' theologians. See also: Tavard, *The Pilgrim Church*, 34f; Congar, 'D'une Ecclesiologie', 370; and Ratzinger, *Zweite Sitzungsperiode*, 25: 'In order to characterize the text offered by the Council fathers it may be useful to realize that in all essentials it emerged from the work of the Belgian theologians close to Cardinal Suenens, and that the standpoint of these theologians represented a balanced middle position between the scholastic treatises of a Roman or Spanish stamp on the one hand, and, on the other, the decidedly modern works of German and French theologians'.

4. For the texts, see Alberigo and Magistretti (edd.), *Constitutionis Dogmaticae Lumen Gentium Synopsis Historica*. See also: Geremia, *I primi due capitoli della 'Lumen Gentium'*, who includes in his analysis relevant

speeches and interventions by the Council fathers. See further: Sigurbjörnsson, *Ministry within the People of God;* and Anton, 'Estructura Teandrica de la Iglesia'. In these two works the focus is not so much the question of the central term: Anton concentrates on the first part of section 8, while Sigurbjörnsson's main concern is whether *Lumen Gentium* 'signifies a break with the pre-Conciliar *societas* conception' (29).

I.1.1

1. Katholiek Archief I, 9, 11f.
2. *Acta* I.iv, 12–91 (esp. 12–17); Alberigo, 2:4–8:223.
3. See *Acta* I.iv 122 for the comment on chapter 1 in Franic's *relatio*.
4. See Valeska, 160ff.
5. For occurrences of *corpus* and *corpus Christi* in the rest of the schema, see Alberigo, 14: 46f, 52, 83, 100f, 125–7, 141; 15: 65, 70, 80, 84, 113; 23: 99, 118f, 121; 30: 51, 53, 63f, 80, 92; 32: 112, 121; 33: 14, 36, 43f; 35: 57; 38: 6, 13; 45: 38f, 128.
6. In chapter I; Alberigo, 2: 54, 66; 3: 41, 54, 83. The other occasions on which *populus* occurs can be found in the chapter on the laity (chapter III); Alberigo, 30: 50; 31: 13, 29; 32: 95, 102, 125, 131; (32: 91).
7. Section 5 (end); Alberigo, 7: 357–67.
8. For this discussion, see also Ardelt, 'Anmerkungen zur antimodernistischen Ekklesiologie'.

I.1.2.1

1. For the distribution of material and chapter-headings, see Alberigo, xxvii–xxxvi; for the text, see Alberigo, 1: 1–27, 213.
2. 'Suadetur ut servetur textus a Commissione propositus, qui pluribus placet...'; Alberigo, 30: 29.
3. New are: Alberigo, 16: 6f, 16, 101; 21: 153–5. Also new are the following passages in which *corpus*, etc. is used for bishops and pope: 20: 107, 110; 22: 142; 23: 45–62, 79; 24: 3; 25: 245; 27: 51. Quoted from the first schema are: 14: 127, 142; 15: 79f, 84; 23: 99–101. From 30: 1 onwards the text quotes the first schema in full (see note 5 of Section I.1.1 above).

I.1.2.2

1. Betti, 136f; Alberigo, xxiiif.
2. See Alberigo, 1: 1–29: 53.
3. 'De unitate Patris et Filii et Spiritus Sancti plebs adunata'.
4. Alberigo, 8: 29–45; see also 8: 110ff.
5. New are: Alberigo, 18: 8 (see note 6), 18; 22: 137; (24: 33). Quoted from the previous version are: 21: 157; (26: 55; 27: 192). 27: 192 adds *populus* to a phrase from the first schema.

6. New are: Alberigo, 18: 9 (see note 5), 17; 22: 24 (section heading). Quoted from schema 1 are: 14: 110 *(membra Ecclesiae* becomes *Ecclesiae societatem incorporantur)*, 125 (also in version 1 of schema 2); 23: 100 (also in version 1 of schema 2), 118. Quoted from schema 2 version 1 are: 16: 3, 19, 101; 21: 153–5; and, in the context of bishops and pope: 18: 76; 20: 107; 22: 102, 109, 139f, 148; 23: 79, 127; 25: 210, 252 (see schema 1).

I.1.2.3
1. *Acta* II.i 339 (Cardinal Browne's *relatio*).
2. The official commentary divides the text into three parts, taking sections 7–10 together: *Acta* II.i 229–31. For the text of the schema, see: *Acta* II.i 215–28 (chapter 1); Alberigo, 1: 1–16: 176.
3. *Acta* II.i 230.
4. The importance of 'body of Christ' is also clear in the rest of the schema. The third version quotes the second version on this point and adds: Alberigo, 32: 6, 13, 30, 87f; 33: 5, 8; 35: 58; 38: 6, 13. Of these, 32: 87; 33: 5, 8; 35: 58; 38: 6, 13 are quotes from the first schema. The following are concerned with bishops and pope: Alberigo, 22: 78, 193.
5. Alberigo, 3: 90; see also 32: 95 and the parallel text in the first schema.
6. Alberigo, 16: 24 (refers to the Jews); 25: 20 (the second version gives *fidelibus suis*, i.e., of the bishops); 30: 5 (title), 12, 23; 32: 10 (connected with body of Christ), 48, 55f, 80–82, 102 (quoting 1 Pet); 33: 4 (connected with body of Christ; 41: 22; 45: 10. See also 19: 24. Of these, 32: 80, 95, 102; 33: 4 are quotations or near-quotations from the first schema. The other occasions on which *populus* occurs are all quotations from the second version (see note 5 to section I.1.2.2 above).

I.1.2.4
1. *Acta* II.i 229.

I.1.3
1. Dufort, 'Histoire et theologie du VIIe chapître de la constitution Lumen Gentium'; Philips I, 57–60; Betti, 148ff.
2. *Acta* III.i 395, 458, 497, 516. See also Kloppenburg, 'Stemmingen over de laatste verbeteringen aan de Constitutie', 193–7.
3. *Acta* III.i 158–70 (chapter 1), 181–92 (chapter 2); Alberigo, 1: 1–17: 37.
4. *Acta* III.i 173.
5. *Acta* III.i 209f.
6. *Acta* III.1 209: 'Si autem haec materia in ipso Capite I reponetur, moles huius Capitis I nimis excresceret'.
7. *Acta* III.i 210: '*Aptior distributio materiae* obtinetur si in Capite I *de Ecclesiae mysterio* agatur de Ecclesia in tota sua amplitudine ab initio creationis in proposito Dei, usque ad consummationem coelestem. Deinde in Capite II, de eodem ipso mysterio quatenus "inter tempora", scilicet Ascensionis Domini Eiusque Gloriosae Parousiae, ad beatum finem progreditur'.
8. *incorporare:* Alberigo, 11: 11; 14: 110, 150, 185; 17: 16; 21: 21; see also 31: 12. *membrum:* Alberigo, 21: 21; 23: 101; 31: 7; 32: 5–9 (quoting Rom

12:4f), 13; 33: 8; 36: 52; 44: 113. *corpus (mysticum):* 23: 99f, 118; 26: 17; 28: 68, 75, 202; 30: 94–103 (quoting Eph 4:15f); 32: 5–9 (quoting Rom 12:4f), 46, 60; 33. 56; 43: 88; 45: 31. See also, in chapter 2, 14: 17; 17: 23, 28. It is remarkable that the whole discussion of collegiality is conducted in terms of 'body'. In view of these data, Congar's remark that 'the subcommission and the theological commission had deliberately avoided speaking in terms of "members"' ('D'une Ecclésiologie', 375) is only partially correct. The replacement of *membrum* by *incorporare* does not eliminate the associations or problems evoked by *membrum.*

9. The final version: *corpus:* Alberigo, 48: 34; 49: 101; 50: 8; see also 49: 34, 75f; *populus:* 50: 179 (which is an allusion to *Mystici Corporis!).*

10. The commission quotes, in favour of the insertion of the second chapter in the schema, the remark: '"Populus" est terminus biblicus, cum aliis imaginibus connexus. In illo clarescit continuitas historica Ecclesiae' (*Acta* III.i 209).

11. For the use of *corpus,* etc., see the passages cited in notes 8 and 9 above, and see also: Alberigo, 18: 17; 21: 92, 135; 22: 64, 79, 103, 130, 147, 193; 23: 79, 127; 25: 203, 253, 266; 28: 208; 31: 31. For *populus,* see Alberigo, 18: 8, 25; 22: 137; 24: 43; 25: 20; 26: 12, 34, 55; 28: 111, 227; 29: 9; 30: 67; 31: 13; 32: 10, 47; 33: 4; 40: 61; 44: 117; 45: 10. 'People' is not always used in the full biblical sense: see, e.g., 25: 20; 26: 34, 55.

12. See Sigurbjörnsson, 120ff for ambiguities in the chapter on the bishops; see also 148ff. Mühlen, *Una Mystica Persona,* 360–65 recognizes the 'broadness' of the text and the problems this causes for finding out the basic intentions of the Council. Although indications can only be found in the text with difficulty, the importance of certain statements, the inner structure, and the comments of the theological commission together show, according to Mühlen, that section 8 – and especially the analogy between incarnation and church – is to be considered as the centre of gravity of the first chapter.

13. McDonnell, 'The Ecclesiology of Calvin and Vatican II'; Persson, 'Die Endzeitliche Character der pilgernden Kirche und ihre Einheit mit der himmlischen Kirche'; Skydsgaard, 'The Church as Mystery and as People of God'. See also: Lindbeck, 'Die Kirchenlehre des Konzils ist ein Uebergang'; and Gilkey's analysis of history in his *Reaping the Whirlwind.*

I.2

1. Since *Lumen Gentium* is our central starting-point, the emphasis in this section lies on theology during and after the Council: the pre-conciliar period is only mentioned insofar as it illuminates these later arguments. This explains why (e.g.) Mersch, Tromp, and the theology reacting upon *Mystici Corporis* are not discussed explicitly. Moreover, since our analysis focuses on the arguments used, theologians who merely mention the synthesis in passing are not discussed explicitly either.

I.2.1.1

1. Congar, 'The Church as the People of God'; Beumer, 'Die Kirche, Leib Christi oder Volk Gottes'; Harvey, 'Le Peuple de Dieu, sacrament du dessein de Dieu'; Küng, *Die Kirche*, 131–80; McNamara, 'The Idea of the Church: Modern Developments in Ecclesiology'; Ratzinger, *Das Neue Volk Gottes*, 75–104; Ratzinger, 'Kirche', part III; Ratzinger, 'Demokratisierung der Kirche'; Schmaus, *Der Glaube der Kirche* I, 8ff, 41ff; Schmaus, 'Das Gegenseitige Verhältnis von Leib Christi und Volk Gottes im Kirchenverständnis'.
2. Congar, 'People of God', 10f. See also: Congar, '*L'Eglise* de Hans Küng', 695, 702; Beumer, 'Die Kirche', 261, 264; Harvey, 92 (and see too 104 and 106, where Harvey says that the use of 'people of God' implies a real continuity); Küng, *Die Kirche*, 151–6, 160–80; McNamara, 108; Schmaus, *Glaube*, 9; Schmaus, 'Verhältnis', 27.
3. Congar, 'People of God', 11f; Küng, *Die Kirche*, 156–8; Schmaus, *Glaube*, 56.
4. Congar, 'People of God', 11f; Harvey, 107; Küng, *Die Kirche*, 158–60.
5. Congar, 'People of God', 12; Küng, *Die Kirche*, 139–41; McNamara, 107f; Ratzinger, 'Demokratisierung', 27; Schmaus, 'Verhältnis', 24. See also Backes, 'Gottes Volk im Neuen Bund', 92 for a critical remark on Schmaus, *Katholische Dogmatik III/1: Die Lehre von der Kirche*, where Schmaus argues similarly.
6. Congar, 'People of God', 12f; Küng, *Die Kirche*, 269f; McNamara, 110; Ratzinger, 'Kirche', part III.
7. Congar, 'People of God', 13f; Beumer, 'Die Kirche', 265; Harvey, 92; Ratzinger, 'Demokratisierung', 27–9. See also: Ratzinger, *Neue Volk*, 84; Schmaus, *Glaube*, 9.
8. Beumer, 'Die Kirche', 261; McNamara, 106f; Schmaus, 'Verhältnis', 25f.
9. Congar, 'People of God', 12; Beumer, 'Die Kirche', 264; McNamara, 108; Schmaus, 'Verhältnis', 24.
10. Congar, 'People of God', 14–16.
11. Ratzinger, *Neue Volk*, 84, 97; 'Demokratisierung', 28f.
12. Schmaus, *Glaube*, 43; 'Verhältnis', 16, 27.
13. Philips, G., II, 322.
14. Küng, *Die Kirche*, 269.
15. McNamara, 108.
16. Beumer, 'Die Kirche', 264.
17. Harvey, 104–6. There are also other theologians who mention or employ a synthesis view or quote Congar, but who do not present an extensive analysis or argument. Bouyer (e.g.) takes Vatican II as the starting-point for the synthetic part of his *L'Eglise de Dieu*. He sets out to answer problems not settled by the Council, but the problem of which term is central is not mentioned among these (207–11). From the

way in which Bouyer argues and uses 'people of God' and 'body of Christ' one may conclude that he works within the synthesis, although there are strong indications that 'mystical body of Christ' eclipses 'people of God'. He understands 'people of God' as an Old Testament concept and as referring to a certain phase, now past, in God's plan: there is a transition from people of God to body of Christ, people of God has become body of Christ (196f, 293). The title of his book is an allusion to *Lumen Gentium* 17, but Bouyer has changed 'people' into 'church': given his understanding of 'people of God', this change does not appear accidental.

Betz, 'Die Theologie und das Zweite Vatikanische Konzil' sees 'people of God' as referring to the sinfulness and provisional character of the church – as a corrective to a possibly triumphalistic interpretation of 'body of Christ', which refers to the inner aspect of the church (98). Similar remarks are made by Courth, 'Kirche als Gottesvolk unterwegs', who sees 'people of God' as a corrective to Bellarmine's view, and as complementary to and a further development of 'body of Christ' (274).

See also: Fransen, 'L'Eglise comme peuple de Dieu', 106; Schillebeeckx, *De Zending van de Kerk*, 21; Willems, 'Der sakramentele Kirchenbegriff', 283; Malmberg, *Eén Lichaam en één Geest*, 63, 89ff (see also 23f) (there is a close resemblance between Congar's and Malmberg's formulations). See further Keller, 276ff.

18. *Mystici Corporis* n. 13, p. 15.
19. Schmaus, 'Verhältnis', 27.
20. Congar, *Sainte Eglise*, 43f; Congar, *Le Mystère du Temple;* Schmaus *Dogmatik* III/1, 46, 202–4, 239f.
21. Beumer, 'Die Kirche', 261.
22. Keller, 276.
23. Congar, 'People of God', 14f. He mentions Deuteronomy, Jeremiah, Isaiah, Proverbs, Psalms, and Lamentations.
24. Congar, 'People of God', 15. He refers to his own *Mystère*, in which he devotes a chapter to the Christian as a temple (18ff).
25. This remark in particular reveals why Congar insists upon 'body of Christ' as a necessary complement. For him, the difference between 'people of God' and 'body of Christ' is related to the difference between the church as congregation of sinful men and the church as a suprapersonal and infallible institution (see his earlier remarks in the context of 'people of God'; see also his more recent article 'Die Wesenseigenschaften der Kirche', 458–77).
26. For *tertium genus*, see: Damme, 'Gottesvolk und Gottesreich in der Christliche Antike'; Mohrmann, '"Tertium genus": Les relations judaisme, antiquité, christianisme reflétées dans la langue des chrétiens'. For developments in the understanding of *corpus (mysticum)*, see Lubac, *Corpus Mysticum*.
27. See Keller, 249ff.

28. See also McNamara, 107–9, who follows Congar and presents similar arguments. On p. 110 he provides a description of the church (of 'what the church really is') in which 'body of Christ' does not occupy a central place.
29. Schmaus, 'Verhältnis', 27.
30. *Mystici Corporis*, esp. 16f. The change from 'organic' to 'organizational' in Schmaus' own writing is particularly interesting in this context (*Glaube*, 51f.).
31. Schmaus, 'Verhältnis', 26f.
32. Ratzinger, 'Kirche'. See also: Ratzinger, *Neue Volk*, 97; Beumer, 'Die Kirche', 267f.
33. Küng, *Die Kirche*, 244, 253, 269; see also 133–5.

I.2.1.2

1. Koster, 'Zum Leitbild von der Kirche auf dem II Vatikanischen Konzil'.
2. Koster, 'Leitbild', 176–8.
3. Koster, 'Leitbild', 178–80; see also 175.
4. Koster, 'Leitbild', 193.
5. Köhler and Baumgartner (edd.), *Hebraisches und Aramaisches Lexicon zum AT; TWAT* s.v. *goi; THAT* s.v. *am/goi;* Lohfink, 'Beobachtungen zum Geschichte des Ausdrucks (am JHWH)'.
6. Koster, 'Leitbild', 178.
7. Koster, 'Leitbild', 177f.
8. Koster, 'Leitbild', 179.
9. Koster, 'Leitbild', 176, 179.
10. Frege, 'Ueber Sinn und Bedeutung'.
11. For a criticism of Koster's understanding of 'people of God', see Keller, 131–4.
12. Luneau and Bobichon, *Eglise ou Troupeau?*.
13. Luneau I, 20.
14. These are the elements relevant to our discussion. He and Bobichon deal also with scripture and tradition.
15. Luneau I, 7–10.
16. Luneau II, 13–17.
17. Luneau I, 11–21; II, 11–19.
18. Luneau II, 21.
19. Luneau II, 22f.
20. Luneau II, 23–8.
21. Luneau II, 28–32.

I.2.1.3

1. Aymans, '"Volk Gottes" und "Leib Christi" in der communio-Struktur der Kirche'.

2. Aymans, 321f, 324. Despite his repeated statements that 'people of God' is the leading image, he also refers to *Lumen Gentium* 8, 1 as 'the central passage for the description of the nature of the Church' (331).
3. Aymans, 323, 332.
4. Aymans, 322–7.
5. Aymans, 327–9.
6. Aymans, 331, 332–4. See also Saier, *'Communio' in der Lehre des Zweiten Vatikanischen Konzils*.
7. King, 'Towards an adequate concept of the Church'.
8. King, 11.
9. King, 15. See also Keller, 249ff.
10. King, 13f.
11. King, 15–18.
12. King, 19.
13. King, 23.
14. King, 24.
15. Feiner and Löhrer (edd.), *Mysterium Salutis IV: Das Heilsgeschehen in der Gemeinde I*, 17. Later in this work, Fries, 'Wandel des Kirchenbilds und dogmengeschichtliche Entfaltung' says that 'people of God' is the leading image of *Lumen Gentium* (276).
16. Semmelroth, 'Um die Einheit des Kirchenbegriffes'.
17. See Chapter IV, section 3 for a fuller discussion.
18. Semmelroth, 'De kerk, het nieuwe Godsvolk', 458ff.
19. Dulles, *Models of the Church*, 48f.
20. Dulles, 49–51.
21. Dulles, 51.
22. Mühlen, *Una Mystica*, Introduction viiff (1st edition). Unless otherwise indicated, the 2nd edition is referred to.
23. Mühlen, *Una Mystica*, 72f.
24. Mühlen, *Una Mystica*, 104–9.
25. Mühlen, 'Der Kirchenbegriff des Konzils', 309.
26. Mühlen, *Una Mystica*, 386.
27. King, 29.

I.2.2
1. Koster, 'Ekklesiologie', 199, 203, 208, 210f, 223, 225f, 241f, 247, 254, 262f, 265ff; 'Leitbild', 176, 179, 193.
2. Luneau II, 26. See also Betz, 98.
3. Philips, G., I, 105. See also Arietta, 'Die Heilsgeschichtliche Schau der Kirche auf dem Zweiten Vatikanischen Konzil', who makes a similar remark when he writes 'if we may call it (i.e., the people of God) a metaphor and no longer a reality' (335). See further Ratzinger, *Neue Volk*, 83 for a similar remark concerning 'body of Christ'. (See also note 4 to section I.1.3 above).

4. Philips, G., I, 105.
5. Ratzinger, 'Kirche', part III; *Neue Volk*, 84.
6. Beumer, 'Die Kirche', 264. See also Malmberg, 24.
7. Mühlen, *Una Mystica*, 12–14. Bouyer, however, seems not to fall in with this consensus, since he argues that in Paul's letters 'body of Christ' becomes less metaphorical and more real (*L'Eglise*, 197, 360f); see also his 'Où en est la théologie du Corps Mystique', 328f. See further Ratzinger, *Neue Volk*, 83 (note 3 above).
8. Schmaus, *Glaube*, 9, 43, 51, 57; 'Verhältnis', 13, 27.
9. Dulles, 50.
10. Semmelroth, 'Einheit', 320, 324f; 'De Kerk', 455–7.
11. Aymans, 321; see also 324.
12. Mühlen, *Una Mystica*, 12–14.
13. Koster, 'Ekklesiologie', 241–3, 262–3.
14. Koster, 'Ekklesiologie', 266.
15. Beumer, 'Die Kirche', 258.
16. Philips, G., I, 99f (see the discussion in Chapter III, section 3).
17. Semmelroth, 'Einheit', 320; 'De Kerk', 451f.
18. Aymans, 321.
19. Dulles, 7f, 16.
20. Koster, 'Ekklesiologie', 244–55.
21. Beumer's link between analogy and graphical language is, at least on Aquinas' understanding of analogy, incorrect.

I.2.3
1. See (e.g.) Lindbeck, 361 and Przywara, 131. Przywara criticises Scheeben for starting with 'mystical body of Christ' rather than, as he should have done, with the church.

Notes to Chapter II

II.1.1
1. For the following, see Ricoeur, *La métaphore vive*, esp. 87–100. An extensive bibliography on metaphor can be found in Shibbles, *Metaphor: An Annotated Bibliography and History*. For a survey of the recent appreciation of metaphor in philosophy, see Bücher, 'Die heutige Einschätzung der Metapher in der Philosophie'.
2. For accounts of different conceptions and theories, see: Stutterheim, *Het Begrip Metaphoor;* Lieb, *Der Umfang des historischen Metaphernbegriffs;* Lieb, 'Was bezeichnet der herkömmliche Begriff "Metapher"?'; and Hawkes, *Metaphor*.
3. Some writers (e.g., Black, Mooij) use this procedure. A justification can be found in the so-called 'constructivist' theory: Kamlah and Lorenzen, *Logische Propädeutik*, esp. chapter 3. See also the discussion in Chapter IV, section 1 below.

4. The examples are taken from poetry and drama for the sake of clarity; this does not imply that metaphors are only to be found in literature. The quotations are as follows: (a) Shakespeare, *Anthony and Cleopatra*, III, x; (b) Shakespeare, *Macbeth*, V, v; (c) Dylan Thomas, *Especially when the October wind;* (d) T. S. Eliot, *The Love Story;* (e) T. S. Eliot, *Burnt Norton* IV; and (f) T. S. Eliot, *Morning at the Window.*

Black, 'More about Metaphors' remarks that the discussion of metaphor is 'thwarted' by the use of 'relatively trivial examples' or 'excitingly suggestive but obscure examples from Shakespeare, Donne, Hopkins, or Dylan Thomas'; and he concludes that 'it may well be a mistaken strategy to treat profound metaphors as paradigms' (434). Although some of my examples are drawn from works by these proscribed authors, they do not appear too profound or too obscure. The remarks provoked by them hold for so-called 'trivial' metaphors as well. The advantage of starting with non-trivial metaphors is that the important distinction between metaphorical sense and metaphorical use is not obscured from the very beginning.

5. See Charlton, 'Living and Dead Metaphors'; Yoos, 'A Phenomenological Look at Metaphor', exp. 84f; Stewart, 'Metaphor and Paraphrase', esp. 112–4; and Erwin, *The Concept of Meaninglessness*, chapter 5.

II.1.2

1. Culler, *Saussure*, 79.
2. Culler, 29.
3. Chomsky, *Current Issues in Linguistic Theory*, 23.
4. Chomsky, *Aspects of the Theory of Syntax*, 4.
5. Chomsky, *Aspects*, 4. See also Schlesinger, 'On Linguistic Competence'.
6. Bickerton, 'Prolegomena to a Linguistic Theory of Metaphor'.
7. Bickerton is here correct (see later). See also Reddy, 'A Semantic Approach to Metaphor'.
8. Bickerton, 41.
9. Bickerton, 42.
10. Bickerton, 48.
11. Matthews, 'Concerning a "Linguistic Theory" of Metaphor', 413.
12. Matthews, 415.
13. Bickerton, 50.
14. Matthews, 415.
15. Matthews, 417.
16. Matthews includes the violation of subcategorial rules in this general term.
17. Matthews, 419.
18. Bickerton, 41.
19. Bickerton, 34.
20. Bolinger, 'The Atomization of Meaning', 566f.

21. Bickerton, 42. This concern also explains why he lists among the false asumptions of non-linguistic writers on metaphor the assumption 'that words have fixed and definite meanings' (36).
22. The metaphors are all quotations, and that explains why he can use them, although no metaphorical meaning is involved: they have a marked sign.
23. Matthews, 424.
24. Price, 'Linguistic Competence and Metaphorical Use', 254.
25. Loewenberg, 'Identifying Metaphors', 325f.
26. Loewenberg, 'Identifying Metaphors', 328.
27. See note 1 of this subsection above.
28. Loewenberg, 'Identifying Metaphors', 324.

II.2.1

1. See: Austin, *How to do Things with Words;* and Searle, *Speech Acts*.
2. Austin calls these the phonetic and phatic aspects respectively (94).
3. Searle, 24.
4. Searle, 24. 'Frame' is not used here in the sense that Black uses it (see section 3.2 below).
5. Warner, 'Black's Metaphors', 370.
6. Warner, 370.
7. Warner, 370. This reveals another point which will be discussed more fully in section 3.2 below: Warner's criticism of Black fails because he shares the same explanation of metaphor.
8. Warner, 370.
9. The first of these examples is taken from William Blake's *The Tyger*. The second and third refer back to the examples quoted in section 1.1 above (see note 4 of that subsection).
10. Manns, 'Metaphor and Paraphrase' makes a similar point when he talks about the ground of the illocutionary force, 'that is, the manner in which it manages to exert the force it does' (362).
11. For this reason 'metaphorical expressions' are not mentioned separately in the rest of the argument. Predication is not to be understood in terms of universals, but in the way Searle understands and uses it (26). See also Ricoeur, 92ff. If predication is understood in this way, there is no need for a discussion about indication-metaphors and description-metaphors (Mooij, *A Study of Metaphor*, 130–32).
12. Goodman, *Language of Art* makes a similar point when he says that 'metaphor typically involves a change not merely of range but also of realm' (72).
13. See the discussion in section 3.1 below.
14. See Warner's earlier-mentioned suggestion. The criticism there was not concerned with this point, but with the confusion of the two main questions. See also Loewenberg, 'Identifying Metaphors', 331–8.

II.2.2

1. See Wittgenstein, *The Blue and Brown Books;* Wittgenstein, *Remarks on the Foundations of Mathematics;* Wittgenstein, *Philosophical Investigations;* Wittgenstein, *Zettel;* Wittgenstein, *On Certainty;* and Wittgenstein, *Philosophical Remarks.* See also: Hacker, *Insight and Illusion;* and Kamlah, chapter 2.
2. The possible objection that this criticism obliterates the distinction between natural and social reality employs a rather limited conception of reality.
3. This argument is borrowed from S. Stenlund, who uses it in an unpublished paper 'Remarks on Some Problems of Meaning'.
4. See (e.g.): Henle (ed.), *Language, Thought and Culture*, chapter 1; and Brower (ed.), *On Translation* (especially the contribution by Nida).
5. Hacker, 150–53.
6. Wittgenstein, *Blue and Brown*, 24.
7. Hacker, 153–66.
8. Wittgenstein, *Zettel*, 331.
9. Wittgenstein, *Philosophical Remarks*, I, 7.
10. Hacker, 163.
11. Wittgenstein, *Investigations*, 230.
12. See Pitkin, *Wittgenstein on Justice;* and Philips, D. C., *Wittgenstein and Scientific Knowledge.* See also (e.g.) Kamlah, 46 for similar remarks.
13. Wittgenstein, *Investigations*, 415 (*Foundations*, I, 141). See also Philips, D. C., 80ff.
14. Wittgenstein, *Certainty*, 558.
15. Wittgenstein, *Investigations*, 206; see also 241f; and *Foundations*, VI, 39.
16. Wittgenstein, *Investigations*, 174; see also 466ff, 650. See further: Hallett, *A Companion to Wittgenstein's Philosophical Investigations* (on *Investigations*, 650); and Wittgenstein, *Zettel*, 469.
17. Wittgenstein, *Certainty*, 204; see also 541.
18. Part of this aspect is the role of tradition: one learns an already existing language. (See below.)
19. Wittgenstein, *Investigations*, 312. See also Strawson, 'Review of Wittgenstein's Philosophical Investigations', 47f.
20. Wittgenstein, *Foundations*, I, 148. See also I, 147: 'And why should they not hand it over for a price which is independent of all this; each buyer pays the same price however much he takes (they have found it possible to live like that)? And is there anything to be said against giving the wood away?'.
21. Wittgenstein, *Zettel*, 383f.
22. Wittgenstein, *Zettel*, 387f.
23. Wittgenstein, *Zettel*, 390.
24. Hallett, 242.

25. See Wittgenstein, *Foundations*, I, 22.
26. Wittgenstein, *Investigations*, 185f. See also *Blue and Brown*, 142: 'Your idea really is that somehow in the mysterious act of *meaning* the rule you made the transitions without making them. You crossed all the bridges before you were there.'
27. Wittgenstein, *Blue and Brown*, 130.
28. Wittgenstein, *Investigations*, 186.
29. Wittgenstein, *Investigations*, 201.
30. Wittgenstein, *Investigations*, 201.
31. See Wittgenstein, *Blue and Brown*, 33.
32. Wittgenstein, *Investigations*, 217.
33. Wittgenstein, *Blue and Brown*, 14f; see also 110f.
34. Wittgenstein, *Blue and Brown*, 143.
35. Wittgenstein, *Certainty*, 110.
36. Wittgenstein, *Zettel*, 355; see also *Investigations*, 185.
37. In the case of a lexical gap, not all the consequences might be considered, since the word receives another meaning.
38. Wittgenstein, *Certainty*, 262.
39. See Ricoeur, 13–61 (esp. 13–18); and IJsseling, *Retoriek en Filosofie*, who presents a historical survey of the tensive relation between philosophy and the art of persuasion, rhetoric, in which metaphors play an important role.

II.3

1. These three headings are not intended as a classification scheme into which all theories of metaphor can be put: they could not be used for such a purpose, since they are of unequal value. The category-mistake-approach can be used within a word-approach and within a sentence-approach. The category-mistake-approach is discussed here since at first sight it resembles the theory proposed in section 2 above.

II.3.1

1. For this subsection, see: Lucas, *Aristotle Poetics;* Ricoeur, 13–61; and Jüngel, 'Erwägungen zur theologischen Relevance der Metapher als Beitrag zur Hermeneutik einer narrativen Theologie', 86–103.
2. Aristotle, *De Poetica*, 1457b 6–9. The translation is Bywater's. See also Aristotle, *Ars Rhetorica*, Book III.
3. Lucas, 109.
4. See Lucas' commentary for placing *arthron* here, and for an explanation.
5. See also Aristotle, *De Interpretatione*, 16f.
6. Ricoeur, 22f provides a slight modification of the observation that the sentence does not occupy a privileged place. See also Jüngel, 87.
7. Lucas, 204.

8. See Aristotle, *Poetica*, 1457b 31. Jüngel's interpretation (88f) does not appear to be correct: Aristotle does not talk about 'acceptance', but about the usefulness of particular words, about the types of words one ought and ought not to use. The criterion here is the type of words everyone uses, i.e., current words and metaphors. The 'acceptance' Jüngel talks about is related to other criteria, such as aptness.
9. Aristotle, *Poetica*, 1458a 23; 1458b 3.
10. Ricoeur, 27.
11. The metaphor definition also contains a classification: see Ricoeur, 30–34.
12. Ricoeur, 63–86.
13. Ricoeur, 64–6.
14. Ricoeur, 173–220.
15. Ullmann, *The Principles of Semantics;* and Ullmann, *Semantics: An Introduction to the Science of Meaning.*
16. Ullmann, *Semantics*, 57.
17. See Ricoeur, 150ff for a discussion of other points connected with Ullmann's view of metaphor; and 155–61 for a discussion of the influence of the theory of metaphor on the Saussurian postulates.
18. E.g., Henle, 173–95 takes the Aristotelian position as his starting-point and then modifies it somewhat. According to him, the metaphorical word appears in a double role: in its conventional or literal sense, and in its metaphorical or figurative sense (174). In Henle's theory, Aristotle's transference becomes the shift from literal to metaphorical or figurative sense: the basis for this shift is an analogy, or parallelism (175–7). Henle also believes that a complete paraphrase is possible, albeit with a loss of effect (194).

    Alston, *Philosophy of Language* agrees with Henle, and finds his analysis illuminating. Another example is Weinrich, who employs two rather different definitions in his 'Semantik der kühnen Metapher': 'the metaphor is a contradictory predication' (337), and 'a metaphor – and this, at the bottom, is the only possible definition of metaphor – is a word in a given context by which it is determined in such a way that it signifies something other than what it means' (340). The translation is by Henel, 'Metaphor and Meaning', 94f: Henel points to several problems connected with Weinrich's semantics (or logic), and himself chooses the latter definition, which he calls 'true' (95).
19. Ryle, *Collected Papers*, II, 311, 313.
20. Frege, *Die Grundlagen der Arithmetik*, par. 60: 'We must always keep the whole proposition in view. Only in that do words properly have meaning'. See also p. x: 'the meaning of a word must be sought, not in its isolation, but in its context within the proposition'.
21. Dummett, *Frege: Philosophy of Language*, 3.
22. Dummett, 4.
23. Dummett, 4.

24. Dummett, 4.
25. Frege saw this explanation in terms of truth-conditions. Whether stating the truth-conditions will suffice for every sentence is a matter of debate. See (e.g.) Platts, *Ways of Meaning*, esp. chapters 1 and 2.
26. See Ricoeur, 167: 'The movement of a word from potential sense to actual sense requires the mediation of a new sentence, even though the potential sense emerges from the sediment and institutionalization of the values endued by past uses'.
27. See Ricoeur, 168. See also the discussion of Richards in the next subsection (II.3.2).
28. See Wittgenstein, *Investigations*, 199.
29. See Charlton, 173. See also, Ryle, *Collected Papers*, II, 408: 'Sentences are not things of which I have a stock or fund'; and 312: 'Words and phrases are there in the bin, for people to avail themselves of when they want to say things. But the saying of these things is not some more things which are there in the bin for people to avail themselves of, when they want to say things'.
30. Ricoeur, 92f: 'all discourse is produced as an event . . .'; see also 127.

II.3.2
1. Mooij, 72f considers that Hermogenes of Tarsus was the first author to advance the interaction view.
2. Richards, *The Philosophy of Rhetoric*. See the theories of Black and Beardsley; see also Ricoeur, 100–09.
3. Richards, 23.
4. Richards, 11.
5. Richards, 51.
6. Richards, 34.
7. Richards, 9.
8. Richards, 39.
9. Richards, 35.
10. Richards, 57ff.
11. Richards, 55.
12. Richards, 93.
13. Richards, 97.
14. Richards, 100.
15. Richards, 100. Similar statements are made by other authors: Jüngel, 77; Bücher, 727–37.
16. Richards, 93.
17. Richards, 92; see also 90, 94, 116f.
18. Richards, 102.
19. See Ricoeur, 100–09 for a different analysis.

20. The emphasis on the difference between tenor and resultant meaning is correct is resultant meaning is understood as 'sentence meaning'.
21. See Richards, 105, 121 (the examples). See also: Black, *Models and Metaphors*, 47 n.23; Beardsley, 'The Metaphorical Twist', 295; and Beardsley, 'Metaphor' for remarks about the terminology.
22. Black, *Models;* see also his later 'More about Metaphors'.
23. Black, *Models*, 27.
24. Black, *Models*, 39–42.
25. Black, *Models*, 10f.
26. For a development of this suggestion, see the discussion of Beardsley below.
27. Black, *Models*, 41, 44: 'If to call a man a wolf is to put him in a special light, we must not forget that the metaphor makes the wolf seem more human than he otherwise would be'.
28. Olscamp, 'How Some Metaphors may be True or False' maintains this.
29. Black, *Models*, 27.
30. Black, *Models*, 39.
31. Black, 'More', 422. There are other differences as well (441–3); and see 439f for 'emphasis' and 'resonance'.
32. Black, 'More', 446.
33. Black, 'More', 442.
34. Black, 'More', 448; see also 451 and 443. The introduction of 'creative rule violations' (336, 338) does not improve the theory. Black, who read a draft of this subsection, probably still thinks that this account does not adequately express his theory. Black's *Models and Metaphors* has exercised great influence (see also the next chapter), and most who quote and use his article 'Metaphor' (*Models*, 25–47) – even those who are critical of some aspects of his analysis or of his own view – share his basic definition and explanation. See, e.g., Khatchadourian, 'Metaphor'; Berggren, 'The Use and Abuse of Metaphor'; Martin, *Language, Truth and Poetry*, esp. 203f (his reference to G. Stern in the context of 'change of meaning' is revealing: see Bickerton, 40); and McCormack, *Metaphor and Myth in Science and Religion*, who strongly emphasizes the change in meaning, treats the metaphor as a word (see, e.g., 74, the discussion of 'particle'), and shifts constantly from a synchronic to a diachronic study.
35. Apart from the literature cited in note 21 above, see: Beardsley, *Aesthetics;* and Beardsley, 'Metaphorical Senses'. See also Ricoeur, 116–28.
36. Beardsley, 'Twist', 293.
37. Beardsley, 'Twist', 295.
38. Beardsley, 'Twist', 295.
39. See Mooij, 55f.

40. Beardsley, *Aesthetics*, 138f.
41. Beardsley, 'Twist', 299: his own summary of his original version.
42. Beardsley, 'Twist', 294. See Ricoeur, 126f for a criticism of the origins of the new intensions.
43. Beardsley, 'Twist', 299.
44. Beardsley, 'Twist', 300. In the first revised version he adds further a distinction between kinds of metaphors.
45. In fact Beardsley refers to the central meanings, but this shows how incoherent or impossible his notion of shift is. See also the discussion about 'inconstant' ('Twist', 301f).
46. Beardsley, 'Twist', 294.
47. See Beardsley's remark: 'properties that a speaker can, in appropriate contexts, show that he attributes to an object by using that term without claiming to follow a rule that he would not apply the term to that kind of object if it did not have that property' ('Twist', 299). See also Beardsley, 'Metaphor', 286, where he raises this objection to his own theory, but does not answer it.
48. Beardsley, 'Twist', 299 (italics added).
49. Mackie, 'A Structure of Aesthetically Interesting Metaphors', 42 n.2.
50. Beardsley, 'Senses', 5. Beardsley uses this formulation to characterize 'conversion theories'; the theories which 'hold that when an expression enters into a metaphorical combination as a metaphorical segment, it brings along one of its standard senses and retains it in that metaphorical posture' are called 'constancy theories' by Beardsley (5). This distinction is a revision of Mooij's distinction between dualistic and monistic theories (Mooij, 31). Given the difference between constancy and conversion theories, one has to suppose that the standard sense (or one of the standard senses) is not 'brought along' and 'retained' in the conversion theories.
51. Beardsley, 'Senses', 8.
52. Beardsley, 'Senses', 8; Mackie, 41f.
53. Beardsley's remark that his second revision is clearly a conversion theory ('Senses', 8) is therefore not correct. (See note 50 above.)

II.3.3

1. Ryle, 'Categories' (*Collected Papers*, II, 170–84); Ryle, *The Concept of Mind*, 10, 19ff.
2. Ryle, *Papers*, II, 179.
3. Ryle, *Papers*, II, 179; see also *Concept*, 19.
4. Ryle, *Papers*, II, 179.
5. Turbayne, *The Myth of Metaphor*, esp. chapter 1. For his judgement of the Aristotelian definition, see 18.
6. Turbayne, 22. Ryle of course does not regard metaphors as mistakes; he does not even connect metaphors to category mistakes.

7. Turbayne, 15. Duality of sense is not something special that occurs exclusively in metaphors: tropes such as metonymy and synechdoche are also sort-crossings, and also have a duality of sense. Turbayne calls these tropes 'potential metaphors'; they only become actual metaphors if the user fuses the two senses 'by making believe there is only one sense' (18).
8. 'The use of metaphors involves both the awareness of the duality of sense and the pretence that the two different senses are one' (Turbayne, 17).
9. 'When one of the different senses confused is metaphorical and this is taken for the literal' (Turbayne, 23).
10. Turbayne, 23f.
11. Drange, *Type Crossings*.
12. Drange, 135; see also 97.
13. Drange, 142.
14. Drange, 13f.
15. Drange, 212. See Bickerton, 36 *n.* 3, for some critical comments on 'unthinkability'.
16. See also Beardsley, 'Twist', 299, and 'Senses', 7 (concept of 'barring'); Berggren, 239–41 (see the discussion in the following section, 4.1); McCormack, 72–101, esp. 80f. Yoos, 83 does not consider this view correct: 'it is not the case that we usually *first* grasp it as false or paradoxical. It requires some effort to see alternative meaning in metaphor.'
17. See Yoos, 83–6.
18. Erwin, 115f is sceptical about the change of meaning in metaphors, and thinks it wrong to define metaphors in terms of category-mistakes (109). His own solution – viz., that the same sentence is used for making two statements – turns interpretation around, and is thus open to the above criticism.

II.4.1

1. Berggren, 244.
2. Berggren, 253.
3. Berggren, 244.
4. Berggren, 243.
5. Olscamp, 81f. Olscamp's own discussion rests upon a misconstruction of what the interaction-theorists intend, and he does not deal with metaphor (see, e.g., his use of Wheelwright's distinction diaphor-epiphor and his appeal to two layers of meaning). See also the criticism of Loewenberg, 'Truth and the Consequences of Metaphor', 33–36.
6. Loewenberg, 'Truth', 41. In her 'Identifying Metaphors', 333ff she maintains that metaphors are false – she discusses 'metaphorical statements which look like assertions' – and employs a two-stage procedure.

7. Ricoeur, 312f; see also 320.
8. Ricoeur, 320.
9. 'False' on its own is as helpful as 'deviant'.

II.4.2
1. Paul, 'Metaphor and the Bounds of Expression'; Manns; Stewart; Warner.
2. Black, *Models*, 46.
3. Berggren, 243f; see also 250.
4. See Richards' earlier quoted statement that 'the co-presence of the vehicle and tenor results in a meaning . . . which is not obtainable without their interaction' (100).
5. This formulation removes the ambivalence of 'loss', which might imply that there is not cognitive content whatsoever in the paraphrase.
6. Warner, 368.
7. Warner, 368.
8. Warner, 368.
9. Warner adds later (372) that sentences embodying metaphors do not have assertive force, and that this is the reason why the thesis about the cognitive content cannot be sustained. See also the discussion of his suggestion in section 2.1 above.
10. Manns, 359–62.
11. Black, *Models*, 46.
12. See Warner's conclusion: 'with rich metaphors one can never know that one has exhausted them and hence be sure one has grasped all their potential "cognitive content"'.
13. Paul, esp. 145–51.
14. Paul, 145.
15. Paul qualifies 'consensus' by allowing for degrees of it, and by admitting that consensus among the 'literate and sensitive is more significant than consensus among the illiterate and insensitive' (146).
16. Paul, 148.
17. Paul, 150.
18. Paul, 150. See also the discussion of Beardsley in section 3.2 above.
19. Paul, 151.
20. Paul, 151.
21. See also section 2.2 above.
22. Loewenberg, 'Truth', 42.
23. Manns, 363.
24. Stewart, 115.
25. Stewart, 115–17.

Notes to Chapter III

III.1

1. See Stroup, 'A Bibliographical Critique'.
2. See, e.g.: Wilder, *Early Christian Rhetoric: The Language of the Gospel;* Funk, *Language, Hermeneutics and the Word of God;* Via, *The Parables: Their Literary and Existential Dimension;* Beardslee, *Literary Criticism of the New Testament;* Weinrich, 'Narrative Theology'; TeSelle, *Speaking in Parables: A Study in Metaphor and Theology.*
3. See: Dunne, *A Search for God in Time and Memory;* Dunne, *The Reasons of the Heart;* Novak, *Ascent of the Mountain, Flight of the Dove;* McClendon, *Biography as Theology: How Life Stories can Remake Today's Theology;* Metz, *Glaube in Geschichte und Gesellschaft.*
4. Crites, 'The Narrative Quality of Experience', 291. Crites discusses the three modalities with reference to Augustine's *Confessions*, XI, 20. See Jones, 'The Concept of Story and Theological Discourse', 429. See also Danto, *Analytical Philosophy of History.* See further Kliever, 'Story and Space: The Forgotten Dimension', who argues that, as far as narrative is concerned, space is more important than time.
5. See: TeSelle; Cone, 'The Story Context of Black Theology', 145; Wachinger, *Erinnern und Erzählen. Reden von Gott aus Erfahrung.*

III.1.1

1. See note 2 to section 1 above.
2. TeSelle, 1.
3. TeSelle, 4.
4. TeSelle, 50.
5. Teselle, 64.
6. TeSelle, 50.
7. TeSelle, 58.
8. TeSelle, 59.
9. TeSelle, 60.
10. TeSelle, 62.
11. TeSelle, 62f.
12. TeSelle, 58.
13. Another consequence of the imprecision of this definition of metaphor can be seen in a comment such as: 'This is technically a simile, not a metaphor, for it has the "as . . . so" construction; but that is really incidental, because metaphorical power is present' (49).
14. TeSelle, 88.
15. TeSelle, 83.
16. TeSelle, 23.
17. TeSelle, 7.
18. TeSelle, 86.

19. TeSelle, 84; see also 139.
20. TeSelle, 83–5.
21. TeSelle, 87f.
22. TeSelle, 38, 87f, 139; see also 21.
23. TeSelle, 2.
24. TeSelle, 1f, 82; see also 39, 64.
25. TeSelle, 1.

III.1.2
1. Metz, *Glaube*, 187.
2. For the presentation which follows, see Metz, *Glaube*, 3–74. Metz here corrects his earlier views on some points (see 15, 45). For a chronological survey, see Bauer, *Christlicher Hoffnung und menschlicher Forschritt*; Lehmann, 'Wandlungen der neuen "politischen Theologie"'; and Lehmann, 'Emanzipation und Leid'.
3. Metz, *Glaube*, 29–43.
4. Metz, *Glaube*, 13–28.
5. Metz, *Glaube*, 44–74.
6. Metz, *Glaube*, 102, 110–12.
7. Metz, *Glaube*, 47f.
8. Metz, *Glaube*, 48.
9. Metz, *Glaube*, 48f.
10. Metz, *Glaube*, 136–48.
11. Metz, *Glaube*, 145.
12. Metz, *Glaube*, 145.
13. Metz, *Glaube*, 145f.
14. Metz, *Glaube*, 147.
15. Metz, *Glaube*, 188f.
16. Metz, *Glaube*, 118; see also 192f.
17. Weinrich, 'Narrative', 51f. See also Steendam, 'De nacht van duizend-en-één verhalen', 6–8 for a summary of Weinrich's *Tempus: Besprochene Zeit und erzählte Welt*.
18. It is therefore not surprising to find Weinrich arguing that theology is too preoccupied with historical scholarship, i.e., that it is only interested in stories that are true rather than just relevant to one individual. The important feature of a biblical story is that it evokes a response in its hearers to that they become 'doers of the Word' ('Narrative', 56, 50). Nor is it surprising to find Weinrich arguing that the 'unholy alliance' between theology and the sciences, between theology on the one hand and argumentation and scholarship on the other, should be brought to an end ('Narrative', 54f, 50f). Christianity began as a story-telling community, but lost its narrative innocence when it was invaded by a Hellenistic culture dominated by the *logos*, i.e., by reason and argument.

Doctrine therefore is not necessary in theology, and even appears a diversion; whereas narrative and practical (political) theology is concerned with what is necessary, i.e., with action ('Narrative', 55f)

19. See Metz, 'Introduction'. See also Metz, *Glaube*, 174 and Steendam, 11–14.
20. Metz, *Glaube*, 183.
21. See Steendam, 14–20.
22. Metz, *Glaube*, 118f; see also 147.
23. Metz, *Glaube*, 48; see also 63f.
24. Metz, *Glaube*, 190.
25. Metz, *Glaube*, 190.
26. Metz, *Glaube*, 193.
27. Metz, *Glaube*, 190; see also his insistence on the cognitive primacy of narrative.
28. It is therefore understandable that some authorities take Metz as advocating a radical view: see, e.g., Steendam, 23 and Mieth, *Moral and Erfahrung*, 60–90.

III.1.3

1. TeSelle, 62f.
2. For an internal discussion, the terminological and conceptual vagueness of 'narrative' (see, e.g., the difference between Weinrich and Metz) would be a normal subject of critical inquiry. For the reconstruction of a metaphorical theology, however, this subject is not relevant. What is relevant is the vagueness of the definition and theory of metaphor employed by TeSelle, but that has already been discussed. See Steendam, 21f for more interpretations of 'narrative'. See also Mieth, *Dichtung, Glaube and Moral*, who calls a statue a narrative (49).

III.1.3.1

1. Weinrich, 'Narrative', 49. Paul does not mention stories, however.
2. Weinrich, *Literatur für Leser*, 137–49. Mieth, *Dichtung*, 41 *n*. 4, also refers to Cancik, *Mythische und Historische Wahrheit*.
3. Weinrich, 'Narrative', 50.
4. Weinrich, 'Narrative', 54.
5. TeSelle, 140f.
6. TeSelle, 141. Later, however, she uses the order argument against S. Keen (172).
7. The novel is not a particularly old form in the history of literature. Theologians who wish to make use of the form should carry out an investigation into its origins.
8. Estess, 'The Inenarrable Contraption: Reflections on the Metaphor of Story', 431.
9. Estess, 432.

10. Estess, 433.
11. Mieth, *Moral*, 64f; see *n*. 18 for other literature.

III.1.3.2
1. TeSelle, 126; see also 96, 97, 116f, 145, 177; see further 23, 86f. See Mieth, *Moral*, 62 for remarks on theology and literature.
2. TeSelle, 104.
3. The sentence that follows the last quotation (TeSelle, 104; see *n*. 2 above) reads: 'But the problems of discriminating between what is and what is not Christian are less acute than the problems of the desiccated imagination'.
4. Weinrich, 'Narrative', 50.
5. The ambivalence is nicely illustrated by Metz's own use of the hedgehog tale: he acknowledges that he reads it against the grain (*Glaube*, 143). See Mieth's use of the same story (*Moral*, 138f).
6. TeSelle, 111.
7. See Het Utrechts Theologencollectief, *Wat hier gebeurt is macht*, 11–24.
8. Metz, *Glaube*, 118.
9. This is not to say that a (speculative) argument may not influence or facilitate the way one goes about solving the problem.
10. Metz, *Glaube*, 48.
11. See, e.g.: Stroup, 140; Weinrich, 'Narrative', 52–4; Mieth, *Moral*, 67ff.

III.1.3.3
1. See: Gallie, *Philosophy and the Historical Understanding*: Danto; Louch, 'History as Narrative'; Mandelbaum, 'A Note on History as Narrative'; Ely, Gruner, and Dray, 'Mandelbaum on Historical Narrative: A Discussion'; Dray, 'On the Nature and Role of Narrative in Historiography'. See also Jones, esp. 422–7.
2. See, e.g., Gallie, 71. See also Gruner (in Ely, Gruner and Dray, 285) for the argument which follows.
3. Louch, 59.
4. Danto, 141.
5. Danto, 11.
6. Danto, 143.
7. Tuchman, *The Guns of August*, 489.
8. Danto, 12.
9. Danto, 142.
10. Danto, 142.
11. Mandelbaum, 417.
12. See Ely (in Ely, Gruner and Dray, 278).
13. Mandelbaum, 416.
14. Mendelbaum, 415, see Ely, 278ff.
15. Ely, 278ff.

16. Danto, 7.
17. Danto, 14.
18. Danto, 9.
19. 'Theologisch gesehen *wird* die Geschichte eigentlich wenn sie Hoffnung, wenn sie Zukunft hat' (Mieth, *Moral*, 109). See also Mieth, *Moral*, 69–72. See further Weinrich, 'Narrative', 52–4. For a conceptual criticism of the nature of historical explanation as defended by (e.g.) Danto, see Gilkey, 91–114.
20. Baumgartner, *Kontinuität und Geschichte*, 269–94 prefers 'construction' to 'organization', since it more clearly expresses the fact that the coherence is read into the data.
21. Jones, 426f. Jones discusses 'story' in reference to works by Barr and Wharton. Compare Jones's comment 'It may be that even confessional stories like those in the Bible were often *argued* into acceptance' with Metz's plea for a reconsideration of the distinction between canonical and apocryphal stories ('In Defence of the Story', 96). This plea is not repeated in *Glaube*.
22. Metz, *Glaube*, 5.

III.2

1. Apostel, 'Towards the Formal Study of Models in the Non-formal Sciences', 4.
2. Harré, *The Philosophies of Science*, 174.
3. Black, *Models*, 219–43.
4. Black, *Models*, 220.
5. Black, *Models*, 222.
6. Black, *Models*, 229.
7. Bertels and Nauta, *Inleiding tot het modelbegrip*, esp. 114–44.

III.2.1

1. Black, *Models*, 228, 236. Black refers in this context to Hutten, 'The Role of Models in Physics'. See also Toulmin, *The Philosophy of Science*, 38f. See further Bertels and Nauta, 36f: on page 167 they refer to chapter 17 of Rapoport, *Operational Philosophy*.
2. Black, *Models*, 228.
3. Black, *Models*, 228.
4. Black, *Models*, 235f.
5. Black, *Models*, 237.
6. Black, *Models*, 238.
7. Hesse, *Models and Analogies in Science*, 161f.
8. Hesse, 162.
9. Black, *Models*, 239.
10. Hesse, 170.
11. Hesse, 161f.

III.2.2

1. For the following, see: Harré, *Philosophies*; Harré, 'Images of the World and Societal Icons'; Harré, 'Metaphysics and Science'; Harré. 'The Constructive Role of Models'.
2. Harré, 'Images', 268–71; 'Metaphysics', 82–4.
3. Harré, 'Metaphysics', 84.
4. Harré, 'Metaphysics', 79–81. The quotation is from S. T. Coleridge, *Biographia Literaria*, XIII.
5. Harré, 'Images', 265f., 277–9; 'Constructive', 39.
6. See Harré, 'Constructive', 22.
7. Harré refers to Pettit, *The Concept of Structuralism*, chapter 4.
8. Black, *Models*, 238.
9. Harré, 'Metaphysics', 84ff.

III.2.3

1. These authors (Ramsey, Ferré, and Barbour) have influenced others: see, e.g., Tracy, *Blessed Rage for Order*, chapter 6.

III.2.3.1

1. Ramsey, *Models and Mystery*, 47ff.; Ramsey, *Christian Discourse*, 29, 54, 60. See also Ramsey, *Religious Language,* esp. chapter 2. See further: Pater, *Taalanalytische Perspektieven op Godsdienst en Kunst, 11–55;* and Gill, *Ian Ramsey,* chapters 4 and 5.
2. Ramsey, *Models*, 2, 9.
3. Ramsey, *Models*, 10.
4. Ramsey, *Models*, 13f. A second condition concerns the verification, which differs in the two cases.
5. Ramsey, *Models*, 50.
6. Ramsey, *Models*, 51f.
7. Ramsey, *Models*, 54.
8. Ramsey, 'Talking about God', 222 *n.* 2.
9. See Ramsey, *Religious Language,* 19f.
10. Ferré, 'Mapping the Logic of Models in Science and Theology'; Ferré, *Basic Modern Philosophy of Religion*; Ferré, 'Metaphor, Models and Religion'.
11. Ferré, 'Metaphors', 333; see also 330.
12. Barbour, *Myth, Models and Paradigms*.
13. Barbour, 42–5.
14. Barbour, 12.
15. Barbour, 13.

III.2.3.2

1. Ramsey, *Models*, 61.
2. Ramsey, *Religious Language*, 53, 62.

3. Ramsey, *Models*, 60.
4. Ramsey, *Models*, 61.
5. Ramsey, *Models*, 62.
6. Ramsey, *Models*, 63.
7. Barbour, 171 and 49–70 (esp. 69).
8. Barbour, 49–70 (esp. 68f). He refers to Ramsey (and Evans) for self-involvement, and to Ferré for the metaphysical models.
9. Ferré, 'Mapping', 79; see also 60–63.
10. Ferré, 'Mapping', 81f, 92ff; see also 64f.
11. Ferré, 'Metaphors', 341.
12. Ferré, 'Mapping', 92.
13. Ferré, 'Mapping', 91; see also 81.
14. Ferré, 'Mapping', 91.
15. Ferré, 'Mapping', 85.
16. Ramsey, *Models*, 62.
17. See Ramsey, *Christian Discourse;* and *Religious Language*.
18. See final chapter.
19. If the remarks about 'religious language' are not intended to be about theology, but about religious language in the sense just mentioned, it is not clear why religious language should then be compared to scientific language.
20. Ferré, 'Mapping', 77–9. See also his qualification that biblical parables are models, and his statement that 'for Christians, of course, the models of the Old Testament – however helpful or even essential – all take second place to what they believe to be the supremely reliable model for God, Jesus of Nazareth' (78). This seems to contradict his later argument that theology uses only conceptual models (80).
21. Ferré, 'Mapping', 75ff.
22. Ferré, 'Mapping', 89.
23. Ferré, 'Mapping', 74. See also 75: 'If we continue to understand by "model" that which provides epistemological vividness and immediacy to the theory by offering as an interpretation of the abstract or unfamiliar theory-structure ...'. See further 83.
24. Ferré, 'Mapping', 54–74.
25. Ferré, 'Mapping', 81.
26. See, however, Ferré, 'Mapping', 65.
27. Auer, 'Die Bedeutung der "Modell-idee" für die "Hilsbegriffe" des katholischen Dogmas'. See also his 'Das "Leib-Modell" und der "Kirchenbegriff" der Katholischen Kirche: Ein Betrag zum Verständnis der Kirche und ihre Aemter'.

III.3.1

1. See Busa (ed.), *Index Thomisticus*, sectio secunda, concordantia prima, vol. 13, 946–51.
2. See, e.g., *In IV Sent.*, d.17, q.1, a.1c; *ST* I–II, q.33, a.1, as 1.
3. *De verit.*, q.10, a.7, 10; *In I Sent.*, d.34, q.3.
4. Manthey, *Die Sprachphilosophie des hl. Thomas von Aquin*; McInerny, *The Logic of Analogy*; McInerny, *Studies in Analogy*, esp. chapters 1 and 2; Pinborg, *Die Entwicklung der Sprachtheorie im Mittelalter*, esp. chapter 1; Pinborg, 'Textsemantische Probleme in der Sprachtheorie und Logik des Mittelalters'; Es, *Spreken over God*, 7–44. See also Burrell, *Aquinas*, 1–11.
5. 'Dicendum quod in quolibet nomine est duo considerare: scilicet id a quo imponitur nomen, quod dicitur qualitas nominis, et id cui imponitur, quod dicitur substantia nominis. Et nomen, proprie loquendo, dicitur significare formam sive qualitatem a qua imponitur nomen; dicitur vero supponere pro eo cui imponitur' (*In III Sent.*, d.6, q.1, a.3). See McInerny, *Logic*, 54ff for a discussion of the 'id a quo'.
6. McInerny, *Logic*, 51–4; Pinborg, *Entwicklung*, 30–45.
7. See McInerny, *Logic*, 49ff; *Studies*. 73ff; Burrell, 8–10.
8. McInerny, *Logic*, 65f; Pinborg, 'Probleme', 138. See Manthey, 84–6 for more elaborate distinctions.
9. 'Ad secundum dicendum quod aliter dividetur aequivocum, analogum et univocum. Aequivocum enim dividetur secundum res significatas, univocum vero dividetur secundum differentias: sed analogum dividetur secundum diversos modos' (*In I Sent.*, d.22, q.1, a.3; see also *ST* I, q.13, a.5).
10. See *ST* I, q.13, a.10c. The formulation 'things are said to be named' expresses the point that the discussion of analogy, univocity, and equivocity form part of the discussion of how we name things, and do not belong to the discussion of how things are: i.e., problems concerning analogy, etc., are logical problems. McInerny, *Logic*, 68, 71, 75, 77. See also his introduction to *Studies*. See further McCabe, 'Note on "Analogy"'; Es, 8.
11. *In IV Metaph.*, lect. 1, n. 535; *In XI Metaph.*, lect. 3, n. 2197.
12. McInerny, *Logic*, 74.
13. See *ST*, I, q.13, a.5 and a.6.
14. *SCG*, IV, 49; see also *QD: De unione verbi*, a.2, ad 4.
15. See McInerny, *Logic*, esp. 147–53; *Studies*, chapter 1 and 77f.
16. *In II Sent.*, d.13, q.1, a.2; see also *ST*, I, q.67, a.1. See McInerny, *Logic*, 147–9 for analysis and commentary.
17. See, e.g., *In II Sent.*, d.16, q.1, a.2, ad 5; *In I Sent.*, d.34, q.3, a.1, ad 2.
18. See McInerny, *Studies*, 82–4 for the possible relationship between metaphor and analogy, but this is accomplished by a change of meaning of 'metaphor'. Es, who treats metaphors as a kind of analogy

in his analysis of Aquinas's view, can only do this because he fails to thematize the difference between *significatio* and *suppositio*.
19. McInerny, *Logic*, 65.
20. See, e.g., *In VII Ethic.*, lect. 6 (commentary on 1149b 30).

III.3.2
1. Corbin, *Le chemin de la théologie chez Thomas d'Aquin* will be used as the principal guide for these analyses. Corbin's overall conclusion accords with the results in other fields of research on Aquinas. As Pesch writes: 'In the middle ages Greek thought did not divert the course of theology into that of a science, but on the contrary theology used Greek thought as an implement or tool, making it follow its own course. Anyone who thinks differently falls behind the present level of research . . . Aristotle's philosophy, and with it the Aristotelian model of scientific knowledge, provided theologians of the 13th century with ready new tools, by which the saving events, and the reality of those saving events – of which faith alone knows, not Greek philosophy – could be better "read off" *(intus legere)* as Anselm was able to do. Again, Anselm's *intellectus fidei* was precisely the 13th century's scientific understanding of faith, fruit of the same endeavour and the same rational courage, but with different, Augustinian means.' ('Um den Plan der Summa Theologiae', 429f.)

III.3.2.1
1. See: Chenu, *Introduction à l'étude de Saint Thomas d'Aquin*, 223–40; Chenu, *La Théologie au douzième siècle*, 223–398; Chenu, *La théologie comme science au XIIIe siècle*; Köpf, *Die Anfänge der theologischen Wissenschaftstheorie im 13.Jahrhundert*. Weisheipl, *Friar Thomas d'Aquino*, 49ff argues for 1252–6 as Aquinas's *baccalaureus* years: see *Rassegna* 9 (1974), 292 for a comment on 1254–6.
2. Mandonnet and Moos (edd.), *Scriptum super Libros Sententiarum Magistri Petri Lombardi*. For a commentary on the first *quaestio*, see Corbin, 113–290.
3. *In I Sent.*, Prol., q.1., a.5, ad 3.
4. See also *In I Sent.*, Prol., q.1, a.5, ad 4.
5. *In I Sent.*, d.11, q.1, a.1; *In I Sent.*, d.34, q.3, a.1; *In III Sent.*, d.11 in expos. textus; *De Verit.*, q.22, a.11 ad 8m; *Super Ioann.*, 12, lect. 8.
6. On Lombard's remark 'sed ex tropicis locutionibus non est recta argumentationis processio', Aquinas comments: 'cuius ratio est quia non sunt simpliciter verae sed secundum quid' (*In III Sent.*, d.11, in expos. textus).
7. See Chenu, *XIIIe siècle*, 44 for some kind of reconciliation. See also Corbin, 280ff.
8. See Chenu's remark: 'In his commentary on the *Sentences* (1254), St Thomas brings the theory of literary modes back into his reckoning; but he situates and measures the various elements of this theory on the epistemological principle according to which a science obtains its rules and method from its specific object.' (*XIIIe siècle*, 42.)

9. 'We may describe the work of the medieval theologians of the 12th and 13th centuries as the progressive transition from dialectics to science, at once adding that, insofar as this transition progressed, technically and historically, it involved a change of level – a change of a fundamental kind; for the transition was one from dialectics, the modest liberal art of the *trivium*, which was only a technique of verbal and conceptual processing, to a philosophy of the spirit which, over and above its rational organization and formulation, comprises a knowledge of the world and of man.' (Chenu, *XIIIe siècle*, 18.) See also his *XIIe siècle*, chapter 15 for the development in the 12th century. See further Smalley, *The Study of the Bible in the Middle Ages*, esp. chapter 5, for the consequences that this greater specialization had for the reading of Scripture. On p. 280 she draws attention to the difference between Paris and Oxford. See also Corbin, 283–90.
10. Chenu, *XIIIe siècle*, 25; Köpf, 13–26.
11. 'Sed ad defensionem fidei et inventionem veritatis in quaestionibus ex principiis fidei oportet argumentis uti.' Concerning this response, Chenu remarks: 'All speculative theology will take this route, truly an "invention" based on the principles of faith' (*XIIIe siècle*, 43).
12. See Corbin, 113–273.
13. 'Utrum praeter physicas disciplinas alia doctrina sit homini necessaria.'
14. 'Contemplatio autem Dei est duplex.'
15. See Chenu, *XIIIe siècle*, esp. chapters 1 and 2.
16. Corbin uses the plural, but Aquinas the singular. (Corbin, 144.)
17. See Corbin, 179–90.
18. See Corbin, 180–83. The anonymous reviewer of Corbin's book in the *Rassegna di letteratura Thomistica* 9 (1974) argues that a.3, q^a.1 is the point of reference. This does not appear correct, for the *quaestio* on the *sacra doctrina* as *scientia* is presupposed in the discussion whether the *scientia* is a practical or a speculative *scientia*.
19. See Corbin, 193, 200, 233, 237.
20. 'Plenius comprehendat . . . quodammodo intelligit.'
21. See Corbin, 219–29 for an outline: see also 838ff.
22. See Corbin, 231f.
23. See Corbin, 233
24. See Corbin, 236–9.
25. See Corbin, 287f.

III.3.2.2

1. See Corbin, 681–903 for the analysis which follows.
2. 'Conveniens est Sacrae Scripturae divina et spiritualia sub similitudine corporalium tradere . . . Unde convenienter in Sacra Scriptura nobis spiritualia sub metaphoris corporalium.'
3. *ST*, I, q.1, a.9, ad 2m.

4. Aquinas twice uses 'Sacra Scriptura' in the previous articles: *ST*, I, q.1., a.2, ad 2m; *ST*, I, q.1, a.8c. But these uses do not constitute a counter-argument. In the first case the identity is not exclusive. The emphasis is on revelation which is the basis of *Sacra Scriptura* and/or *sacra doctrina*. That 'Sacra Scriptura' is mentioned separately is due to the objection which is concerned with the examples from Scripture. In the second case, the way in which Scripture argues is taken as the example for the argumentation in the *sacra doctrina*, which is the topic under discussion. Corbin does not discuss these passages explicitly, and in the case of a.8c he translates 'Sacra Scriptura' as 'science sacrée', although he adds in a footnote that he does not follow those manuscripts that read 'sacra doctrina' (811f). The Blackfriars translation does not acknowledge the transition from *Sacra Scriptura* to *disputamus*.
5. 'Quia igitur Sacra Scriptura considerat aliqua secundum quod sunt divinitus revelata, secundum quod dictum est, omnia quaecumque sunt divinitus revelabilia communicant in una ratione formali objecti huius scientiae.' (*ST*, I, q.1, a.3c.)
6. See Corbin, 706–09.
7. See Corbin, 694.
8. As (e.g.) in his commentary on Boethius' *De Trinitate:* see Corbin, 373–85 and 713–17. See also 202–05 for a commentary on a section of *In I Sent., Prol. a.3, qa. 2 sol.*, in which the notion of the *scientia subalternata* ocurs. See Köpf, 145–50, who also refers to further literature.
9. See Corbin, 717–20 and 836ff; see also note 1 of section 3.2 above.
10. 'Et hoc ipsum quod sic utitur eis non est propter defectum vel insufficientiam eius, sed propter defectum intellectus nostri; qui ex eis quae per naturalem rationem ex qua procedunt aliae scientiae cognoscuntur, facilius manuducitur in ea quae sunt supra rationem quae in hac scientia traduntur.' (*ST*, I, q.1, a.5, ad 2m.) See Corbin, 738–43. See also Schillebeeckx, *Openbaring en Theologie*, 82f.
11. Corbin refers to Congar's article 'Théologie', 382. (Corbin, 814f.)
12. See Corbin, 815f; see also Schillebeeckx, 99–105. Schillebeeckx remarks: 'In other words, the syllogism is raised to the level of a psychological activity, when in fact it only acts as a logical check on reasoning as a psychological activity. Human knowledge comes into contact with reality only in and through a knowledge in which experience and conceptuality form a unity. If the concept is isolated from experience, then one is excluded by the fact itself from reality.' (*Openbaring*, 103.)
13. See Schillebeeckx, *Openbaring*, 100–02; Corbin, 812f.
14. 'Quandam coaptationem aliquarum partium distinctarum.' (*ST*, II–II, q.1, a.6c.)
15. 'Unde et credibilia fidei Christianae dicuntur per articulos distingui inquantum in quasdam partes dividantur habentes aliquam coaptationem ad invicem.' (*ST*, II–II, q.1, a.6c.)

16. *ST*, II–II, q.1, a.7c. Or as Aquinas puts it in a text in *De Veritate* (q.14, a.12c) to which Schillebeeckx refers (*Openbaring*, 100), a process of plurification occurs in the way that faith is expressed. See also *ST*, II–II, q.1, a.5, ad 2m, where Aquinas refers back to the very first *quaestio* of the *Summa*.
17. *ST*, I, q.79 and qq.84–9; *In Post. Analyt.*, Lib. II, lect. XX.
18. *ST*, I, q.79, a.8c.
19. See Corbin, 840; see also note 1 of section 3.2 above.
20. See *ST*, II–II, q.1, a.9, ad 1m.
21. See Lubac, *Exégèse Mediévale*, II, chapter 9 (esp. 272–302), for Aquinas' view of the theory of the senses and for the various interpretations of the relevant texts. See Corbin, 867–74.
22. See Corbin, 856f, 860.
23. See *ST*, II–II, q.1, a.9, ad 1m.

III.3.3
1. Corbin, 857–67 (esp. 857–60).
2. Corbin, 857; see also *ST*, I, q.13, a.6c.
3. Corbin, 857f.
4. For a recent discussion, see Burrell, see also McInerny, *Logic and Studies*.
5. 'Unde ea quae in uno loco Scripturae traduntur sub metaphoris in aliis locis expressius exponuntur.' (*ST*, I, q.1, a.9, ad 2m.)
6. Corbin, 863. He refers to *In Ioann.*, chapter 1, lect. 1, 41.
7. See, e.g., Aquinas's discussion of memory in his *In Post. Analyt.*, Lib. II, lect. XX.
8. See the *sed contra:* 'Tradere autem aliquid sub similitudine est metaphoricam'.
9. McInerny, *Studies*, 83.
10. A reconstruction may lead to a new view of the question of analogical knowledge about God, but any statement about this requires not only a thorough analysis of Aquinas's theoretical comments, but also of the way in which he works. See Burrell, 55.
11. *ST*, II–II, q.1, a.9, ad 1m (Blackfriars translation).
12. Corbin, 879f.
13. Corbin, 720, 726, 880; see also note 1 of section 3.2 above.
14. See, e.g., *ST*, II–II, q.1, a.7, a.9, a.10. See also Gilby, 'Doctrinal Development'.

Notes to Chapter IV
IV.1.1
1. See Ladrière, 'Le discours théologique et le symbole'; see also Ricoeur, 376ff.

IV.1.2

1. Since this discussion is invoked to clarify the paraphrase of metaphors, only points relevant to this particular problem are mentioned.
2. See Hempel and Oppenheim, 'Studies in the Logic of Explanation'; and see Wright, *Explanation and Understanding*, 11 for a somewhat different formulation. Puntel, 'Wissenschaftstheorie und Theologie' points out that there are some problems with the term *explanandum* as used in the outline of the theory. The conclusion of a deduction is not an *explicandum*, as suggested by the theory, but the *explicatum*. (281).
3. Hempel, *Aspects of Scientific Explanation:* 'A scientific explanation may be regarded as an answer to a why question such as "why do the planets move in elliptical orbits with the sun at one focus?" . . . "why did Hitler go to war against Russia?"' (334f). These questions, all of the form 'why is it the case that p?, are called 'explanation-seeking why-questions' by Hempel, who contrasts them with 'reason-seeking why-questions (epistemic questions) which ask for the ground to belief that p. The answers to these two types of question is different: to the first it is 'an explanation of a presumptive empirical phenomenon', to the second a validation or justification of grounds in support of a statement.
4. Wright, 59; see also 55–60.
5. Wright, 27: 'Broadly speaking, what the subsumption-theoretical model is to causal explanation and explanation in the natural sciences, the practical syllogism is to teleological explanations and explanations in history and the social sciences.'
6. Melden, quoted by Wright, 195 *n*. 14. Wright argues for this view via verification, 107–17.
7. Wright, 121.
8. Wright, 118f.
9. Wright, 124.
10. Wright, 124.
11. Wright, 135.
12. Wright, 134.
13. See the views of Aristotle and Aquinas (set out in Chapter III above).
14. Pannenberg, *Wissenschaftstheorie und Theologie*, 142f. See Puntel's remark (*n*. 2) that the obscurity which gives rise to the explanation is not sufficiently recognised by the use of *explanandum*.
15. Pannenberg, 149–52.
16. Pannenberg, 154f.
17. There are differences as well, of course, and not only in emphasis. Von Wright does not appear as concerned about rejection of the division, and Pannenberg (151) makes some critical remarks concerning intentionality.
18. See Grijs, 'Didache en Theologie'.

19. See Harré, 'Metaphysics', 84ff.
20. Gilkey, chapters 3 and 4.
21. For what follows, see Kamlah, esp. chapter 3, 70–116 ('Erste Bausteine der wissenschaftlichen Aussagen'). See also the discussion in the context of the theory of metaphor in chapter II (2.2) above.
22. Kamlah, 70–80.
23. Kamlah, 101, 104.
24. Swinburne, *The Coherence of Theism*, 12.
25. Swinburne, 38.
26. Swinburne, 39.
27. Swinburne, 39ff.
28. Swinburne, 45–9.

IV.2

1. Congar, *Sainte Eglise*, 21–44 ('Peut-on définir l'Eglise? Destin et valeur de quatre notions qui s'offrent à le faire'); Holböck, 'Das Mysterium der Kirche in dogmatischer Sicht'; Semmelroth, *Die Kirche als Ursakrament*; Semmelroth, 'De Kerk'; Koster, 'Ekklesiologie'; Koster, 'Leitbild'; Schmaus, *Dogmatik*; Schmaus, *Glaube;* Dulles. See also Valeske, 25–9.
2. Congar, *Sainte Eglise*, 21.
3. William of Ockham is said to have been the first to make the distinction: 'Definitio autem dupliciter accipitur. Quaedam est definitio exprimens quid rei, quaedam est definitio exprimens quid nominis.' (*Summa totius logicae*, Pars I, c. XXVI; quoted by Menne, 'Definition'.) See Robinson, *Definition*, 12–148 for further distinctions and a discussion of nominal definition.
4. Congar, *Sainte Eglise*, 42. For his first argument Congar refers to Journet, *L'Eglise du Verbe Incarné*, II, 49f. But Journet is there talking about 'names': 'synonyms for the name "Church"' (49), and 'the word 'Church"' which signifies summons or convocation' (50). Later Journet discusses the 'main definitions of "Church"' and deals with 'the constitutive elements of the nature of the Church' (580ff).
5. Commer, *Die Kirche im ihren Leben und Wesen Dargestellt*, 9f (chapter 1: 'Vom Wesen der Kirche'). See also 65ff.
6. Commer, *Die Kirche*, 9f. See also 65ff.
7. Commer, 'Das Leben der Kirche. Grundlegung', 173.
8. See Koster, 'Ekklesiologie', 244–7, who refers to Ternus and Feckes and shows their dependence on Commer.
9. Holböck, 214.
10. Holböck, 215f.
11. Holböck, 216f: he refers to Semmelroth, *Ich Glaube an die Kirche*. 35.
12. Schmaus, *Dogmatik*, 40f; *Glaube*, 9. See also Semmelroth, 'De Kerk', 452.
13. Dulles, 15.

14. Dulles, 14.
15. Similar elements can be found in the work of other theologians. See, e.g., Adam, 'Ekklesiologie im Werden?', esp. 150, 166; Betz, 98; Beumer, 'Die Kirche', 257f; Boff, *Die Kirche als Sakrament im Horizont der Welterfahrung*, 38 (Boff refers both to Vatican II and to Pope Paul's encyclical, *Ecclesiam Suam*); Bouyer, 'Où en est la théologie', 314; Kress, 'The Church as *Communio*' 131; Malmberg, 48.
16. 'Ad definiendam describendamque hanc veram Christi ecclesiam quae sancta, catholica, apostolica Romana Ecclesia est, nihil nobilius, nihil praestantius, nihil denique divinius invenitur sententia illa qua eadem nuncupatur "mysticum Jesu Christi corpus"' (*n*.13, p.15).
17. Holböck, 216.
18. Semmelroth, *Ursakrament*, 27f. See also Schmaus' solution (in *Glaube*) discussed in chapter I.2.1 above.
19. Congar, *Sainte Eglise*, 42. See also Fenton, '*Mystici corporis* and the Definition of the Church'.
20. Hamer, on the other hand, who calls the pope's declaration the 'axis' of the whole encyclical, does not question the possibility of a definition; nor, in a chapter devoted to the definition of the church, does he discuss arguments concerning the mystery-character of the church. In his view, the four requirements that a definition of the church has to fulfil are all concerned with 'content', and these are met by 'the church is the mystical body of Christ'. But he acknowledges that the first two of his requirements – continuity with the Old Covenant, and movement towards the kingdom of God – are not explicitly expressed by this definition. (*L'Eglise est une communion*, 87–100, esp. 95–8.) See also, Lialine, who also does not question the possibility of a definition.
21. Koster, 'Ekklesiologie', 244–55; see also his 'Leitbild', 193, where he says that time is not yet ripe for a theological determination of the church.
22. Koster, 'Ekklesiologie', 245f.
23. Koster, 'Ekklesiologie', 247.
24. Koster, 'Ekklesiologie', 253–5.
25. Koster, 'Ekklesiologie', 254; see also 255.
26. Koster, 'Ekklesiologie', 253.
27. Koster, 'Ekklesiologie', 201, 241–3, 260–63.

IV.2.2

1. Wittgenstein, *Zettel*, 331.
2. Since the other aspect of the conventionality of language – the aspect of the human activity stressed – is less important in this context, it is not mentioned explicitly here.
3. Just, 'Definitionen in der Theologie' appears incorrect in his argument and to oversimplify the issue.

4. For what follows, see: Robinson, 149–92; Abelson, 'Definition'; Hospers, *An Introduction to Philosophical Analysis*, 18–67; Brümmer, *Wijsgerige Begripsanalyse*, 65–84.
5. Hornby (ed.), *The Oxford Advanced Learner's Dictionary of Current English*.
6. Robinson distinguishes two further meanings of analysis: one mostly used in mathematics and logic, and one referring to the translation of symbols into symbols (188f).
7. Robinson, 171.
8. Robinson (162) and Hospers (27f) disagree about the value of the specification of the cause as a valid answer.
9. For these rules, see: Robinson, 140–48; and Abelson, 322f.
10. See Abelson, 322.

IV.2.3

1. See, e.g., the discussion of Beardsley's view in Chapter II.3.2 above. This formulation does not, of course, exclude the discussion about which of the characteristics are defining characteristics, and which are accompanying characteristics.
2. Koster, 'Ekklesiologie', 246.
3. For what follows, see: Bochenski, *The Logic of Religion*, 89–117; and Katz, 'The language and logic of "mystery" in Christology'.
4. Katz, 242f.
5. Holböck, 214 quotes Braun, *Handlexicon der Katholische Dogmatik*, 217: 'A truth revealed by God whose sense, even in the terms in which it was revealed, remains cut off from human understanding'. See also Scheeben, *Die Mysterien des Christentums*, 445: 'A [unity] so sublime and so full of mystery that no human understanding can achieve a glimmering, let alone a grasp, of it . . . This applies too to that particular mystery which surpasses all human meaning and conception, and from which we must conclude that we can never think deeply enough about the essence and signification of the church'. Katz, 252 remarks that one does not usually find a consistent use of the first alternative.
6. See Scheeben, 445; see also Commer, *Die Kirche*, 68ff.
7. Congar, *Sainte Eglise*, 42f.
8. Scheeben, 9.
9. Scheeben, 8: 'The essence of anything and *everything* does not lie open before our eyes'.
10. In Paul's letters the connection between 'mystery' and revelation and preaching is clear: 1 Cor 2:6–16 (see also 4:1); Rom 16:25f; Eph 1:9; 3:3–5; 6:19; Col 1:7, 26–8; 4:3–4. See also: Lubac, *Paradoxe et Mystère de l'Eglise*, 30–59; and Barauna (esp. Rigeaux, 'Het Mysterie van de Kerk in het licht van de Bijbel'; and Smulders, 'De Kerk als sacrament van het heil').
11. Smulders, 379.

12. Smulders, 378.
13. Küng, Congar, and O'Hanlon, *Council Speeches of Vatican II*, 15f. Dulles, 26, quotes this remark, and continues by drawing the methodological consequences already noted.
14. Dulles, 7f; Mühlen, *Una Mystica*, 13f.
15. Koster, 'Ekklesiologie', 247.
16. Ramsey, *Models*, chapter 1.
17. Mühlen, *Una Mystica*, 11f. See also the remarks of G. Phillips mentioned in *n.* 16 to section 2.2 of Chapter I above. See further IJsseling, 144–57 for the reactions of philosophers.
18. The insistence on a number of metaphors is understood in terms of complementarity, which seems to be the most obvious view, and which implies that the metaphors are not too different, as there is no special feature about the application of very different predicates to a subject. See also Barbour, chapter 5; and Ramsey, chapter 3.
19. See the criticism of Metz (section 1.3.3 of Chapter III above).

IV.3

1. Schmaus, *Glaube*, 10; *Dogmatik*, 48; 'Verhältnis', 27.
2. Schmaus, 'Verhältnis', 27; see also *Dogmatik*, 204.
3. Congar, 'People of God', 16.
4. Dulles, 8.
5. Dulles, 185. Dulles's scepticism about finding a super-model is founded on his view of the mystery-character of the church, but apparently also derives from his understanding of model. In model-theory there is no decisive argument for a kind of necessary pluralism: on the contrary, the realism of models forms the driving force behind the search for a perfect model (Hesse). As argued earlier, the mystery of the church does not provide an argument either.
6. Dulles, 185.
7. Dulles, 187.
8. Dulles, 68. See also his remarks about its attractions to theologians, and his defence of 'sacrament' (68f).
9. Semmelroth, 'Einheit', 319ff.
10. Semmelroth, 'Einheit', 321–3.
11. Semmelroth, 'Einheit', 323–5.
12. Semmelroth, 'Einheit', 326.
13. 'Symbolum esse rei sacrae et invisibilis gratiae formam visibilem' (D–S 1639).
14. Holböck, 220–24. On 221f he makes his remark about 'bride of Christ', quoting Tromp, but provides no argument for his verdict.
15. Holböck, 221; he again quotes Tromp.

16. Holböck, 224: 'Die Kirche ist jene christusförmige, hierarchisch geordnete, universelle Gemeinschaft, die durch, mit und in Christus in der Einheit des Heiligen Geistes Gott der Vater alle Ehre und Verherrlichung, den Menschen und der Welt aber die Wahrheit und das Heil zu vermitteln hat'.
17. For the translation of 'Gemeinschaft' by 'society', see p. 224, where Holböck translates 'societas' by 'Gemeinschaft'. See also 225.
18. The rest of the article devotes little attention to 'people of God'. Holböck's argument against the use of metaphors in a definition is an inconsistent element in his argumentation as a whole. On the one hand, he denies the possibility of a definition and of concepts, and allows only a 'circumscription' by means of images; and, on the other, he criticizes descriptions using images – i.e., instances of just such 'circumscriptions' – because they use images, and proposes a quasi-definition without images. As argued earlier, the appeal to the rule about images is not valid in its generality, and as such is not a valid criticism of the synthesis view. Moreover, the qualification of metaphors as 'only sensible circumscriptions of rational concepts' ('nur sinnenfällige Umschreibungen verstandnismässiger Begriffe', 223) undermines the whole previous argument that the mystery can only be expressed in images and metaphors.
19. Mühlen, *Una Mystica*, 17.
20. Mühlen, *Una Mystica*, 72f.
21. For a criticism of their arguments insofar as they concern the content of 'people of God' and 'body of Christ', see Chapter I, sections 2.1 and 2.3 above, where similar arguments are discussed.
22. Aymans, 332; see also 331. See further Boff, 41f, who says that it is precisely the task of theology to penetrate the images of the church in order to disclose the internal linking principle. Boff does not discuss explicitly the methodological problems involved in the use of images and metaphors, but refers to Semmelroth's 'Einheit' and to Mühlen.
23. *Mystici Corporis*, n. 14, 24, 58 (see also 35, 51, 57), where this process of analysis can be seen.
24. Hamer, esp. 97f.
25. Koster, 'Leitbild', 175ff.
26. Luneau, I, 11–21; and II, 13–30. See Chapter I, section 2.1.2 above.
27. See Chapter I, section 2.2 above. See also Semmelroth, 'Einheit', 324–6, who contrasts 'sacrament' with 'concept of church', and then refers to 'people of God' and 'body of Christ', where previously he has used 'images', etc.
28. See the analysis of *Lumen Gentium* in Chapter I, section 1.1 above.
29. *Mystici Corporis*, n. 25ff.
30. Koster, 'Ekklesiologie', 239–41, 207; see also his remark about the codex of 1918, 206. See further 'Leitbild', 180–4, and his discussion of 'bride' and 'family'.

31. Valeske, 245; Keller, 131–4. But Koster is not the only one: see Keller, 85–136; Keller concludes that, certainly up to the middle of this century, most attempts to use 'people of God' in ecclesiology employ the term under the term understood as *societas* (135f).
32. Especially revealing is Przywara's criticism (131) of Scheeben: in common with the 'mystical body' theologians of about 1940, Scheeben starts from mystical body, whereas, according to Przywara, the proper starting-point is the church.
33. See also the rather limited ways in which Holböck and Semmelroth ('Einheit') understand 'people of God'; or Mühlen's conclusion that 'people of God' looms in the background of Bellarmine's definition because he discusses structure.
34. Dulles, despite his use of 'sacrament', does not belong to this category. His scepticism about finding a super-model is not the only factor that determines the harmonizing process: the other factor is the way in which he classifies his material. Dulles does not take seriously the formal methodological claims which Semmelroth makes when he proposes 'sacrament'. It is not Semmelroth's intention to understand 'sacrament' as a rival to 'mystical body' or 'people of God' (or as a rival to 'servant' and 'herald', to use two of Dulles' own models). Semmelroth's claim may be incorrect, but Dulles does not show this to be the case; nor does he discuss this possibility.

    A similar point arises when Dulles discusses the church as mystical communion. Following a discussion of the advantages and disadvantages of 'people of God' and 'body of Christ', he concludes that 'both illuminate from different angles the notion of the church as a communion or community' (51). Since he calls 'people of God' and 'body of Christ' models, this conclusion suggests that 'community' is a super-model, or at least a more basic notion. And in the evaluation (179ff) there are elements which can be seen as some kind of differentiation between the models: his own preference for 'sacrament', and his exclusion of 'institution' as a primary model. But these various elements and suggestions are not developed further.

IV.4

1. See, e.g., Congar, *L'Eglise*, 269ff.
2. See, e.g., Keller, 83ff, esp. 187ff for the period.
3. Semmelroth, 'Die Kirche als Sakrament des Heils', 309f; see also 328.
4. Semmelroth, *Ursakrament*, 328f.
5. 'Sacrament' can be understood in different ways, or with different emphases. For the development over the last two centuries, see Bernards, 'Zur Lehre von der Kirche als Sakrament'. See also Boff, 182–375, who analyzes the use of 'the church as sacrament' in the official teachings of the church (from the First Vatican Council to the Second) and in the works of theologians since Scheeben. In

Semmelroth's understanding there seems to be a shift from an emphasis on the combination of visible–invisible to an emphasis on the sacrament as sign or instrument: in both cases, however, the criticism is valid.

6. Boff, 45f, where he indicates that he will develop this basic statement in future works.
7. Boff, 17ff.
8. Boff, 28ff.
9. Boff, 43; see 42–4 for the other conditions.
10. Mühlen's comment that Bellarmine's definition is dominated by a metaphor is also applicable to his own formula, which is dominated by *una mystica persona*. Another difficulty with his view is that 'many' is too vague to establish a specifically ecclesiological approach (see below). Mühlen has to maintain this vagueness, since 'many' refers to Christ and us.
11. See Przywara, 123, who cites Pelz, *Der Christ als Christus*. See also Valeske, 160ff (esp. 165–7) for the literature. See further Mühlen, *Una Mystica*, 173ff.
12. This implies that the way in which Congar uses the distinction between *ecclesia congregans* and *ecclesia congregata* cannot be accepted ('Wesenseigenschaften', 458–77). The starting-point of the outline also calls into question the usefulness of the distinction itself.
13. See *n*. 13 to Chapter I, section 1.3 above; see also Metz's criticism of certain views of history (Chapter III, section 1.2 above).
14. See, e.g., the way in which the *Lineamenta* for the special synod of the Dutch bishops (January 1980) uses 'communio'.

Bibliography

Only works cited in the text and notes are included in this bibliography. The bibliography is arranged alphabetically under the names of authors (and editors); where two or more works by the same author are listed, they are given in order of publication.

Full titles of periodicals, normally abbreviated in this bibliography, are given in the Table of Abbreviations on pp. xivff above.

ABELSON, R., 'Definition', *The Encyclopedia of Philosophy* (ed. P. Edwards), New York 1967.

Acta Synodalia Sacrosancti Concilii Oecumenici Vaticani Secundi, Vatican City State 1970–78.

ADAM, K., 'Ekklesiologie im Werden? Kritische Bemerkungen zu M. D. Kosters Kritik an den ekklesiologischen Versuchen der Gegenwart', *TQ* 122 (1941), 145–66.

ALBERIGO, G., and F. Magistretti (edd.), *Constitutionis Dogmaticae Lumen Gentium Synopsis Historica*, Bologna 1975.

ALSTON, W., *Philosophy of Language*, Englewood Cliffs 1964.

ANON., review of M. Corbin (q.v.), *RLT* IX (1977: literature for the year 1974), 291–303.

ANTON, A., 'Estructura Teándrica de la Iglesia: Historia y significando ecclesiologico del numero 8 de la Lumen Gentium', *EE* 42 (1967), 39–72.

APOSTEL, L., 'Towards the Formal Study of Models in the Non-formal Sciences', *The Concept and Role of Models in Mathematics and Natural and Social Sciences* (ed. H. Freudenthal), Dordrecht 1961, 1–37.

AQUINAS, St Thomas, *Expositio super librum Boethii de Trinitate* (ed. B. Decker), Leiden 1959 (orig. 1955).

— *In duodecim libros Metaphysicorum Aristotelis expositio* (ed. Marietti), Turin 1950.

— *Quaestio disputata De unione verbi* (ed. Marietti), Turin 1953.

— *Quaestio disputata De veritate* (3 vols.) (ed. Leonina), Rome 1970–76.

— *Scriptum super libros sententiarum magistri Petri Lombardi* (ed. Mandonnet and Moos), Paris 1919ff.

— *Sententia libri Ethicorum* (2 vols.) (ed. Leonina), Rome 1969.

— *Summa contra Gentiles* (3 vols.) (ed. Leonina), Rome 1918–30².

— *Summa Theologiae* (9 vols.) (ed. Leonina), Rome 1888–1906².

— *Super Evangelium S. Johannis lectura* (ed. Marietti), Turin 1952.

ARDELT, R., 'Anmerkungen zur antimodernistischen Ekklesiologie', *Der Modernismus* (ed. E. Weinzierl), Graz/Vienna/Cologne 1974, 257–82.

ARIETTA, J., 'Die Heilsgeschichtliche Schau der Kirche auf dem Zweiten Vatikanischen Konzil', *Oikonomia: Heilsgeschichte als Thema der Theologie. Oscar Cullmann zum 65. Geburtstag gewitmet* (edd. F. Christ et al.), Hamburg 1967, 322–41.

ARISTOTLE, *De Arte Poetica* (ed. I. Becker), Berlin 1960ff (orig. 1831ff).

— *De Arte Rhetorica* (ed. I. Becker), Berlin 1960ff (orig. 1831ff).

— *De Interpretatione* (ed. I. Becker), Berlin 1960ff (orig. 1831ff).

AUER, J., 'Die Bedeutung der "Modell-idee" für die "Hilfsbegriffe" der katholischen Dogmas', *Einsicht und Glaube* (edd. J. Ratzinger and H. Fries), Freiburg 1962, 259–79.

— 'Das "Leib-Modell" und der "Kirchenbegriff" der katholischen Kirche: Ein Betrag zum Verständnis der Kirche und ihre Aemter', *MTZ* 12 (1961), 14–38.

AUGUSTINE, St., *Confessions* (ed. M. Skutella), Stuttgart 1969² (orig. 1934).

AUSTIN, J., *How to Do Things with Words* (edd. J. Urmson and M. Sbisà), Oxford 1975².

AYMANS, W., '"Volk Gottes" und "Leib Christi" in der communio-Struktur der Kirche', *TTZ* 81 (1972), 321–34.

BACKES, I., 'Gottes Volk im Neuen Bund', *TTZ* 70 (1961), 80–93.

BARAUNA, G. (ed.), *De Kerk van Vaticanum II: Commentaren op de Concilie-constitutie over de Kerk* (2 vols.), Bilthoven 1966.

BARBOUR, I., *Myths, Models and Paradigms: The Nature of Scientific and Religious Language*, London 1974.

BAUER, B. G., *Christliche Hoffnung und menschlicher Forschritt: Die politische Theologie von J. B. Metz als theologische Begründung gesellschaftlicher Verantwortung der Christen*, Mainz 1976.

BAUMGARTNER, H. M., *Kontinuität und Geschichte: Zur Kritik und Metakritik der historischen Vernunft*, Frankfurt-am-Main 1972.

BEARDSLEE, W., *Literary Criticism of the New Testament*, Philadelphia 1970.

BEARDSLEY, M., *Aesthetics*, New York 1958.

— 'The Metaphorical Twist', *PPR* 22 (1962), 293–307.

— 'Metaphor', *The Encyclopedia of Philosophy* (ed. P. Edwards), New York 1967.

— 'Metaphorical Senses', *Nous* 12 (1978), 3–16.

BERGGREN, D., 'The Use and Abuse of Metaphor', *RM* 16 (1962/3), 237–58; 450–72.

BERNARDS, M., 'Zur Lehre von der Kirche als Sakrament', *MTZ* 20 (1969), 29–54.

BERTELS, K., and D. Nauta, *Inleiding tot het modelbegrip*, Amsterdam 1974.

BETTI, U., 'Geschiedenis van de Constitutie', *De Kerk van Vaticanum II* (ed. G. Barauna) (q.v.), Bilthoven 1966, I, 130–55.

BETZ, J., 'Die Theologie und das Zweite Vatikanische Konzil', *TTZ* 75 (1966), 89–107.

BEUMER, J., 'Das für das Erste Vatikanische Konzil entworfene Schema De Ecclesia im Urteil der Konzilsväter', *Scholastik* 38 (1963), 392–401.

— 'Die Kirche, Leib Christi oder Volk Gottes', *TG* 53 (1963), 255–68.

BICKERTON, D., 'Prolegomena to a Linguistic Theory of Metaphor', *FL* 5 (1969), 34–52.

BLACK, M., *Models and Metaphors*, New York 1962.

— 'More about Metaphors', *Dialectica* 31 (1977), 431–57.

BOCHENSKI, J., *The Logic of Religion*, New York 1865.

BOFF, L., *Die Kirche als Sakrament im Horizont der Welterfahrung: Versuch einer Legitimation und einer struktur-funktionalistischen Grundlegung der Kirche im Anschluss an das II. Vatikanische Konzil*, Paderborn 1972.

BOLINGER, D., 'The Atomization of Meaning', *Language* 41 (1965), 555–73.

BOUYER, L., 'Où en est la théologie du Corps Mystique', *RSR* 22 (1948), 313–33.

— *L'Eglise de Dieu: Corps du Christ et Temple de l'Esprit*, Paris 1970.

BROWER, R. (ed.), *On Translation*, Cambridge (Mass.) 1959.

BRÜMMER, V., *Wijsgerige Begripsanalyse: Een inleiding voor theologen en belangstellenden*, Kampen 1975.

BÜCHER, T., 'Die heutige einschätzung der Metaphern in der Philosophie', *TF* 34 (1972), 704–60.

BURRELL, D., *Aquinas: God and Action*, London 1979.

BUSA, R. (ed.), *Index Thomisticus: Sancti Thomae Aquinatis Operum Omnium Indices et concordantiae*, Stuttgart 1974.

BUTLER, C. B., *The Theology of Vatican II*, London 1967.

CANCIK, H., *Mythische und historische Wahrheit*, Stuttgart 1970.

CHARLTON, W., 'Living and Dead Metaphors', *BJA* 15 (1975), 172–8.

CHENU, M.-D., *La Théologie comme science au XIIIe siècle*, Paris 1957³ (orig. 1927).

— *Introduction à l'Etude de saint Thomas d'Aquin*, Paris 1974 (3rd edition). [ET: *Toward Understanding Saint Thomas*, Chicago 1964.]

— *La Théologie au douzième siècle*, Paris 1976 (3rd edition). [ET: *Nature, Man and Society in the Twelfth Century*, Chicago/London 1968.]

CHOMSKY, N., *Current Issues in Linguistic Theory*, Den Haag 1964.
— *Aspects of the Theory of Syntax*, Cambridge (Mass.) 1965.
COLERIDGE, S. T., *Biographia Literaria* (ed. G. Watson), London 1906.
COMMER, E., *Die Kirche im ihrem Leben und Wesen dargestellt: I. Vom Wesen der Kirche*, Vienna 1904.
— 'Das Leben der Kirche: Grundlegung', *DT* 6 (1919), 167–88.
CONE, J., 'The Story-Context of Black Theology', *TT* 32 (1975), 144–50.
CONGAR, Y., 'Théologie', *DThC*.
— *Le Mystère du Temple* (lectio divina 22), Paris 1958. [ET: *The Mystery of the Temple*, London 1962.]
— *Vatican II: Le Concile au jour le jour*, Paris 1963–6.
— 'The Church: The People of God', *Concilium* 1 (1965) 1, 7–19.
— *Sainte Eglise: Etudes et approches ecclésiologiques*, Paris 1964.
— '*L'Eglise* de Hans Küng', *RSPT* 53 (1969), 693–706.
— *L'Eglise: De saint Augustin à l'époque moderne* (Histoire des Dogmes), Paris 1970.
— 'D'une "Ecclésiologie en gestation" à Lumen Gentium Chap. I et II', *FZPT* 18 (1971), 366–77.
— 'Die Wesenseigenschaften der Kirche', *Mysterium Salutis. Grundriss einer heilsgeschichtlichen Dogmatik: IV/1. Das Heilsgeschehen in der Gemeinde* (ed. J. Feiner and M. Löhrer) (q.v.), Einsiedeln/Zurich/Cologne 1972, 357–502; 535–94.
CORBIN, M., *Le chemin de la théologie chez Thomas d'Aquin*, Paris 1974.
COURTH, F., 'Kirche als Gottesvolk unterwegs: Zur Begegnung mit einer menschlichen Kirche', *GL* 47 (1974), 271–84.
CRITES, S., 'The Narrative Quality of Experience', *JAAR* 39 (1971), 291–311.
CULLER, J., *Saussure*, Glasgow 1975.
DAMME, D. van, 'Gottesvolk und Gottesreich in der christliche Antike', *Judentum und Kirche: Volk Gottes* (Theologische Berichte III), Zurich/Einsiedeln/Cologne 1974, 157–68.

DANTO, A., *Analytical Philosophy of History*, Cambridge 1965.

DRANGE, T., *Type Crossings: Sentential Meaninglessness in the Border Area of Linguistics and Philosophy*, Den Haag 1966.

DRAY, W., 'On the Nature and Role of Narrative in Historiography', *HT* 10 (1971), 153–71.

DUFORT, J.-H., 'Histoire et théologie du VIIe chapitre de la constitution Lumen Gentium', *SE* 20 (1968), 77–94.

DULLES, A., *Models of the Church: A Critical Assessment of the Church in all its Aspects*, Dublin 1976.

DUMMETT, M., *Frege: Philosophy of Language*, London 1973.

DUNNE, J., *A Search for God in Time and Memory*, London/New York 1967.

— *The Reasons of the Heart*, London 1978.

ELY, R., R. Gruner, and W. Dray, 'Mandelbaum on Historical Narrative: A Discussion', *HT* 8 (1969), 275–94.

ERWIN, E., *The Concept of Meaninglessness*, Baltimore/London 1970.

ES, J. VAN, *Spreken over God: letterlijk of figuurlijk?*, Amsterdam 1979.

ESTESS, T., 'The Inenarrable Contraption: Reflections on the Metaphor of Story', *JAAR* 42 (1974), 415–34.

FEINER, J., and M. Löhrer (edd.), *Mysterium Salutis: Grundriss einer heilsgeschichtlichen Dogmatick: IV. Das Heilsgeschehen der Germeinde* (2 vols.), Einsiedeln/Zurich/Cologne, 1972–3.

FENTON, J., '*Mystici Corporis* and the Definition of the Church', *AER* 128 (1953), 448–59.

FERRÉ, F., *Basic Modern Philosophy of Religion*, London 1967.

— 'Metaphors, Models, and Religion', *Soundings* 51 (1968), 327–45.

— 'Mapping the Logic of Models in Science and Theology', *New Essays on Religious Language* (ed. D. High), New York 1969, 54–96.

FESQUET, H., *Le Journal du Concile*, Forcalquier 1966.

FRANSEN, P., 'L'Eglise comme peuple de Dieu', *La nouvelle image de l'Eglise: Bilan du Concile Vatican II* (ed. B. Lambert), Paris 1967, 102–24.

FREGE, G., *Die Grundlagen der Arithmetik: eine logisch-mathematische Untersuchung über den Begriff der Zahl*, Breslau 1884. [ET: *The Foundations of Arithmetic: A Logico-mathematical Enquiry into the Concept of Number* (ed. J. Austin), Oxford/New York 1953 (2nd revised edition).]
— 'Ueber Sinn und Bedeutung', *ZPPK* 100 (1892), 25–50. [ET: 'On Sense and Reference', *Translations from the Philosophical Writings of Gottlob Frege* (ed. P. Geach and M. Black), Oxford/New York 1960 (2nd revised edition), 56–78.]
FRIES, H., 'Wandel des Kirchenbilds und dogmengeschichtliche Entfaltung', *Mysterium Salutis: Grundriss einer heilsgeschichtlichen Dogmatik: IV/2. Das Heilsgeschehen in der Gemeinde* (ed. J. Feiner and M. Löhrer) (q.v.), Einsiedeln/Zurich/Cologne 1973, 223–86.
FUNK, R., *Language, Hermeneutics, and the Word of God*, New York/London 1966.

GALLIE, W., *Philosophy and the Historical Understanding*, New York 1964.
GEREMIA, F., *I primi due capitoli della 'Lumen Gentium': Genesi ed elaborazione del testo conciliare*, Rome 1971.
GILBY, T., 'Doctrinal Development', *Christian Theology* (vol. 1 of the Blackfriars edition of the *Summa Theologiae*), London 1964, 102–23.
GILKEY, L., *Reaping the Whirlwind: A Christian Interpretation of History*, New York 1976.
GILL, J., *Ian Ramsey: To Speak Responsibly of God*, London 1976.
GOODMAN, N., *Languages of Art*, Indianapolis/New York 1968.
GRIJS, F. de, 'Didache en Theologie (notitie)', *Bijdragen* 36 (1975), 302–07.

HACKER, P., *Insight and Illusion: Wittgenstein on Philosophy and the Metaphysics of Experience*, London/Oxford/New York 1972.
HALLETT, G., *A Companion to Wittgenstein's Philosophical Investigations*, Ithaca 1977.
HAMER, J., *L'Eglise est une communion*, Paris 1962. [ET: *The Church is a Communion*, London 1964.]

HAMPE, J. C. (ed.), *Die Autorität der Freiheit: Gegenwart des Konzils und Zukunft der Kirche im ökumenischen Disput* (3 vols.), Munich 1967.

HARRÉ, R., *The Philosophies of Science*, London/Oxford/New York 1972.

— 'Images of the World and Societal Icons', *Determinants and Controls of Scientific Development* (ed. K. Knorr, H. Strasser, and H. Zilian), Dordrecht 1975, 257–83.

— 'Metaphysics and Science', *Philosophica* 15 (1975), 79–98.

— 'The Constructive Role of Models', *The Use of Models in the Social Sciences* (ed. L. Collins), London 1976, 14–43.

HARVEY, J., 'Le Peuple de Dieu, sacrement du dessein de Dieu', *LTP* 22 (1966), 89–108.

HAWKES, T., *Metaphor*, London 1972.

HEMPEL, C. G., *Aspects of Scientific Explanation and other Essays in the Philosophy of Science*, New York 1965.

HEMPEL, C. G., and P. Oppenheim, 'Studies in the Logic of Explanation', *PS* 15 (1948), 135–75. [Reproduced in Hempel, C. G., *Aspects of Scientific Explanation* (q.v.), 245–95, with some changes and a postscript.]

HENEL, H., 'Metaphor and Meaning', *The Disciplines of Criticism: Essays in Literary Theory, Interpretation, and History* (ed. P. Demetz et al.), New Haven/London 1968.

HENLE, P. (ed.), *Language, Thought, and Culture*, Ann Arbor 1958.

HESSE, M., *Models and Analogies in Science*, Notre Dame 1970 (2nd enlarged edition).

HOLBÖCK, F., 'Das Mysterium der Kirche in dogmatischer Sicht', *Mysterium Kirche in der Sicht der theologischen Disziplinen* (ed. F. Holböck and T. Sartory) (2 vols.), Salzburg 1962, I, 201–346.

HORNBY, A. (ed.), *The Oxford Advanced Learner's Dictionary of Current English*, Oxford 1977.

HORST, F. van der, *Das Schema über die Kirche auf dem I. Vatikanischen Konzil*, Paderborn 1963.

HOSPERS, J., *An Introduction to Philosophical Analysis*, London 1967².

HUTTEN, E. H., 'The Role of Models in Physics', *BJPS* 4 (1953–5).

IJSSELING, S., *Retoriek en Filosofie: Wat gebeurt er wanneer er gesproken wordt*, Bilthoven 1975. [ET: *Rhetoric and Philosophy in Conflict*, The Hague 1976.]

JAKI, S., *Les tendances nouvelles de l'ecclésiologie*, Rome 1957.

JONES, H., 'The Concept of Story and Theological Discourse', *SJT* 29 (1976), 415–33.

JOURNET, C., *L'Eglise du Verbe Incarné: I. La hiérarchie apostolique*, Paris 1941. [ET: *The Church of the Word Incarnate: The Apostolic Hierarchy*, London/New York 1955.]; *II. Sa structure interne et son unité catholique*, Paris 1951; *III. Essai de théologie de l'histoire du salut*, Paris 1969.

JÜNGEL, E., 'Erwagungen zur theologischen Relevanz der Metapher als Beitrag zur Hermeneutik einer narrativen Theologie', *Zur Hermeneutik religiöser Sprache* (P. Ricoeur and E. Jüngel) (Sonderheft Evangelische Theologie), Munich 1976, 71–122.

JUST, W., 'Definitionen in der Theologie', *ZEE* 21 (1977), 257–75.

KAMLAH, W., and P. Lorenzen, *Logische Propädeutik: Vorschule des vernünftigen Redens*, Mannheim 1973 (2nd revised and augmented edition).

KATHOLIEK Archief, *Het Concilie*, Amersfoort 1962–6.

KATZ, S., 'The Language and Logic of "Mystery" in Christology', *Christ, Faith, and History* (ed. S. Sykes and J. Clayton), Cambridge 1972, 239–61.

KELLER, M., *'Volk Gottes' als Kirchenbegriff: Eine Untersuchung zum neueren Verständnis*, Zurich/Einsiedeln/Cologne 1970.

KHATCHADOURIAN, H., 'Metaphor', *BJA* 8 (1968), 227–43.

KING, J., 'Towards an Adequate Concept of the Church', *Thomist* 27 (1963), 11–29.

KLIEVER, L., 'Story and Space: The Forgotten Dimension', *JAAR* 45 (1977), 2nd suppl. 579–613.

KLOPPENBURG, B., 'Stemmingen over de laatste verbeteringen aan de Constitutie', *De Kerk van Vaticanum II* (ed. G. Barauna) (q.v.), Bilthoven 1966, I, 193–224.

KÖHLER, L., and A. Baumgartner (edd.), *Hebraisches und Aramaisches Lexicon zum AT*, Leiden 1967.

KÖPF, U., *Die Anfänge der theologischen Wissenschaftstheorie im 13. Jahrhundert*, Tübingen 1974.

KOSTER, M. D., 'Ekklesiologie im Werden', *Volk Gottes im Werden: Gesammelte Studien* (ed. H.-D. Langer and O. H. Pesch), Mainz 1971, 195–272 (orig. Paderborn 1940).

— 'Zum Leitbild von der Kirche auf dem II. Vatikanischen Konzil', *Volk Gottes im Werden: Gesammelte Studien* (ed. H.-D. Langer and O. H. Pesch), Mainz 1971, 172–93 (orig. *TQ* 145 [1965], 13–42).

KRESS, R., 'The Church as *Communio:* Trinity and Incarnation as the Foundation of Ecclesiology', *Jurist* 36 (1976), 127–58.

KÜNG, H., *Die Kirche*, Freiburg/Basle/Vienna 1967. [ET: *The Church*, London 1968.]

KÜNG, H., Y. Congar, and D. O'Hanlon (edd.), *Council Speeches of Vatican II*, Glen Rock/London 1964.

LADRIÈRE, J., 'Le discours théologique et le symbole', *RSR* 49 (1975), 116–41.

LAURENTIN, R., *L'Enjeu du Concile* (4 vols.), Paris 1962–5.

LEHMANN, K., 'Wandlungen der neuen "politischen Theologie"', *IKZ* 2 (1973), 383–99.

— 'Emanzipation und Leid', *IKZ* 3, (1974), 42–63.

LIALINE, D. C., 'Une étape en ecclésiologie: Reflexions sur l'encyclique "Mystici Corporis"', *Irenikon* 19 (1946), 129–52; 283–317; 20 (1947), 34–54.

LIEB, H.-H., *Der Umfang des historischen Metaphernbegriffs*, Cologne 1964.

— 'Was bezeichnet der herkommliche Begriff "Metapher"', *Literaturwissenschaft und Linguistik* (ed. J. Ihwe), Frankfurt-am-Main 1971, I, 334–48.

LINDBECK, G. A., 'Die Kirchenlehre des Konzils ist ein Uebergang', *Die Autorität der Freiheit* (ed. J. Hampe) (q.v.), (Munich 1967, I, 359–72.

LOEWENBERG, I., 'Truth and the Consequences of Metaphors', *PR* 6 (1974), 30–46.

— 'Identifying Metaphors', *FL* 12 (1975), 315–18.

LOHFINK, N., 'Beobachtungen zum Geschichte des Ausdrucks (am JIIWH)', *Probleme biblische Theologie* (ed. H. Wolff), Munich 1971, 275–305.

LOUCH, A., 'History as Narrative', *HT* 8 (1969), 54–70.

LUBAC, H. de, *Corpus Mysticum: L'Eucharistie et l'Eglise au Moyen Age*, Paris 1949 (2nd revised edition).

— *Exégèse Médiévale: Les quatre sens de l'Ecriture*, Seconde Partie (2 vols.), Paris 1961 and 1964.

— *Paradoxe et Mystère de l'Eglise*, Paris 1967. [ET: *The Church: Paradox and Mystery*, Shannon 1969.]

LUCAS, D., *Aristotle: Poetics*, Oxford 1968.

LUNEAU, A., and M. Bobichon, *Eglise ou Troupeau? Du troupeau fidèle au peuple de l'Alliance: I. Ecriture et Histoire; II. Une Volonté de Renouveau*, Paris 1972.

MCCABE, H., 'Note on "Analogy"', *Knowing and Naming God* (vol. 3 of the Blackfriars edition of the *Summa Theologiae*), London 1964, 106–07.

MCCLENDON, *Biography as Theology: How Life Stories can Remake Today's Theology*, Nashville 1974.

MCCORMACK, E., *Metaphor and Myth in Science and Religion*, Durham (North Carolina) 1976.

MCDONNELL, K., 'The Ecclesiology of Calvin and Vatican II', *RL* 36 (1967), 542–56.

MCINERNY, R., *The Logic of Analogy: An Interpretation of St Thomas*, The Hague 1961.

— *Studies in Analogy*, The Hague 1968.

MACKIE, A., 'The Structure of Aesthetically Interesting Metaphors', *APQ* 12 (1975), 41–9.

MCNAMARA, K., 'The Idea of the Church: Modern Developments in Ecclesiology', *ITQ* 33 (1966), 99–113.

MALMBERG, F., *Eén Lichaam en één Geest: Nieuwe gezichtspunten in de Ecclesiologie*, Utrecht 1958.

MANDELBAUM, 'A Note on History as Narrative', *HT* 6 (1967), 413–19.

MANNS, J., 'Metaphor and Paraphrase', *BJA* 15 (1975), 358–66.

MANTHEY, F., *Die Sprachphilosophie des Hl. Thomas von Aquin und ihre Anwendung auf Probleme der Theologie*, Paderborn 1937.

MARTIN, G. D., *Language, Truth and Poetry: Notes towards a Philosophy of Literature*, Edinburgh 1975.

MATTHEWS, R., 'Concerning a "Linguistic Theory" of Metaphor', *FL* 7 (1971), 413–25.

MENNE, A., 'Definition', *Handbuch Philosophischer Grundbegriffe* (ed. H. Krings, H. M. Baumgartner, and C. Wild) (3 vols.), Munich 1973.

MERSCH, E., *Le Corps Mystique du Christ. Etudes de théologie historique* (2 vols.), Paris/Brussels 1936².

METZ, J. B., 'A Short Apology of Narrative', *Concilium* 9 (1973) 5, 84–96.

— 'Introduction', *Concilium* 12 (1976) 5, 3–6.

— *Glaube in Geschichte und Gesellschaft*, Mainz 1977. [ET: *Faith in History and Society*, London 1980.]

MIETH, D., *Dichtung, Glaube und Moral: Studien zur Begründung einer narrativen Ethik*, Mainz 1976.

— *Moral und Erfahrung: Beiträge zur theologisch-ethischen Hermeneutik*, Freiburg/Vienna 1977.

MOELLER, C., 'Het rijpen van de ideeën bij de voorbereiding van de Constitutie', *De Kerk van Vaticanum II* (ed. G. Barauna) (q.v.), Bilthoven 1966, I, 193–224.

MOHRMANN, C., '"Tertium genus": Les relations judaisme, antiquité, christianisme reflétées dans la langue des chrétiens', *Etudes sur le latin des chrétiens* IV, Rome 1977, 195–210.

MOOIJ, J., *A Study of Metaphor: On the Nature of Metaphorical Expressions, with Special Reference to their Reference*, Amsterdam/New York/Oxford 1976.

MÜHLEN, H., *Una Mystica Persona: Die Kirche als das Mysterium der Identität des heiligen Geistes in Christus und den Christen – Eine Person in vielen Personen*, Munich/Paderborn/Vienna 1967 (2nd revised and augmented edition) (orig. 1964).

— 'Der Kirchenbegriff des Konzils', *Die Autorität der Freiheit* (ed. J. Hampe) (q.v.), Munich 1967, I, 291–313.

Mystici Corporis. See PIUS XII.

NÉDONCELLE, M. (ed.), *L'Ecclésiologie au XIXe siècle*, Paris 1960.
NOVAK, M., *Ascent of the Mountain, Flight of the Dove*, New York 1971.
OCKHAM, William of, *Summa Logicae* (2 vols.) (ed. P. Boehner), New York/Louvain/Paderborn 1967.
OLSCAMP, P., 'How Some Metaphors may be True or False', *JAAC* 29 (1970), 77–86.
PANNENBERG, W., *Wissenschaftstheorie und Theologie*, Frankfurt-am-Main 1977. [ET: *Theology and the Philosophy of Science*, London 1980.]
PATER, W. de, *Taalanalytische Perspektieven op Godsdienst en Kunst*, Antwerp 1970.
PAUL, A., 'Metaphor and the Bounds of Expression', *PR* 5 (1973), 143–58.
PAUL VI, *Ecclesiam Suam* (in *AAS* 46 [1964], 609–59).
PELZ, K., *Der Christ als Christus* (unpublished manuscript).
PERSSON, P., 'Die Endzeitliche Character der pilgernden Kirche und ihre Einheit mit der himmlischen Kirche', *Die Autorität der Freiheit* (ed. J. Hampe) (q.v.), Munich 1967, I, 338–43.
PESCH, O., 'Um den Plan der Summa Theologiae des Hl. Thomas von Aquin', *Thomas von Aquin* (ed. K. Bernath) (2 vols.), Darmstadt 1978, 411–37.
PETTIT, P., *The Concept of Structuralism: A Critical Analysis*, Dublin 1975.
PHILIPS, D. C., *Wittgenstein and Scientific Knowledge*, London 1977.
PHILIPS, G., *Dogmatische Constitutie over de Kerk Lumen Gentium. Geschiedenis, tekst, kommentaar* (2 vols.), Antwerp 1967–8.
PINBORG, J., *Die Entwicklung der Sprachtheorie im Mittelalter*, Münster 1967.
— 'Textsemantische Probleme in der Sprachtheorie und Logik des Mittelalters', *Sprache und Sprachverständnis in religiöser Rede: Zum Verhältnis von Theologie und Linguistik* (ed. T. Michels and A. Paus), Salzburg/Munich 1973, 135–69.
PITKIN, H., *Wittgenstein on Justice*, Berkeley/London 1972.

Pius XII, *Mystici Corporis* (ed. S. Tromp), Rome 1963⁴ (orig. *AAS* 35 [1943], 193–248).

Platts, M., *Ways of Meaning: An Introduction to a Philosophy of Language*, London 1979.

Price, J., 'Linguistic Competence and Metaphorical Use', *FL* 11 (1974), 253–6.

Przywara, E., 'Corpus Christi Mysticum: Ein Bilanz', *Katholische Krise* (ed. B. Gertz), Düsseldorf 1967, 123–52.

Puntel, L., 'Wissenschaftstheorie und Theologie: Zu Wolfhart Pannenbergs gleichnamigen Buch', *ZKT* 98 (1976), 271–92.

Ramsey, I. T., *Models and Mystery*, London/New York/Toronto 1964.

— *Christian Discourse*, London/New York/Toronto, 1965.

— 'Talking about God', *Words about God: The Philosophy of Religion* (ed. I. T. Ramsey), London 1971, 202–23.

— *Religious Language: An Empirical Placing of Theological Phrases*, London 1973 (orig. 1957).

Rapoport, A., *Operational Philosophy: Integrating Knowledge and Action*, New York 1953.

Ratzinger, J., *Die Erste Sitzungsperiode des Zweiten Vatikanischen Konzils: Ein Rückblick*, Cologne 1963.

— *Das Konzil auf dem Weg: Rückblick auf die Zweite Sitzungsperiode*, Cologne 1964.

— *Ergebnisse und Probleme der dritte Konzilsperiode*, Cologne 1965.

— *Die Letzte Sitzungsperiode des Konzils*, Cologne 1966.

— *Das neue Volk Gottes*, Düsseldorf 1970².

— 'Kirche', *LTK* (2nd edition).

— 'Demokratisierung der Kirche', *Demokratie in der Kirche: Möglichkeiten, Grenzen, Gefahren* (ed. J. Ratzinger and H. Maier), Limburg 1970, 9–46.

Reddy, M., 'A Semantic Approach to Metaphor', *Papers from the Fifth Regional Meeting of the Chicago Linguistics Society*, Chicago 1969, 240–51.

Richards, I. A., *The Philosophy of Rhetoric*, London/Oxford/New York 1971 (orig. 1936).

RICOEUR, P., *La métaphore vive*, Paris 1975. [ET: *The Rule of Metaphor*, London 1978.]
RIGEAUX, B., 'Het mysterie van de Kerk in het licht van de Bijbel', *De Kerk van Vaticanum II* (ed. G. Barauna) (q.v.), Bilthoven 1966, I, 324–44.
ROBINSON, R., *Definition*, Oxford 1972 (orig. 1950).
RYLE, G., *The Concept of Mind*, London 1949.
— *Collected Papers, 2: Collected Essays 1929–68*, London 1971.
RYNNE, X., *Vatican Council II*, New York 1968.

SAIER, O., *'Communio' in der Lehre des Zweiten Vatikanischen Konzils: Eine rechtsbegriffliche Untersuchung* (Münchener Theologische Studien), Munich 1973.
SCHEEBEN, M., *Die Mysterien des Christentums: Wesen Bedeutung und Zusammenhang derselben nach der in ihrem übernatürlichen Charakter gegebenen Perspektive dargestellt* (Ausgabe letzter Hand herausgegeben von Josef Höfer), Freiburg-im-Breisgau 1941. [ET: *The Mysteries of Christianity*, New York 1947.]
SCHILLEBEECKX, E., *Het Tweede Vatikaans Concilie* (2 vols.), Tielt/Den Haag 1964–6. [ET (vol. 2): *Vatican II: The Real Achievement*, London 1967.]
— *Openbaring en Theologie* (Theologische Peilingen, I), Bilthoven 1964. [ET (part 1): *Revelation and Theology*, London 1967; (part 2): *The Concept of Truth and Theological Renewal*, London 1968.]
— *De Zending van de Kerk* (Theologische Peilingen, IV), Bilthoven 1968. [ET: *The Mission of the Church*, London 1973.]
SCHLESINGER, J. M., 'On Linguistic Competence', *Pragmatics of Natural Languages* (ed. B. Y. Bar-Hillel), Dordrecht 1971, 150–72.
SCHMAUS, M., *Katholische Dogmatik: III/1. Die Lehre von der Kirche*, Munich 1978 (3rd–5th editions).
— 'Das gegenseitige Verhältnis von Leib Christi und Volk Gottes im Kirchenverständnis', *Volk Gottes: Festgabe für J. Höfer* (ed. R. Bäumer and H. Dolch), Freiburg 1967, 13–27.

SCHMAUS, M., *Der Glaube der Kirche: Handbuch Katholischer Dogmatik* (2 vols.), Munich 1970.

SEARLE, J., *Speech Acts: An Essay in the Philosophy of Language*, Cambridge 1969.

SEMMELROTH, O., *Die Kirche als Ursakrament*, Frankfurt-am-Main 1963 (orig. 1953).

— 'Um die Einheit der Kirchenbegriffes', *Fragen der Theologie Heute* (ed. J. Feiner, J. Trütsch and F. Böckle), Einsiedeln 1957, 319–35.

— *Ich Glaube an die Kirche*, Düsseldorf 1959.

— 'De Kerk, het nieuwe Godsvolk', *De Kerk van Vaticanum II* (ed. G. Barauna) (q.v.), Bilthoven 1966, I, 451–65.

— 'Die Kirche als Sakrament des Heils', *Mysterium Salutis: Grundriss einer heilsgeschichtlichen Dogmatik: IV/1. Das Heilsgeschehen der Gemeinde* (ed. J. Feiner and M. Löhrer) (q.v.), 309–56.

SHIBBLES, W., *Metaphor: An Annotated Bibliography and History*, Whitewater (Wisc.) 1971.

SIGURBJÖRNSSON, E., *Ministry within the People of God: The Development of the Doctrines on the Church and on the Ministry in the Second Vatican Council's "De Ecclesia"*, Lund 1974.

SKYDSGAARD, K., 'The Church as Mystery and as People of God', *Dialogue on the Way* (ed. G. Lindbeck), Minneapolis 1965, 145–74.

SMALLEY, B., *The Study of the Bible in the Middle Ages*, Notre Dame (Ind.) 1952².

SMULDERS, P., 'De Kerk als sacrament van het heil', *De Kerk van Vaticanum II* (ed. G. Barauna) (q.v.), Bilthoven 1966, I, 372–95.

STEENDAM, G. VAN, 'De nacht van de duizend-en-één verhalen: Orientatie bij de narratieve theologie', *TvT* 19 (1979), 3–27.

STENLUND, S., 'Remarks on some Problems of Meaning' (unpublished paper).

STEWART, D., 'Metaphor and Paraphrase', *PR* 4 (1972), 111–23.

STRAWSON, P., 'Review of Wittgenstein's "Philosophical Investigations"', *Wittgenstein* (ed. G. Pitcher), London 1966, 22–64.

STROUP, G., 'A Bibliographical Critique', *TT* 3 (1975), 133–43.
STUTTERHEIM, C., *Het Begrip Metaphoor: Een taalkundig en wijsgerig onderzoek*, Amsterdam 1941.
SWINBURNE, R., *The Coherence of Theism*, Oxford 1977.

TAVARD, G., *The Pilgrim Church*, London 1967.
TESELLE, S., *Speaking in Parables: A Study in Metaphor and Theology*, London 1975.
TOULMIN, S., *The Philosophy of Science*, London 1953.
TRACY, D., *Blessed Rage for Order: The New Pluralism in Theology*, New York 1975.
TUCHMAN, B., *The Guns of August: August 1914*, London 1962.
TURBAYNE, C., *The Myth of Metaphor*, Columbia (S. Carolina) 1970 (2nd revised edition).

ULLMANN, S., *The Principles of Semantics*, Glasgow 1951.
— *Semantics: An Introduction to the Science of Meaning*, Oxford 1967 (orig. 1962).
UTRECHTS Theologencollectief, Het, *Wat hier gebeurt is macht. Een actueel-theologisch onderzoek*, Hilversum 1975.

VALESKE, U., *Votum Ecclesiae: I. Das Ringen um die Kirche in der neueren römisch-katholischen Theologie. Dargesstelt auf dem Hintergrund der evangelischen und ökumenischen Parallel-Entwicklung; II. Interkonfessionelle ekklesiologische Bibliographie*, Munich 1962.
VIA, D., *The Parables: Their Literary and Existential Dimension*, Philadelphia 1967.

WACHINGER, L., *Erinnern und Erzählen: Reden von Gott aus Erfahrung*, Munich 1974.
WACKER, B., *Narrative Theologie?*, Munich 1974.
WARNER, M., 'Black's Metaphors', *BJA* 13 (1973), 367–72.
WEINRICH, H., 'Semantik der kühnen Metapher', *DVLG* 37 (1963), 325–44.
— *Tempus: Besprochene Zeit und erzählte Welt*, Stuttgart 1972 (2nd revised edition).

WEINRICH, H., *Literatur für Leser: Essays und Aufsätze zur Literaturwissenschaft*, Stuttgart 1972.
— 'Narrative Theology', *Concilium* 9 (1973) 5, 46–56.
WEISHEIPL, J., *Friar Thomas d'Aquino: His Life, Thought and Works*, Oxford 1975.
WILDER, A., *Early Christian Rhetoric: The Language of the Gospel*, Cambridge (Mass.) 1971 (orig. 1964).
WILLEMS, B., 'Der sakramentele Kirchenbegriff', *FZPT* 5 (1958), 274–96.
WITTGENSTEIN, L., *Philosophical Investigations*, Oxford 1967³ (orig. 1953).
— *The Blue and Brown Books*, Oxford 1969² (orig. 1958).
— *Remarks on the Foundations of Mathematics*, Oxford 1964.
— *Zettel*, Oxford 1967.
— *On Certainty*, Oxford 1969.
— *Philosophical Remarks*, Oxford 1975.
WRIGHT, G. H. VON, *Explanation and Understanding*, London 1971.
YOOS, G., 'A Phenomenological Look at Metaphor', *PPR* 32 (1972), 78–88.
'ZWEITE Vatikanische Konzil', *LTK*.

Index of Names

ADAM, K., 273
Abelson, R., 274
Anselm, 178
Annas, J., 7
Ambrose, 169f
Alberigo, G., 240–43
Alston, W., 253
Anton, A., 241
Apostel, L., 149, 263
Aquinas, St Thomas, 6, 63, 123, 159, 167–191, 218, 267, 269f, 271
Ardelt, R., 241
Arietta, J., 247
Aristotle, 94f, 159, 168, 171f, 176, 178, 181, 183, 185f, 189f, 252f, 271
Aubert, R., 239
Auer, J., 167, 265
Augustine, 46, 169
Austin, J., 250
Aymans, W., 56f, 59, 62–64, 246–248, 276

BACKES, I., 244
Barauna, G., 240, 274
Barbour, I., 160–163, 165, 264f, 275
Barr, J., 263
Bauer, B. G., 260
Baumgartner, H. M., 246, 263
Beardsley, M., 103–107, 111, 113, 254–257, 259, 274
Bellarmine, R., 224, 277f
Berggren, D., 112–115, 255, 257f
Bernards, M., 277
Bertels, K., 149, 263
Betti, U., 240f
Betz, J., 245, 247, 273
Beumer, J., 42, 44, 61, 63f, 239, 244, 248, 273
Bickerton, D., 71–76, 249f, 255, 257
Black, M., 4, 69, 100–103, 107, 115f, 149–153, 157f, 161f, 248–250, 254f, 258, 263f

Blake, W., 250
Bobichon, M., 246
Boccaccio, 138
Bochenski, J., 274
Boff, L., 273, 276–278
Bolinger, D., 74, 249
Bonhoeffer, D., 139
Bouyer, L., 244f, 248, 273
Braun, 274
Brower, R., 251
Brümmer, V., 274
Bücher, T., 248, 254
Burrell, D., 266, 270
Busa, R., 266
Butler, C. B., 240

CHARLTON, W., 249, 254
Chenu, M.-D., 174, 267f
Chomsky, N., 70f, 73, 75, 249
Coleridge, S. T., 154, 264
Commer, 206f, 218, 272, 274
Cone, J., 259
Congar, Y., 39–43, 45–47, 61, 64, 206, 208, 220, 239, 244–246, 269, 272–275, 277
Corbin, M., 171, 174f, 177, 179, 186–189, 267–270
Courth, F., 245
Crites, S., 259
Culler, J., 249
Cyprian, 31

DAMME, D. van, 245
Danto, A., 143, 145, 259, 262f
Davis, H., 239
Dionysius, 169, 170, 173, 180
Drange, T., 110–112, 257
Dray, W., 262
Dufort, J.-H., 242
Dulles, A., 58f, 62–64, 123, 207f, 218, 221, 247f, 272f, 275, 277
Dummett, M., 96, 253f
Dunne, J., 259

Eliot, T. S., 249
Ely, R., 144, 256, 262
Erwin, E., 249, 257
Estess, T., 146, 261f

Feckes, 272
Feiner, J., 247
Fenton, J., 273
Ferré, F., 160, 162–166, 264f
Fesquet, H., 240
Fransen, P., 245
Frege, G., 96, 246, 253f
Fries, H., 247
Funk, R., 259

Gallie, W., 143, 256
Geiselmann, J., 239
Geremia, F., 240
Gilby, T., 270
Gilkey, L., 201, 243, 263, 272
Gill, J., 264
Goodman, N., 250
Grijs, F. de, 271
Gruner, R., 256

Hacker, P., 251
Hallett, G., 251
Hamer, J., 224, 273, 276
Hampe, J., 240
Harré, R., 7, 153–159, 201, 263f, 272
Harvey, J., 41, 44, 244
Hawkes, T., 248
Hempel, C., 271
Henle, P., 251, 253
Hesse, M., 151–153, 157f, 162, 263
Holböck, F., 207–209, 222–224, 272–277
Hornby, A., 274
Horst, F. van der, 239
Hospers, J., 274
Huizinga, J., 142
Hutten, E., 263

Ijsseling, S., 252, 275

Jaki, S., 239
Jones, H., 146, 259, 263
Journet, C., 272
Jüngel, E., 252–254
Just, W., 273

Kamlah, W., 248, 251, 272
Katz, S., 274
Keen, S., 261

Keller, M., 46, 239, 245, 247, 277
Khatchadourian, H., 255
King, J., 57–60, 247
Kliever, L., 259
Kloppenburg, B., 242
Köhler, L., 246
Köpf, U., 267, 269
Koster, M., 49–52, 55, 60–64, 123, 209f, 214f, 218f, 224f, 227f, 239, 246f, 272–277
Kress, R., 273
Küng, H., 39, 40, 44, 48, 244, 275

Ladrière, J., 270
Laurentin, R., 240
Lehmann, K., 260
Lialine, D., 239, 273
Lieb, H., 248
Lindbeck, G., 243, 248
Loewenberg, I., 75–77, 113, 250, 257f
Löhrer, M., 247
Lombard, 171f, 267
Lorenzen, P., 248
Louch, A., 143, 262
Löwith, 145
Lubac, H. de, 270, 274
Lucas, D., 252
Luneau, A., 52–55, 61, 64, 225, 227, 246f, 276

McCabe, H., 266
McClendon, 259
McCormack, E., 255, 257
McDonnell, K., 243
McInerny, R., 171, 188, 266f, 270
McNamara, K., 40–42, 244–246
Mackie, A., 106f, 256
Malmberg, F., 245, 273
Mandelbaum, 144, 146, 262
Mandonnet, 267
Manns, J., 116, 118, 250, 258
Manthey, F., 266
Martin, G., 255
Matthews, R., 72–77, 249f
Maxwell, 150
Melden, 271
Menne, A., 272
Mersch, E., 239
Metz, J.-B., 124, 128–135, 139, 141f, 146–148, 205, 259–263, 275–278
Mieth, D., 136, 145, 261–263
Moeller, C., 240
Möhler, J. A., 2, 224

Index of Names

Mohrmann, C., 245
Mooij, J., 248, 250, 254–256
Moos, 267
Mühlen, H., 59–64, 123, 218, 222–224, 231, 243, 247f, 275–278

NAUTA, D., 149, 263
Nédoncelle, M., 239
Newman, J. H., 2
Novak, M., 259

OCKHAM, William of, 272
O'Hanlon, 275
Olscamp, P., 255, 257
Oppenheim, 271
Ottaviani, Cardinal, 11

PANNENBERG, W., 198, 200f, 271
Pater, W. de, 264
Paul, St, 14, 17, 46f, 50, 57, 62, 116f, 138, 184, 210, 217, 258, 261, 274
Paul VI, 217, 273
Pelz, K., 278
Persson, P., 243
Pesch, O., 267
Pettit, P., 264
Philips, G., 12, 18, 22, 39, 44, 61, 63f, 123, 240, 244, 247f, 251, 275
Pinborg, J., 266
Pitkin, H., 251
Pius XII, 208, 239
Plato, 135f
Platts, M., 254
Price, J., 75–77, 250
Przywara, E., 239, 248, 277f
Puntel, L., 271

RAMSEY, I., 4, 160–165, 218, 264f, 275
Ratzinger, J., 39–43, 48, 61, 240, 244, 246–248
Richard of St Victor, 178
Richards, I., 98–103, 161, 254f, 258
Ricoeur, P., 4, 84, 95, 98, 113f, 248, 250, 252–254, 256, 258, 270
Rigeaux, B., 274
Robinson, R., 272, 274
Ryle, G., 96, 108–110, 112, 214, 253, 256
Rynne, X., 240

SAUSSURE, F. de, 70f, 156
Scheeben, M., 216, 248, 274, 277
Schillebeeckx, E., 240, 245, 269f

Schmaus, M., 39–45, 47f, 61, 64, 207f, 220, 244, 246, 248, 272, 275
Searle, J., 78, 80, 250
Semmelroth, O., 58–60, 63f, 207, 209, 222, 224, 230, 247f, 272f, 275–278
Shakespeare, W., 92, 249
Shibbles, W., 248
Sigurbjörnsson, E., 241, 243
Skydsgaard, K., 243
Smalley, B., 268
Smulders, 274f
Steendam, G. van, 260f
Stenlund, S., 251
Stern, G., 255
Stewart, D., 118, 249, 258
Stroup, G., 259, 262
Swinburne, W., 204f, 272
Stutterheim, C., 248

TAVARD, G., 240
Ternus, 272
TeSelle, S., 124–128, 132, 134–139, 141, 190, 259–262
Thomas, D., 249
Toulmin, S., 263
Tracy, D., 264
Tromp, S., 275
Tuchman, B., 262
Turbayne, C., 109–112, 114, 256f

ULLMANN, S., 95, 253

VALESKE, U., 239, 241, 272, 277f
Via, D., 259

WACHINGER, L., 259
Warner, M., 79–81, 115–117, 250, 258
Weinrich, H., 69, 132, 135, 138f, 141, 253, 259–263
Weisheipl, J., 267
Wharton, 263
Wheelwright, 114, 257
Wilder, A., 259
Willems, B., 245
Wittgenstein, L., 87–91, 95, 211, 214, 251, 254, 273
Wright, G. von, 196, 198–200, 271

YOOS, G., 249, 257

Index of Subjects

ANALOGY, 61–63, 65, 168f, 209, 266, 270
- and metaphor, 169–171, 187f
- and model(s), 151f, 156f, 162

BODY OF CHRIST (MYSTICAL), 2, 210, 245, 247, 276f
- as central term in ecclesiology, 6, 12, 226f
- content (meaning) of, 6, 41–48, 56–60, 220–225, 228
- linguistic status of, 6f, 45, 61f, 64f, 193
- relation of to People of God, 6, 27, 36–38, 43–45, 47–51, 54, 56–59
- use of in *Lumen Gentium* I, 14–18, 227
  II^1, 19–21, 29
  II^2, 23, 25, 29
  II^3, 26f, 29
  III, 31, 33f

CHURCH
- as *Christus prolongatus*, 15, 27, 29, 37
- as *communio*, communion, community, 7, 19, 32, 57f, 221, 232f, 236, 277
- concept of, 222, 224
- as corporate personality, 59, 224, 231
- as sacrament, 22f, 28, 56–58, 221f, 230f, 235, 277f
- as *societas*, society, 2, 16–19, 23, 32, 37, 59, 206, 223, 233, 276f

COHERENCE OF STATEMENTS, 204, 234

CONCEPT(S), 60–62, 86, 92f, 88–90, 108, 207, 225f
- concept of, 201
- grammar of, 87f
- and metaphor, 63f, 180, 190, 218
- sets (realms) of, 81f, 84, 119, 121, 202f
- theological, 63–65
- transition of to terminus, 202f

DEFINITION, 205f, 210f
- attribution of defining properties, 101–103, 107
- and metaphor(s), 193, 207–210, 213f, 218f, 223, 225f
- real (and nominal), 61, 206, 208–216, 224f

DEFINITION OF THE CHURCH, 42, 45, 49f, 63f, 208, 223
- (im)possibility of, 7, 65f, 193, 205–207, 209f, 215, 217f, 220, 223f, 273, 276

ECCLESIOLOGY
- apologetic approach to, 2f, 231, 233
- basic statement in, 7, 193, 204f, 220–223, 225–227, 229–231, 233
- central term in, 3, 11, 38f, 49–52, 55, 65f, 224, 228f, 236, 244f
- Christocentric approach to, 235
- formal network in, 233–236
- history of, 2f
- models in, 220f
- pneumatocentric approach to, 235
- quintessential approach, 230, 232f
- salvation-historical approach to, 231, 235
- theological approach, 1–4, 7, 38, 229, 236

ENLIGHTENMENT, THE, 129f, 231

EXPLANATION, 197–199
- causal, 153–155, 159, 196–198, 200, 271
- conceptual, 199–201
- teleological, 196–200, 271
- and understanding, 196, 228, 230

FAITH (Aquinas on), 178f, 183–186

LANGUAGE
- argumentative (conceptual), 63f, 126, 132, 134f, 141, 146–148, 173f, 190f, 205, 218, 260
- conventionality of, 86–91, 120, 211, 273
- metaphorical, 6f, 104, 126f, 141, 158f, 173, 180, 187f, 190, 193, 218
- ordinary (everyday), 165, 202, 231
- relation of religious and theological, 4–6
- religious, 165f, 187, 189f, 194, 205, 265
- technical, 159, 165

LANGUAGE RULES, 78f, 84f, 90–92, 97, 120, 203
- changing, 75–77, 83
- following, 82, 85, 91, 119
- relaxation of, 83, 119–121
- violation of, 71, 73f, 77f, 82, 108, 110, 156, 158

LINGUISTIC THEORY, 68, 78, 97–100
- competence/performance, 70, 73–77, 120
- diachronic/synchronic analysis, 74f, 95, 99f, 120
- relation of language to reality, 86–90, 120, 147f, 191, 211, 218
- and the theory of metaphor, 70f, 73–76

LUMEN GENTIUM, 1, 6, 39, 44f, 49, 53f, 56, 58f, 61, 64f, 193, 220, 227, 229
- ambivalence of, 2f, 20f, 24f, 27, 29, 33–37
- apologetic approach of, 12, 18, 20f, 24, 27, 37
- central term in, 3, 6, 11, 15, 21, 25, 27, 29, 34–37, 44f, 47, 56, 65, 247
- open approach of, 18
- salvation-historical approach of, 12, 20, 24, 27f, 33
- theological approach of, 38

MEANING
- change of (in metaphor), 74, 76–78, 85, 89, 95, 97, 100–103, 113, 115, 117, 120, 126, 153–160, 171, 255, 257
- interanimation of words, 98f, 103, 111, 120
- marginal/central, 104–107, 256
- theory of, 94–96

METAPHOR(S), METAPHORICAL
- and absurdity, 105, 108, 112f
- cognitive content of, 5, 114–116, 119, 194, 218f, 258
- conceptual explanation of, 200f
- cultural determination of, 82, 92
- evocative power of, 115, 194f
- extraordinary combination in, 69f, 81–83, 114, 119, 121, 189, 195f, 200, 205
- the function of, 66f, 83f, 92, 120f, 128, 132, 134, 148, 161–163, 167, 171–173, 179f
- 'interpretation', 110–113
- the mechanism (structure) of, 6, 66f, 75, 79, 83, 103, 106, 114f, 117, 120f, 148f, 152f, 161–163, 167–170
- and Revelation, 173, 180, 186
- the semantic indeterminacy (open texture) of, 116f, 119, 195
- transition of to concept/terminus, 203–205, 218, 227, 229
- sense (meaning), 69f, 74f, 92, 107, 109f, 112f, 120, 126, 248, 250, 253
- truth (falsehood) of, 112–115, 121, 152, 257
- use, 69f, 76, 78, 85, 92, 100–103, 119–121, 126, 194f, 248

METAPHOR, THEORY OF, 4, 67, 84, 103, 105, 108, 114, 119f, 125f, 128, 159f, 187–189, 191, 203
- category-mistake approach, 93, 108–110, 112, 121, 256f
- comparison theory, 102, 151f, 157
- conversion theory, 256
- disclosure, 160f
- interaction theory, 98–103, 112, 114f, 117f, 120, 151f, 161f, 254, 257
- linguistic theory, 95, 120, 156, 158
- modern, 66, 98
- proper/improper, 95, 167f
- requirements of, 6, 67, 70, 72, 78
- (traditional) rhetorical theory, 66, 93–97, 100–105, 167f. 194, 203, 218
- semantic theory, 68, 70
- sentence approach, 69, 77, 93, 100, 119, 171, 226
- *suppositio/significatio*, 168–170, 267
- word approach, 93, 100, 111, 120, 171, 225f

METAPHYSICS, 159, 164, 166, 183

Index of Subjects

MODEL(S), 62, 123, 275
- concept of, 149f, 155, 164–166, 191
- function of, 149–151, 163f
- and metaphor(s), 5, 93, 148, 150–153, 157, 159–163, 191
- in science, 148f, 157–161, 163–166
- in theology, 4, 6, 148f, 160–166, 191
- and transcendental realism, 155f

MYSTERY, 61f
- of the church, 19f, 22, 28, 31, 34–36, 63–65, 206–208, 215–217, 219–221, 273–275
- and concepts, 218f
- concept of, 206f, 215–217
- and metaphor(s), 64f, 207f, 217–219, 276

MYSTICI CORPORIS, 2, 45–50, 58–60, 208, 222, 224, 227

NARRATIVE (STORY), 128f, 137–139, 140f, 261
- concept of, 124, 132, 135f, 144, 146f
- criteria and, 136–140, 142, 146–148
- effect of, 131, 134, 137, 142, 260
- 'innocence', 135f, 148, 190, 260f
- language, 132–134, 146
- and (dangerous) memory, 131, 139
- self-explanatory character of, 142–146
- tolerance, 138

NARRATIVE THEOLOGY, 6, 123, 127–129, 139, 145–147, 187, 190f
- moderate version of, 132–135
- radical version of, 127f, 132–135
- relation to argumentative theology, 128
- sources of, 124

PARAPHRASE, 117
- concept of, 117–119
- of metaphor, 112, 114, 116–118, 121, 151, 194–196, 205, 253, 271
- theology as, 195f, 199, 205

PEOPLE OF GOD, THE, 245, 247, 276f
- as central term in ecclesiology, 6, 12, 226
- content (meaning) of, 6, 39–60, 220–225, 227f
- linguistic status of, 6f, 54, 61f, 64f, 193, 227f
- relation of to Body of Christ, 6, 27, 36–38, 43–45, 47–51, 54, 56–59
- use of in *Lumen Gentium* I, 14, 16f
  II^1, 20f, 29
  II^2, 22f, 25, 29
  II^3, 25–27, 29
  III, 29f, 32–36

PHILOSOPHY
- of history, 134, 142–146, 201
- relation of to theology, 175–179, 181–187
- of science, 153, 166

ROMAN CATHOLIC CHURCH, 16f, 20, 23, 26, 32–35, 60

SCIENTIA
- concept of, 172, 175–178, 181–184, 190
- *sacra doctrina* as, 172, 174f, 181–186
- theology as, 5, 174, 176f, 189, 268

SCRIPTURE, 39, 54, 130f, 137, 140, 172f, 174, 180–182, 186–190, 207, 209, 222, 226
- language of, 4, 63–65, 124, 129, 165, 181, 186f, 189
- and metaphor(s), 218
- parable(s) in, 63, 123–129, 136, 265

SPEECH ACT(S), 75, 77, 96, 120
- content aspect, 78, 80f
- illocutionary force/aspect, 78–80, 250
- perlocutionary force/aspect, 79, 81

TERMINUS, 201–203
- formal, 233f
- pivot, 230–233
- transition from concept to, 202f

THEOLOGY, THEOLOGICAL
- argumentative (conceptual), 5, 124, 128, 132f, 135
- conclusion, 184
- function of, 124f, 127–129
- as *intellectus fidei*, 178f, 186, 267
- intermediary, 124f, 127f
- language, 56, 128, 130, 142, 147, 165f, 187, 191, 193f
- and metaphor(s), 3–6, 60–66, 123, 132, 148, 209f
- metaphorical, 124, 128, 134f, 139, 148, 190f, 200, 219, 261
- political, 129, 261
- systematic, 123f, 128, 191

TRANSCENDENTAL REALISM, 153–156, 166, 201

UNDERSTANDING, 196–199

VATICAN COUNCIL, FIRST, 2, 223

VATICAN COUNCIL, SECOND, 1–3, 6, 11f, 38, 53–55, 66, 193, 233, 236